BERLITZ®

GERMAN
for travellers

By the staff of Berlitz Guides

How best to use this phrase book

● We suggest that you start with the **Guide to pronunciation** (pp. 6–8), then go on to **Some basic expressions** (pp. 9–15). This gives you not only a minimum vocabulary, but also helps you get used to pronouncing the language. The phonetic transcription throughout the book enables you to pronounce every word correctly.

● Consult the **Contents** pages (3–5) for the section you need. In each chapter you'll find travel facts, hints and useful information. Simple phrases are followed by a list of words applicable to the situation.

● Separate, detailed contents lists are included at the beginning of the extensive **Eating out** and **Shopping guide** sections (Menus, p. 39, Shops and services, p. 97).

● If you want to find out how to say something in German, your fastest look-up is via the **Dictionary** section (pp. 164–189). This not only gives you the word, but is also cross-referenced to its use in a phrase on a specific page.

● If you wish to learn more about constructing sentences, check the **Basic grammar** (pp. 159–163).

● Note the **colour margins** are indexed in German and English to help both listener and speaker. And, in addition, there is also an **index in German** for the use of your listener.

● Throughout the book, this symbol ☛ suggests phrases your listener can use to answer you. If you still can't understand, hand this phrase book to the German-speaker to encourage pointing to an appropriate answer. The English translation for you is just alongside the German.

Library of Congress Catalog Card No. 85-81372

Second revised edition—8th printing 1989
Printed in Hungary

Contents

Acknowledgments
We are particularly grateful to Eva Bayer for her help in the preparation of this book, and to Dr. T.J.A. Bennett who devised the phonetic transcription.

Guide to pronunciation

You'll find the pronunciation of the German letters and sounds explained below, as well as the symbols we use for them in the transcriptions.

The imitated pronunciation should be read as if it were English except for any special rules set out below. It is based on Standard British pronunciation, though we have tried to take into account General American pronunciation as well. Of course, the sounds of any two languages are never exactly the same; but if you follow carefully the indications supplied here, you'll have no difficulty in reading our transcriptions in such a way as to make yourself understood.

In the transcriptions, letters shown in bold print should be read with more stress (louder) than the others.

Consonants

Letter	Approximate pronunciation	Symbol	Example	
f, h, k, l, m, n, p, t, x	normally pronounced as in English			
b	1) at the end of a word or between a vowel and a consonant like **p** in **up**	p	**ab**	ahp
	2) elsewhere as in English	b	**bis**	biss
c	1) before **e, i, ö** and **ä**, like **ts** in **hits**	ts	**Celsius**	**tsehl**ziuss
	2) elsewhere like **c** in **cat**	k	**Café**	kah**fay**
ch	1) after back vowels (e.g. **ah, o, oo**) like **ch** in Scottish lo**ch**, otherwise more like **h** in **h**uge	kh	**doch**	dokh

ch	2) sometimes, especially before **s**, like **k** in **k**it	k	**Wachs**	vahks
d	1) at the end of a word or between a vowel and a consonant like **t** in ea**t**	t	**Rad**	raat
	2) elsewhere, like **d** in **d**o	d	**durstig**	**door**stikh
g	1) always hard as in **g**o but at the end of a word often more like **ck** in ta**ck**	g k	**gehen** **weg**	**gay**ern vehk
	2) when preceded by **i** at the end of a word like **ch** in Scottish lo**ch**	kh	**billig**	**bil**likh
j	like **y** in **y**es	y	**ja**	yaa
qu	like **k** followed by **v** as in **v**at	kv	**Quark**	kvahrk
r	generally rolled in the back of the mouth	r	**warum**	vah**rum**
s	1) before or between vowels like **z** in **z**oo	z	**sie**	zee
	2) before **p** and **t** at the beginning of a syllable like **sh** in **sh**ut	sh	**spät**	shpait
	3) elsewhere, like **s** in **s**it	s/ss	**es ist**	ehss ist
ß	always like **s** in **s**it	s/ss	**heiß**	highss
sch	like **sh** in **sh**ut	sh	**schnell**	shnehl
tsch	like **ch** in **ch**ip	ch	**deutsch**	doych
tz	like **ts** in hi**ts**	ts	**Platz**	plahts
v	1) like **f** in **f**or	f	**vier**	feer
	2) in most words of foreign origin, like **v** in **v**ice	v	**Vase**	**vaa**zer
w	like **v** in **v**ice	v	**wie**	vee
z	like **ts** in hi**ts**	ts	**zeigen**	**tsigh**gern

Vowels

In German, vowels are generally long when followed by **h** or by one consonant and short when followed by two or more consonants.

a	1) short like **u** in cut	ah	**lassen**	**lah**ssern
	2) long like **a** in car	aa	**Abend**	**aa**bernt
ä	1) short like **e** in let	eh	**Lärm**	lehrm
	2) long like **ai** in hair	ai	**spät**	shpait
e	1) short like **e** in let	eh	**sprechen**	**shpreh**khern
	2) long like **a** in late, but pronounced without moving tongue or lips	ay	**geben**	**gay**bern
	3) in unstressed syllables generally like **er** in other	er*	**bitte**	**bit**ter
i	1) short like **i** in hit	i	**billig**	**bil**likh
	2) long like **ee** in meet	ee	**ihm**	eem
ie	like **ee** in bee	ee	**hier**	heer
o	1) short like **o** in got	o	**voll**	fol
	2) long like **o** in note, but pronounced without moving tongue or lips	oa	**ohne**	**oa**ner
ö	like **ur** in fur (long or short)	ur*	**können**	**kur**nern
u	1) short like **oo** in foot	u	**Nuß**	nuss
	2) long like **oo** in moon	oo	**gut**	goot
ü	like French **u** in **u**ne; round your lips and try to say **ea** as in mean (long or short)	ew	**über**	**ew**ber
y	like German **ü**	ew	**typisch**	**tew**pish

Diphthongs

ai, ay, ei, ey	like **igh** in **high**	igh	**mein**	mighn
au	like **ow** in **now**	ow	**auf**	owf
äu, eu	like **oy** in **boy**	oy	**neu**	noy

* The r should not be pronounced when reading this transcription.

Some basic expressions

Yes.	**Ja.**	yaa
No.	**Nein.**	nighn
Please.	**Bitte.**	**bit**ter
Thank you.	**Danke.**	**dahn**ker
You're welcome.	**Bitte.**	**bit**ter
Thank you very much.	**Vielen Dank.**	**fee**lern dahnk
That's all right/ Don't mention it.	**Gern geschehen.**	gehrn ger**shay**ern

Greetings *Begrüßung*

Good morning.	**Guten Morgen.**	**goo**tern **mor**gern
Good afternoon.	**Guten Tag.**	**goo**tern taag
Good evening.	**Guten Abend.**	**goo**tern **aa**bernt
Good night.	**Gute Nacht.**	**goo**ter nahkht
Good-bye.	**Auf Wiedersehen.**	owf **vee**derrzayern
See you later.	**Bis bald.**	biss bahlt
This is Mr./Mrs./ Miss ...	**Das ist Herr/Frau/ Fräulein ...**	dahss ist hehr/frow/ **froy**lighn
How do you do? (Pleased to meet you.)	**Sehr erfreut.**	zayr ehr**froyt**
How are you?	**Wie geht es Ihnen?**	vee gayt ehss **ee**nern
Very well, thanks. And you?	**Sehr gut, danke. Und Ihnen?**	zayr goot **dahn**ker. unt **ee**nern
How's life?	**Wie geht's?**	vee gayts
Fine.	**Gut.**	goot

I beg your pardon?	**Wie bitte?**	vee **bit**ter
Excuse me. (May I get past?)	**Gestatten Sie?**	ger**shtah**tern zee
Sorry!	**Entschuldigung/ Verzeihung!**	ehnt**shul**diggung/ fehr**tsigh**ung

Questions *Fragen*

Where?	**Wo?**	voa
How?	**Wie?**	vee
When?	**Wann?**	vahn
What?	**Was?**	vahss
Why?	**Warum?**	vah**rum**
Who?	**Wer?**	vayr
Which?	**Welcher/Welche/ Welches?**	**vehl**kherr/**vehl**kher/ **vehl**kherss
Where is ...?	**Wo ist ...?**	voa ist
Where are ...?	**Wo sind ...?**	voa zint
Where can I find/ get ...?	**Wo finde/bekomme ich ...?**	voa **fin**der/ber**kom**mer ikh
How far?	**Wie weit?**	vee vight
How long?	**Wie lange?**	vee **lahn**ger
How much?	**Wieviel?**	vee**feel**
How many?	**Wie viele?**	vee **fee**ler
How much does this cost?	**Wieviel kostet das?**	vee**feel kos**tert dahss
When does ... open/ close?	**Wann öffnet/ schließt ...?**	vahn **urf**nert/shleest
What do you call this/that in German?	**Wie heißt dies/ das auf deutsch?**	vee highst deess/dahss owf doych
What does that mean?	**Was bedeutet das?**	vahss ber**doy**tert dahss
What does this word mean?	**Was bedeutet dieses Wort?**	vahss ber**doy**tert **dee**zerss vort

Do you speak ...? *Sprechen Sie ...?*

Do you speak English?	**Sprechen Sie Englisch?**	**shprehkhern zee ehnglish**
Is there anyone here who speaks English?	**Spricht hier jemand Englisch?**	shprikht heer **yay**mahnt **ehng**lish
I don't speak (much) German.	**Ich spreche kaum Deutsch.**	ikh **shpreh**kher kowm doych
Could you speak more slowly?	**Könnten Sie bitte langsamer sprechen?**	**kurn**tern zee **bit**ter **lahng**zaamerr **shpreh**khern
Could you repeat that?	**Könnten Sie das bitte wiederholen?**	**kurn**tern zee dahss **bit**ter veederr**hoa**lern
Could you spell it?	**Könnten Sie es bitte buchstabieren?**	**kurn**tern zee ehss **bit**ter bookhshtah**bee**rern
Please write it down.	**Schreiben Sie es bitte auf.**	**shrigh**bern zee ehss **bit**ter owf
Can you translate this for me/us?	**Könnten Sie mir/uns das übersetzen?**	**kurn**tern zee meer/uns dahss ewberr**zehts**ern
Please point to the phrase/sentence in the book.	**Bitte zeigen Sie mir den Ausdruck/ den Satz im Buch.**	**bit**ter **tsigh**gern zee meer dayn **ows**druk/ dayn zahts im bookh
Just a moment. I'll see if I can find it in this book.	**Einen Augenblick bitte, ich schaue mal im Buch nach, ob ich es finde.**	**igh**nern **ow**gernblik **bit**ter ikh **show**er maal im bookh naakh op ikh ehss **fin**der
I understand.	**Ich verstehe.**	ikh **fehrshtayer**
I don't understand.	**Ich verstehe nicht.**	ikh fehr**shtay**er nikht
Do you understand?	**Verstehen Sie?**	fehr**shtay**ern zee

Can/May ...? *Kann ...?*

Can I have ...?	**Kann ich ... haben?**	kahn ikh ... **haa**bern
Can we have ...?	**Können wir ... haben?**	**kur**nern veer ... **haa**bern
Can you show me ...?	**Können Sie mir ... zeigen?**	**kur**nern zee meer ... **tsigh**gern
I can't.	**Leider nicht.**	**ligh**derr nikht

Can you tell me ...?	**Können Sie mir sagen ...?**	**kur**nern zee meer **zaa**gern
Can you help me?	**Können Sie mir helfen?**	**kur**nern zee meer **hehl**fern
Can I help you?	**Kann ich Ihnen helfen?**	kahn ikh **ee**nern **hehl**fern
Can you direct me to ...?	**Können Sie mir den Weg nach/ zu ... zeigen?**	**kur**nern zee meer dayn vayg naakh/ tsoo ... **tsigh**gern

What do you want? *Was wünschen Sie?*

I'd like ...	**Ich hätte gern/ Ich möchte ...**	ikh **heh**ter gehrn/ ikh **murkh**ter
We'd like ...	**Wir hätten gern/ Wir möchten ...**	veer **heh**tern gehrn/ veer **murkh**tern
Give me ...	**Geben Sie mir ...**	**gay**bern zee meer
Give it to me.	**Geben Sie es mir.**	**gay**bern zee ehss meer
Bring me ...	**Bringen Sie mir ...**	**bring**ern zee meer
Bring it to me.	**Bringen Sie es mir.**	**bring**ern zee ehss meer
Show me ...	**Zeigen Sie mir ...**	**tsigh**gern zee meer
Show it to me.	**Zeigen Sie es mir.**	**tsigh**gern zee ehss meer
I'm looking for ...	**Ich suche ...**	ikh **zoo**kher
I'm hungry.	**Ich habe Hunger.**	ikh **haa**ber **hung**err
I'm thirsty.	**Ich habe Durst.**	ikh **haa**ber doorst
I'm tired.	**Ich bin müde.**	ikh bin **mew**der
I'm lost.	**Ich habe mich verirrt.**	ikh **haa**ber mikh feh**reert**
It's important.	**Es ist wichtig.**	ehss ist **vikh**tikh
It's urgent.	**Es ist dringend.**	ehss ist **dring**ernt
Hurry up!	**Beeilen Sie sich!**	ber**igh**lern zee zikh

It is/There is ... *Es ist/Es gibt ...*

It is ...	**Es ist ...**	ehss ist
Is it ...?	**Ist es ...?**	ist ehss

It isn't ...	**Es ist nicht ...**	ehss ist nikht
Here it is.	**Hier ist es.**	heer ist ehss
Here they are.	**Hier sind sie.**	heer zint zee
There it is.	**Dort ist es.**	dort ist ehss
There they are.	**Dort sind sie.**	dort zint zee
There is/are ...	**Es gibt ...**	ehss gipt
Is there/Are there ...?	**Gibt es ...?**	gipt ehss
There isn't (any) ...	**Es gibt keinen/Es gibt keine/Es gibt kein ...**	ehss gipt **kigh**nern/ehss gipt **kigh**ner/ehss gipt kighn
There aren't (any) ...	**Es gibt keine ...**	ehss gipt **kigh**ner

Adjectives *Eigenschaftswörter*

big/small	**groß/klein**	groass/klighn
quick/slow	**schnell/langsam**	shnehl/**lahng**zaam
cheap/expensive	**billig/teuer**	**bil**likh/**toy**err
hot/cold	**heiß/kalt**	highss/kahlt
full/empty	**voll/leer**	fol/layr
easy/difficult	**leicht/schwierig**	lighkht/**shwee**rikh
heavy/light	**schwer/leicht**	shvayr/lighkht
open/shut	**offen/geschlossen**	**of**fern/ger**shlos**sern
right/wrong	**richtig/falsch**	**rikh**tikh/fahlsh
old/new	**alt/neu**	ahlt/noy
old/young	**alt/jung**	ahlt/yung
next/last	**nächste/letzte**	**naikh**ster/**lehts**ter
beautiful/ugly	**schön/häßlich**	shurn/**hehs**likh
free (vacant)/ occupied	**frei/besetzt**	frigh/ber**zehtst**
good/bad	**gut/schlecht**	goot/shlehkht
better/worse	**besser/schlechter**	**beh**sserr/**shlehkh**terr
early/late	**früh/spät**	frew/shpait
near/far	**nah/weit**	naa/vight
left/right	**linke/rechte**	**lin**ker/**rehkh**ter

Quantities *Mengen*

a little	**ein wenig**	ighn **vay**nikh
a lot	**eine Menge**	**igh**ner **mehn**ger
few/a few	**wenige/einige**	**vay**nigger/**igh**nigger
much/many	**viel/viele**	feel/**fee**ler
more (than)	**mehr (als)**	mayr (ahlss)
less (than)	**weniger (als)**	**vay**niggerr (ahlss)
enough/too (much)	**genug/zu (viel)**	ger**nook**/tsu (feel)
some/any (sing.)	**etwas**	**eht**vahss
some/any (pl.)	**einige**	**igh**nigger

A few more useful words *Weitere nützliche Wörter*

at	**an/bei**	ahn/bigh
on	**an/auf**	ahn/owf
in	**in**	in
to	**zu**	tsoo
after	**nach**	naakh
before	**vor**	foar
for	**für**	fewr
from	**von**	fon
with	**mit**	mit
without	**ohne**	**oa**ner
through	**durch**	doorkh
towards	**gegen**	**gay**gern
until	**bis**	biss
during	**während**	**vai**rernt
next to	**neben**	**nay**bern
behind	**hinter**	**hin**terr
between	**zwischen**	**tsvi**shern
since	**seit**	zight
above	**oben**	**oa**bern
below	**unten**	**un**tern
over	**über**	**ew**berr
under	**unter**	**un**terr

inside	**drinnen**	**drin**nern
outside	**draußen**	**drow**ssern
up	**hinauf**	hinn**owf**
down	**hinunter**	hinn**un**terr
here	**hier**	heer
there	**dort**	dort
and	**und**	unt
or	**oder**	**oa**derr
but	**aber**	**aa**berr
not	**nicht**	nikht
never	**nie**	nee
nothing	**nichts**	nikhts
none	**kein**	kighn
very	**sehr**	zayr
too (also)	**auch**	owkh
yet	**noch**	nokh
soon	**bald**	bahlt
now	**jetzt**	yehtst
only	**nur**	noor
then	**dann**	dahn
perhaps	**vielleicht**	fee**lighkht**

Pronunciation of the German alphabet

A	aa	**H**	haa	**Ö**	ur	**V**	fow
Ä	ai	**I**	ee	**P**	pay	**W**	vay
B	bay	**J**	yot	**Q**	koo	**X**	eeks
C	tsay	**K**	kaa	**R**	ehr	**Y**	**ewp**sillon
D	day	**L**	ehl	**S**	ehss	**Z**	tseht
E	ay	**M**	ehm	**T**	tay		
F	ehf	**N**	ehn	**U**	oo		
G	gay	**O**	oa	**Ü**	ew		

In addition to these letters there is the **ß** sign, a combination of **s** and **z**. It is pronounced exactly like **ss**.

Arrival

PASSKONTROLLE
PASSPORT CONTROL

Here's my passport.	**Hier ist mein Paß.**	heer ist mighn pahss
I'll be staying ...	**Ich bleibe ...**	ikh **bligh**ber
a few days	**ein paar Tage**	ighn paar **taa**ger
a week	**eine Woche**	**igh**ner **vo**kher
a month	**einen Monat**	**igh**nern **moa**naht
I don't know yet.	**Ich weiß es noch nicht.**	ikh vighss ehss nokh nikht
I'm here on holiday.	**Ich bin auf Urlaub hier.**	ikh bin owf **oor**lowp heer
I'm here on business.	**Ich bin geschäftlich hier.**	ikh bin ger**shehft**likh heer
I'm just passing through.	**Ich bin nur auf der Durchreise.**	ikh bin noor owf derr **doorkh**righzer

If things become difficult:

I'm sorry, I don't understand.	**Es tut mir leid, ich verstehe nicht.**	ehss toot meer light ikh fehr**shtay**er nikht
Is there anyone here who speaks English?	**Spricht hier jemand Englisch?**	shprikht heer **yay**mahnt **ehng**lish

Customs *Zoll*

After collecting your baggage at the airport (*der Flughafen*—derr **floog**haafern) you have a choice: use the green exit if you have nothing to declare. Or leave via the red exit if you have items to declare (in excess of those allowed).

ANMELDEFREIE WAREN
NOTHING TO DECLARE

ANMELDEPFLICHTIGE WAREN
GOODS TO DECLARE

The chart below shows what you can bring in duty-free.

		 Cigarettes	 Cigars	 Tobacco	 Spirits (Liquor)	 Wine
Germany	1)	200 or	50 or	250 g.	1 l. and	2 l.
	2)	300 or	75 or	400 g.	1.5 l. and	5 l.
	3)	400 or	100 or	500 g.	1 l. and	2 l.
Austria		200 or	50 or	250 g.	1 l. and	2 l.
Switzerland		200 or	50 or	250 g.	1 l. and	2 l.

1) Visitors arriving from EEC countries with tax-free items, and visitors from other European countries
2) Visitors arriving from EEC countries with non-tax-free items
3) Visitors arriving from countries outside Europe

I've nothing to declare.	**Ich habe nichts zu verzollen.**	ikh **haa**ber nikhts tsoo fehrt**soll**ern
I've ...	**Ich habe ...**	ikh **haa**ber
a carton of cigarettes	**eine Stange Zigaretten**	**igh**ner **shtahng**er tsiggah**reh**tern
a bottle of gin	**eine Flasche Gin**	**igh**ner **flah**sher "gin"
It's for my personal use.	**Es ist für meinen persönlichen Gebrauch.**	ehss ist fewr **migh**nern pehr**zurn**likhern ger**browkh**
This is a gift.	**Das ist ein Geschenk.**	dahss ist ighn ger**shenk**

Ihren Paß, bitte.	Your passport, please.
Haben Sie etwas zu verzollen?	Do you have anything to declare?
Bitte öffnen Sie diese Tasche.	Please open this bag.
Dies ist zollpflichtig.	You'll have to pay duty on this.
Haben Sie noch mehr Gepäck?	Do you have any more luggage?

Baggage—Porters *Gepäck—Gepäckträger*

These days porters are only available at airports or the railway stations of large cities. Where no porters are available you'll find luggage trolleys for the use of the passengers.

Porter!	**Gepäckträger!**	ger**pehk**traigerr
Please take this luggage.	**Nehmen Sie bitte dieses Gepäck.**	**nay**mern zee **bit**ter **dee**zerss ger**pehk**
That's mine.	**Das gehört mir.**	dahss ger**hurrt** meer
That's my suitcase/ (travelling) bag.	**Das ist mein Koffer/ meine (Reise)tasche.**	dahss ist mighn **kof**ferr/ **migh**ner (**righ**zer)tahsher
There is one piece missing.	**Es fehlt ein Gepäckstück.**	ehss fayIt ighn ger**pehk**shtewk
Please take this to the ...	**Bringen Sie das bitte ...**	**brin**gern zee dahss **bit**ter
bus/taxi	**zum Bus/Taxi**	tsum buss/**tahk**si
luggage lockers	**zu den Schließfächern**	tsoo dayn **shlees**fehkherrn
How much is that?	**Wieviel macht das?**	vee**feel** mahkht dahss
Where are the luggage trolleys (carts)?	**Wo sind die Kofferkulis?**	voa zint dee **kof**ferrkooliss

Changing money *Geldwechsel*

Where's the nearest currency exchange office?	**Wo ist die nächste Wechselstube?**	voa ist dee **naikh**ster **vehk**serlshtoober
Can you change these traveller's cheques (checks)?	**Können Sie diese Reiseschecks einlösen?**	**kur**nern zee **dee**zer **righ**zershehks **ighn**lurzern
I want to change some dollars/pounds.	**Ich möchte Dollar/ Pfund wechseln.**	ikh **murkh**ter **dol**lahr/pfunt **vehk**serln
Can you change this into ...?	**Können Sie das in ... umwechseln?**	**kur**nern zee dahss in ... **um**vehkserln
Austrian shillings	**Schilling**	**shil**ling
German marks	**D-Mark**	day-mahrk
Swiss francs	**Schweizer Franken**	**shvight**serr **frahn**kern
What's the exchange rate?	**Wie ist der Wechselkurs?**	vee ist derr **vehk**serlkoors

BANK—CURRENCY, see page 129

Where is ...? *Wo ist ...?*

Where is the ...?	**Wo ist ...?**	voa ist
booking office	**der Reservierungs-schalter**	derr rehzerr**veer**ungs-shahlterr
car hire	**der Autoverleih**	derr **ow**toffehrligh
duty-free shop	**der Duty-free-Shop**	derr "duty-free-shop"
newsstand	**der Zeitungsstand**	derr **tsigh**tungsshtahnt
restaurant	**das Restaurant**	dahss rehstor**rahng**
shopping gallery	**die Einkaufsgalerie**	dee **ighn**kowfsgahlehree
How do I get to Stuttgart?	**Wie komme ich nach Stuttgart?**	vee **kom**mer ikh nakh **shtut**gahrt
How do I get to the ... Hotel?	**Wie komme ich zum Hotel ...?**	vee **kom**mer ikh tsum hot**tehl**
Is there a bus into town?	**Fährt ein Bus ins Stadtzentrum?**	fairt ighn buss ins **shtaht**tsehntrum
Where can I get a taxi?	**Wo finde ich ein Taxi?**	voa **fin**der ikh ighn **tahk**si
Where can I hire (rent) a car?	**Wo kann ich ein Auto mieten?**	voa kahn ikh ighn **ow**to **mee**tern

Hotel reservation *Hotelreservierung*

Do you have a hotel guide?	**Haben Sie ein Hotel-verzeichnis?**	**haa**bern zee ighn hot**tehl**-fehrtsighkhniss
Could you reserve a room for me at a hotel/boarding house?	**Können Sie mir bitte ein Hotel-/Pensions-zimmer reservieren?**	**kur**nern zee meer **bit**ter ighn hot**tehl**/pehn**zioans**-tsimmerr rehzerr**veer**ern
in the centre	**im Zentrum**	im **tsehn**trum
near the railway station	**beim Bahnhof**	bighm **baan**hoaf
a single room	**ein Einzelzimmer**	ighn **ighn**tserltsimmerr
a double room	**ein Doppelzimmer**	ighn **dop**perltsimmerr
not too expensive	**nicht zu teuer**	nikht tsu **toy**err
Where is the hotel/boarding house?	**Wo liegt das Hotel/ die Pension?**	voa leegt dahss hot**tehl**/ dee pehn**zioan**
Do you have a street map?	**Haben Sie einen Stadtplan?**	**haa**bern zee **igh**nern **shtaht**plaan

HOTEL/ACCOMMODATION, see page 22

Car hire (rental) *Autoverleih*

To hire a car you must produce a valid driving licence (held for at least one year) and your passport. Some firms set a minimum age at 21, other 25. Holders of major credit cards are normally exempt from deposit payments, otherwise you must pay a substantial (refundable) deposit for a car. Third-party insurance is usually automatically included.

I'd like to hire (rent) a car.	**Ich möchte ein Auto mieten.**	ikh **murkh**ter ighn **ow**to **mee**tern
small/medium-sized/ large	**ein kleines/mittleres/ großes**	ighn **kligh**nerss/**mit**lerrerss groasserss
automatic	**mit Automatik**	mit owtom**maa**tik
I'd like it for a day/a week.	**Ich möchte es für einen Tag/eine Woche.**	ikh **murkh**ter ehss fewr **igh**nern taag/**igh**ner **vo**kher
Are there any week-end arrangements?	**Gibt es Wochenend-pauschalen?**	gipt ehss **vo**khernehnt-powshaalern
Do you have any special rates?	**Haben Sie Sonder-tarife?**	**haa**bern zee **zon**derr-tahreefer
How much does it cost per day/week?	**Wieviel kostet es pro Tag/Woche?**	vee**feel ko**stert ehss proa taag/**vo**kher
Is mileage included?	**Ist das Kilometer-geld inbegriffen?**	ist dahss killom**may**terr-gehlt **in**bergriffern
What's the charge per kilometer?	**Wieviel kostet es pro Kilometer?**	vee**feel ko**stert ehss proa killom**may**terr
I want to hire the car here and leave it in ...	**Ich möchte den Wagen hier mieten und in ... zurück-geben.**	ikh **murkh**ter dayn **vaa**gern heer **mee**tern unt in ... tsoo**rewk**gaybern
I want full insurance.	**Ich möchte eine Vollkasko-versicherung.**	ikh **murkh**ter **igh**ner **fol**kahskoffehrzikherrung
What's the deposit?	**Wieviel muß ich hinterlegen?**	vee**feel** muss ikh hinterr**lay**gern
I've a credit card.	**Ich habe eine Kreditkarte.**	ikh **haa**ber **igh**ner kreh**dit**kahrter
Here's my driving licence.	**Hier ist mein Führerschein.**	heer ist mighn **few**rerrshighn

CAR, see page 75

Taxi *Taxi*

A taxi is usually caught at a rank (*der Taxistand*—der **tahk**si-shtahnt). You can also phone for a taxi wherever you are; numbers are listed on a separate page in front of the phone books. All taxis have meters.

Where can I get a taxi?	**Wo finde ich ein Taxi?**	voa **fin**der ikh ighn **tahk**si
Please get me a taxi.	**Besorgen Sie mir bitte ein Taxi.**	ber**zor**gern zee meer **bit**ter ighn **tahk**si
What's the fare to ...?	**Was kostet es bis ...?**	vahss **kos**tert ehss biss
How far is it to ...?	**Wie weit ist es bis ...?**	vee vight ist ehss biss
Take me to ...	**Bringen Sie mich ...**	**brin**gern zee mikh
this address	**zu dieser Adresse**	tsoo **dee**zerr ah**dreh**sser
the airport	**zum Flughafen**	tsum **floog**haafern
the railway station	**zum Bahnhof**	tsum **baan**hoaf
the town centre	**ins Stadtzentrum**	ins **shtahtt**sehntrum
the ... Hotel	**zum Hotel ...**	tsum hot**tehl**
Turn ... at the next corner.	**Biegen Sie an der nächsten Ecke ... ab.**	**bee**gern zee ahn derr **naikh**stern **eh**ker ... ahp
left/right	**links/rechts**	links/rehkhts
Go straight ahead.	**Geradeaus.**	ger**raa**derrowss
Please stop here.	**Halten Sie hier, bitte.**	**hahl**tern zee heer **bit**ter
I'm in a hurry.	**Ich habe es eilig.**	ikh **haa**ber ehss **igh**likh
Could you drive more slowly?	**Bitte fahren Sie langsamer.**	**bit**ter **faa**rern zee **lahng**zaamerr
Could you help me carry my luggage?	**Könnten Sie mir bitte beim Gepäcktragen helfen?**	**kurn**tern zee meer **bit**ter bighm ger**pehk**traagern **hehl**fern
Will you wait for me, please?	**Würden Sie bitte auf mich warten?**	**vewr**dern zee **bit**ter owf mikh **vahr**tern
I'll be back in 10 minutes.	**Ich bin in 10 Minuten zurück.**	ikh bin in 10 min**noo**tern tsoo**rewk**

TIPPING, see inside back-cover

Hotel—Other accommodation

Early reservation and confirmation are essential in most major tourist centres during the high season. Most towns and arrival points have a tourist information office (*Fremdenverkehrsbüro*—**frehm**dernfehrkayrsbewroa), and that's the place to go if you're stuck without a room.

Hotel (hot**tehl**)	Hotel; simple or fancy, your room will be spotless. You'll probably sleep under a quilt filled with duck or goose down. *Hotel garni* means that only a room and breakfast are offered, no other meals.
Schloßhotel (**shlos**hottehl)	Castle or palace converted into a hotel; often located in the countryside.
Rasthof (**rahst**hoaf)	Wayside lodge, motel; most are located just off a motorway (expressway) or principal route.
Gasthaus/Gasthof (**gahst**howss/**gahst**hoaf)	Inn
Pension/Fremdenheim (pehn**zioan**/**frehm**dernhighm)	Boarding-house; offers full or half board. *Zimmer frei* will tell you there's a room to let, sometimes also in a private home.
Jugendherberge (**yoo**gernthehrbehrger)	Youth hostel
Ferienwohnung (**fay**riernvoanung)	Furnished flat (apartment) found in holiday resorts; you'll probably have to reserve it in advance. Otherwise, contact the local tourist office.

Can you recommend a hotel/pension?	**Können Sie mir ein Hotel/eine Pension empfehlen?**	**kur**nern zee meer ighn hot**tehl**/**igh**ner pehn**zioan** ehm**pfay**lern
Do you have a hotel guide?	**Haben Sie ein Hotelverzeichnis?**	**haa**bern zee ighn hot**tehl**-fehrtsighkhniss
Are there any flats (apartments) vacant?	**Gibt es noch freie Ferienwohnungen?**	gipt ehss nokh **frigh**er **fay**riernvoanungern

CAMPING, see page 32

Checking in—Reception *Empfang*

My name is ...	**Mein Name ist ...**	mighn **naa**mer ist
I've a reservation.	**Ich habe reservieren lassen.**	ikh **haa**ber rehzerr**vee**rern **lah**ssern
We've reserved two rooms, a single and a double.	**Wir haben zwei Zimmer reservieren lassen – ein Einzelzimmer und ein Doppelzimmer.**	veer **haa**bern tsvigh **tsim**merr rehzerr**vee**rern **lah**ssern—ighn **ighn**tserltsimmerr unt ighn **dop**perltsimmerr
Here's the confirmation.	**Hier ist die Bestätigung.**	heer ist dee ber**shtai**tig-gung
Do you have any vacancies?	**Haben Sie noch freie Zimmer?**	**haa**bern zee nokh **frigh**er **tsim**merr
I'd like a ...	**Ich hätte gern ein ...**	ikh **heh**ter gehrn ighn
single room	**Einzelzimmer**	**ighn**tserltsimmerr
double room	**Doppelzimmer**	**dop**perltsimmerr
A room ...	**Ein Zimmer ...**	ighn **tsim**merr
with twin beds	**mit zwei Einzelbetten**	mit tsvigh **ighn**tserlbehtern
with a double bed	**mit einem Doppelbett**	mit **igh**nerm **dop**perlbeht
with a bath	**mit Bad**	mit baat
with a shower	**mit Dusche**	mit **du**sher
with a balcony	**mit Balkon**	mit bahl**koan**
with a view	**mit Aussicht**	mit **ows**sikht
facing the lake/ the mountains	**mit Blick auf den See/ auf die Berge**	mit blik owf dayn zay/ owf dee **behr**ger
in the front	**zur Straße**	tsoor **shtraa**sser
at the back	**zum Hof**	tsum hoaf
It must be quiet.	**Es muß ruhig sein.**	ehss muss **roo**ikh zighn
Is there ...?	**Gibt es ...?**	gipt ehss
air conditioning	**Klimaanlage**	**klee**mahnlaager
a radio/a television in the room	**Radio/Fernsehen im Zimmer**	**raa**dio/**fehrn**zayern im **tsim**merr
laundry service	**einen Wäschedienst**	**igh**nern **veh**sherdeenst
room service	**Zimmerbedienung**	**tsim**merrberdeenung
hot water	**warmes Wasser**	**vahr**merss **vah**sserr
running water	**fließendes Wasser**	**flee**sserndess **vah**sserr
a private toilet	**eine eigene Toilette**	**igh**ner **igh**gerner toah**leh**ter
Could you put an extra bed in the room?	**Könnten Sie ein zusätzliches Bett ins Zimmer stellen?**	**kurn**tern zee ighn **tsoo**zehtslikhers beht ins **tsim**merr **shteh**lern

CHECKING OUT, see page 31

How much? *Wieviel?*

What's the price ...?	**Wieviel kostet es ...?**	vee**feel** **kos**tert ehss
per night	**pro Nacht**	proa nahkht
per week	**pro Woche**	proa **vo**kher
for bed and breakfast	**für Übernachtung mit Frühstück**	fewr ewberr**nahkh**tung mit **frew**shtewk
excluding meals	**ohne Mahlzeiten**	**oa**ner **maal**tsightern
for full board (A.P.)	**mit Vollpension**	mit **fol**pehnzioan
for half board (M.A.P.)	**mit Halbpension**	mit **hahlp**pehnzioan
Does that include ...?	**Ist ... inbegriffen?**	ist ... **in**begriffern
breakfast	**Frühstück**	**frew**shtewk
service	**Bedienung**	ber**dee**nung
Value-Added Tax (VAT)*	**Mehrwertsteuer**	**mayr**vayrtshtoyerr
Is there any reduction for children?	**Gibt es Ermäßigung für Kinder?**	gipt ehss ehr**mais**siggung fewr **kin**derr
Do you charge for the baby?	**Berechnen Sie etwas für das Baby?**	ber**rehkh**nern zee **eht**vahss fewr dahss "baby"
That's too expensive.	**Das ist zu teuer.**	dahss ist tsu **toy**err
Haven't you anything cheaper?	**Haben Sie nichts Billigeres?**	**haa**bern zee nikhts **bil**liggerrerss

Decision *Entscheidung*

May I see the room?	**Kann ich das Zimmer sehen?**	kahn ikh dahss **tsim**merr **zay**ern
That's fine. I'll take it.	**Gut, ich nehme es.**	goot ikh **nay**mer ehss
No, I don't like it.	**Nein, es gefällt mir nicht.**	nighn ehss ger**fehlt** meer nikht
It's too ...	**Es ist zu ...**	ehss ist tsu
cold/hot	**kalt/warm**	kahlt/vahrm
dark/small	**dunkel/klein**	**dun**kerl/klighn
noisy	**laut**	lowt
I asked for a room with a bath.	**Ich wollte ein Zimmer mit Bad.**	ikh **vol**ter ighn **tsim**merr mit baat

* Americans note: a type of sales tax in Germany and Austria

NUMBERS, see page 147

Do you have anything ...?	**Haben Sie etwas ...?**	**haa**bern zee **eht**vahss
better/bigger cheaper/quieter higher up/lower down	**Besseres/Größeres Billigeres/Ruhigeres weiter oben/weiter unten**	**beh**sserrerss/**grurs**serrerss **bi**lliggerrerss/**roo**iggerrerss **vigh**terr **oa**bern/**vigh**terr **un**tern
Do you have a room with a better view?	**Haben Sie ein Zimmer mit einer besseren Aussicht?**	**haa**bern zee ighn **tsim**merr mit **igh**nerr **beh**sserrern **ows**sikht

Registration *Anmeldung*

Upon arrival at a hotel or boarding-house you may be asked to fill in a registration form. (*Anmeldeschein*—**ahn**mehl-dershighn).

Name/Vorname	Name/First name
Wohnort/Straße/Nr.	Home address/Street/Number
Nationalität/Beruf	Nationality/Profession
Geburtsdatum/Geburtsort	Date/Place of birth
Letzter Aufenthaltsort/ Reiseziel	Coming from/Going to
Paßnummer	Passport number
Kraftfahrzeugnummer	Car number
Ort/Datum	Place/Date
Unterschrift	Signature

What does this mean?	**Was bedeutet das?**	vahss ber**doy**tert dahss

Kann ich Ihren Paß sehen?	May I see your passport?
Würden Sie bitte den Anmeldeschein ausfüllen?	Would you mind filling in the registration form?
Unterschreiben Sie hier, bitte.	Please sign here.
Wie lange bleiben Sie?	How long will you be staying?

We'll be staying ...	**Wir bleiben ...**	veer **bligh**bern
overnight only	**nur eine Nacht**	noor **igh**ner nahkht
a few days	**einige Tage**	**igh**nigger **taa**ger
a week (at least)	**(mindestens) eine Woche**	(**min**dersterns) **igh**ner **vo**kher
I don't know yet.	**Ich weiß es noch nicht.**	ikh vighss ehss nokh nikht

Hotel staff *Hotelpersonal*

hall porter	**der Portier**	derr por**tyayr**
maid	**das Zimmermädchen**	dahss **tsim**mermaitkhern
manager	**der Direktor**	derr dirr**ehk**tor
page (bellboy)	**der Page**	derr **paa**zher
porter	**der Hausdiener**	derr **hows**deenerr
receptionist	**der Empfangschef**	derr em**pfahngs**shehf
switchboard operator	**die Telefonistin**	dee taylayfoa**nis**tin
waiter	**der Kellner**	derr **kehl**nerr
waitress	**die Kellnerin**	dee **kehl**nerrin

If you want to address members of the staff, don't say *Herr, Frau* or *Fräulein,* but use an introductory phrase such as:

Excuse me. Could you please ...?	**Entschuldigung. Könnten Sie bitte ...?**	ehnt**shul**diggung. **kurn**tern zee **bit**ter

General requirements *Allgemeine Fragen*

What's my room number?	**Welche Zimmernummer habe ich?**	**vehl**kher **tsim**merrnummerr **haa**ber ikh
The key, please.	**Den Schlüssel, bitte.**	dayn **shlew**sserl **bit**ter
Where can I park my car?	**Wo kann ich meinen Wagen parken?**	voa kahn ikh **migh**nern **vaa**gern **pahr**kern
Does the hotel have a garage?	**Gibt es eine Hotelgarage?**	gipt ehss **igh**ner hot**tehl**-gahraazher
Will you have our luggage sent up?	**Bitte schicken Sie unser Gepäck hinauf.**	**bit**ter **shik**kern zee **un**zerr ger**pehk** hinn**owf**
I'd like to leave this in your safe.	**Ich möchte dies in Ihrem Safe lassen.**	ikh **murkh**ter deess in **ee**rerm "safe" **lah**ssern

TELLING THE TIME, see page 153

Is there a bath on this floor?	**Gibt es ein Bad auf dieser Etage?**	gipt ehss ighn baat owf deezerr ay**taa**zher
What's the voltage here?	**Welche Stromspannung haben Sie hier?**	**vehl**kher **shtroam**shpahnung **haa**bern zee heer
Where's the outlet for the shaver?	**Wo ist die Steckdose für den Rasierapparat?**	voa ist dee **shtehk**doazer fewr dayn rah**zeer**ahpahraat
Would you please wake me at ...?	**Würden Sie mich bitte um ... Uhr wecken?**	**vewr**dern zee mikh **bit**ter um ... oor **vehk**ern
Can we have breakfast in our room?	**Können wir im Zimmer frühstücken?**	**kur**nern veer im **tsim**merr **frew**shtewkern
Can you find me a ...?	**Können Sie mir ... besorgen?**	**kur**nern zee meer ... ber**zor**gern
babysitter	**einen Babysitter**	**igh**nern "babysitter"
secretary	**eine Sekretärin**	**igh**ner zaykray**tai**rin
typewriter	**eine Schreibmaschine**	**igh**ner **shrighp**mahsheener
May I have a/an/some ...?	**Kann ich ... haben?**	kahn ikh ... **haa**bern
ashtray	**einen Aschenbecher**	**igh**nern **ah**shernbehkherr
bath towel	**ein Badetuch**	ighn **baa**dertookh
(extra) blanket	**eine (extra) Decke**	**igh**ner (**ek**straa) **deh**ker
envelopes	**Briefumschläge**	**breef**umshlaiger
(more) hangers	**(noch) einige Kleiderbügel**	(nokh) **igh**nigger **kligh**derrbewgerl
hot-water bottle	**eine Wärmflasche**	**igh**ner **vehrm**flahsher
ice cubes	**Eiswürfel**	**ighs**vewrferl
needle and thread	**eine Nadel und etwas Faden**	**igh**ner **naa**derl unt **eht**vahss **faa**dern
(extra) pillow	**ein (extra) Kopfkissen**	**ighn**(**ek**straa) **kopf**kissern
reading-lamp	**eine Leselampe**	**igh**ner **lay**zerlahmper
soap	**Seife**	**zigh**fer
writing-paper	**Schreibpapier**	**shrighp**pahpeer
Where's the ...?	**Wo ist ...?**	voa ist
bathroom	**das Bad**	dahss baat
dining-room	**der Speisesaal**	derr **shpigh**zerzaal
emergency exit	**der Notausgang**	derr **noat**owsgahng
hairdresser's	**der Friseur**	derr fri**zurr**
lift (elevator)	**der Fahrstuhl**	derr **faar**shtool
television room	**der Fernsehraum**	derr **fehrn**zayrowm
toilet	**die Toilette**	dee toah**leh**ter

Telephone—Post (mail) *Telefon – Post*

Can you put me through to Vienna 12 34 56?	**Können Sie mich mit Wien 12 34 56 verbinden?**	**kur**nern zee mikh mit veen 12 34 56 fehr**bin**dern
Do you have stamps?	**Haben Sie Briefmarken?**	**haa**bern zee **breef**mahrkern
Would you post this for me, please?	**Würden Sie das bitte für mich aufgeben?**	**vewr**dern zee dahss **bit**ter fewr mikh **owf**gaybern
Is there any mail for me?	**Ist Post für mich da?**	ist post fewr mikh daa
Are there any messages for me?	**Hat jemand eine Nachricht für mich hinterlassen?**	haht **yay**mahnt **igh**ner **naakh**rikht fewr mikh hinterr**lah**ssern
How much are my telephone charges?	**Wie hoch ist meine Telefonrechnung?**	vee hoakh ist **migh**ner taylay**foan**rehkhnung

Difficulties *Schwierigkeiten*

The ... doesn't work.	**... funktioniert nicht.**	... funktsion**neert** nikht
air conditioner	**die Klimaanlage**	dee **klee**mahahnlaager
fan	**der Ventilator**	derr vehntil**laa**tor
heating	**die Heizung**	dee **high**tsung
light	**das Licht**	dahss likht
radio	**das Radio**	dahss **raa**dio
television	**der Fernseher**	derr **fehrn**zayerr
The tap (faucet) is dripping.	**Der Wasserhahn tropft.**	derr **vah**sserrhaan tropft
There's no hot water.	**Es gibt kein warmes Wasser.**	ehs gipt kighn **vahr**mers **vah**sserr
The wash-basin is blocked.	**Das Waschbecken ist verstopft.**	dahss **vahsh**behkern ist fehr**shtopft**
The window/The door is jammed.	**Das Fenster/Die Tür klemmt.**	dahss **fehn**sterr/dee tewr klehmt
The curtain is stuck.	**Der Vorhang klemmt.**	derr **foar**hahng klehmt
The bulb is burned out.	**Die Birne ist kaputt.**	dee **beer**ner ist kah**put**
My room has not been made up.	**Mein Zimmer ist nicht gemacht.**	mighn **tsim**merr ist nikht ger**mahkht**

POST OFFICE AND TELEPHONE, see page 132

The ... is broken.	**... ist kaputt.**	... ist kah**put**
blind	**das Rollo**	dahss **rollo**
lamp	**die Lampe**	dee **lahm**per
plug	**der Stecker**	derr **shtehk**err
shutter	**der Fensterladen**	derr **fehn**sterrlaadern
switch	**der Schalter**	derr **shahl**terr
Can you get it repaired?	**Können Sie es reparieren lassen?**	**kur**nern zee ehss rehpah**ree**rern **lah**ssern

Laundry—Dry cleaner's *Wäscherei – Reinigung*

I want these clothes ...	**Ich möchte diese Kleider ... lassen.**	ikh **murkh**ter **dee**zer **kligh**derr ... **lah**ssern
cleaned	**reinigen**	**righ**niggern
ironed	**bügeln**	**bew**gerln
pressed	**dampfbügeln**	**dahmpf**bewgerln
washed	**waschen**	**vah**shern
When will they be ready?	**Wann sind sie fertig?**	vahn zint zee **fehr**tikh
I need them ...	**Ich brauche sie ...**	ikh **brow**kher zee
today	**heute**	**hoy**ter
tonight	**heute abend**	**hoy**ter **aa**bernt
tomorrow	**morgen**	**mor**gern
before Friday	**vor Freitag**	foar **fright**aag
Can you ... this?	**Können Sie das ...?**	**kur**nern zee dahss
mend	**ausbessern**	**ows**behsserrn
patch	**flicken**	**flik**kern
stitch	**nähen**	**nai**ern
Can you sew on this button?	**Können Sie diesen Knopf annähen?**	**kur**nern zee **dee**zern knopf **ahn**naiern
Can you get this stain out?	**Können Sie diesen Fleck entfernen?**	**kur**nern zee **dee**zern flehk ehnt**fehr**nern
Is my laundry ready?	**Ist meine Wäsche fertig?**	ist **migh**ner **veh**sher **fehr**tikh
This isn't mine.	**Das gehört nicht mir.**	dahss ger**hurrt** nikht meer
There's one piece missing.	**Es fehlt ein Stück.**	ehss faylt ighn shtewk
There's a hole in this.	**Da ist ein Loch drin.**	daa ist ighn lokh drin

DAYS OF THE WEEK, see page 151

Hairdresser's—Barber's *Damen- und Herrenfriseur*

Is there a hairdresser/ beauty salon in the hotel?	**Gibt es einen Friseur/ Kosmetiksalon im Hotel?**	gipt ehss **igh**nern fri**zurr**/ kos**may**tikzahlong im hot**tehl**
Can I make an appointment for sometime on Thursday?	**Kann ich mich für Donnerstag anmelden?**	kahn ikh mikh fewr **don**nerrstaag **ahn**mehldern
I'd like it cut and shaped.	**Schneiden und Legen, bitte.**	**shnigh**dern unt **lay**gern **bit**ter
The parting (part) left/right, please.	**Den Scheitel links/ rechts, bitte.**	dayn **shigh**terl links/ rehkhts **bit**ter
I want a haircut, please.	**Haare schneiden, bitte.**	**haa**rer **shnigh**dern **bit**ter
bleach	**eine Aufhellung**	**igh**ner **owf**hehlung
blow-dry	**fönen**	**fur**nern
colour rinse	**eine Farbspülung**	**igh**ner **fahrp**shpewlung
dye	**färben**	**fehr**bern
face-pack	**eine Gesichtsmaske**	**igh**ner ger**zikhts**mahsker
manicure	**eine Maniküre**	**igh**ner **mah**nikkewrer
permanent wave	**eine Dauerwelle**	**igh**ner **dow**errvehler
setting lotion	**ein Haarfestiger**	ighn **haar**fehstiggerr
shampoo and set	**Waschen und Legen**	**vah**shern unt **lay**gern
with a fringe (bangs)	**mit Ponyfransen**	mit **pon**nifrahnzern
I'd like a shampoo for ... hair.	**Ein Haarwaschmittel für ... Haar, bitte.**	ighn **haar**vahshmitterl fewr ... haar **bit**ter
normal/dry/ greasy (oily)	**normales/trockenes/ fettiges**	nor**maa**lerss/**trok**kernerss/ **feh**tiggerss
Do you have a colour chart?	**Haben Sie eine Farbtabelle?**	**haa**bern zee **igh**ner **fahrp**tahbehler
Don't cut it too short.	**Nicht zu kurz schneiden.**	nikht tsu koorts **shnigh**dern
A little more off the ...	**Bitte ... etwas kürzer.**	**bit**ter ... **eht**vahss **kewr**tserr
back	**hinten**	**hin**tern
neck	**im Nacken**	im **nah**kern
sides	**an den Seiten**	ahn dayn **zigh**tern
top	**oben**	**oa**bern
I don't want any hairspray.	**Kein Haarspray, bitte.**	kighn **haar**shpray **bit**ter
I'd like a shave.	**Rasieren, bitte.**	rah**zee**rern **bit**ter

DAYS OF THE WEEK, see page 151

Would you please trim my ...?	**Stutzen Sie mir bitte ...**	**shtut**sern zee meer **bit**ter
beard	**den Bart**	dayn baart
moustache	**den Schnurrbart**	dayn **shnoor**baart
sideboards (sideburns)	**die Koteletten**	dee kot**leh**tern

Checking out *Abreise*

May I please have my bill?	**Kann ich bitte die Rechnung haben?**	kahn ikh **bit**ter dee **rehkh**nung **haa**bern
I'm leaving early tomorrow. Please have my bill ready.	**Ich reise morgen früh ab. Bereiten Sie bitte meine Rechnung vor.**	ikh **righ**zer **mor**gern frew ahp. ber**righ**tern zee **bit**ter **migh**ner **rehkh**nung foar
I must leave at once.	**Ich muß sofort abreisen.**	ikh muss zoa**fort** **ahp**righzern
Is everything included?	**Ist alles inbegriffen?**	ist **ah**lerss **in**bergriffern
Can I pay by credit card?	**Kann ich mit Kreditkarte bezahlen?**	kahn ikh mit kreh**dit**kahrter **bert**saalern
You've made a mistake in this bill, I think.	**Ich glaube, Sie haben sich verrechnet.**	ikh **glow**ber zee **haa**bern zikh fehr**rehkh**nert
Can you get us a taxi?	**Können Sie uns ein Taxi bestellen?**	**kur**nern zee uns ighn **tah**ksi ber**shteh**lern
Could you have our luggage brought down, please?	**Würden Sie bitte unser Gepäck herunterbringen lassen?**	**vewr**dern zee **bit**ter **un**zerr ger**pehk** **hehrun**terrbringern **lah**ssern
We're in a great hurry.	**Wir haben es sehr eilig.**	veer **haa**bern ehss zayr **igh**likh
Here's the forwarding address.	**Hier ist meine Nachsendeadresse.**	heer ist **migh**ner **naakh**zehnderahdrehsser
You have my home address.	**Sie haben meine Wohnadresse.**	zee **haa**bern **migh**ner **voan**ahdrehsser
It's been a very enjoyable stay.	**Es war ein sehr angenehmer Aufenthalt.**	ehss vaar ighn zayr **ahn**ger-naymerr **owf**ehnthahlt

TIPPING, see inside back-cover

Camping

There are plenty of authorized camp sites in Germany, many with excellent facilities. Austria and Switzerland also have well-equipped camp sites, some of them high up in the mountains. For information apply to any Tourist Office.

Is there a camp site near here?	**Gibt es hier in der Nähe einen Campingplatz?**	gipt ehss heer in derr **naier ighnern** **kehm**pingplahts
Can we camp here?	**Können wir hier zelten?**	**kur**nern veer heer **tsehl**tern
Have you room for a tent/caravan (trailer)?	**Haben Sie Platz für ein Zelt/einen Wohnwagen?**	**haa**bern zee plahts fewr ighn tsehlt/**igh**nern **voan**vaagern
Is there/Are there (a) ...?	**Gibt es ...?**	gipt ehss
drinking water	**Trinkwasser**	**trink**vahsserr
electricity	**Stromanschluß**	**shtroam**ahnshluss
playground	**einen Spielplatz**	**igh**nern **shpeel**plahts
restaurant	**ein Restaurant**	ighn rehstor**rahng**
shopping facilities	**Einkaufsmöglichkeiten**	**ighn**kowfsmurglikhkightern
swimming pool	**ein Schwimmbad**	ighn **shvim**baat
What's the charge ...?	**Wie hoch sind die Gebühren ...?**	vee hoakh zint dee ger**bew**rern
per day	**pro Tag**	proa taag
per person	**pro Person**	proa pehr**zoan**
for a car	**für ein Auto**	fewr ighn **ow**to
for a caravan (trailer)	**für einen Wohnwagen**	fewr **igh**nern **voan**vaagern
for a tent	**für ein Zelt**	fewr ighn tsehlt
Is the tourist tax included?	**Ist die Kurtaxe inbegriffen?**	ist dee **koor**tahkser **in**bergriffern
Where are the showers/toilets?	**Wo sind die Duschen/die Toiletten?**	voa zint dee **du**shern/dee toah**leh**tern
Where can I get butane gas?	**Wo kann ich Butangas bekommen?**	voa kahn ikh bu**ttaan**gaass ber**kom**mern
Is there a youth hostel near here?	**Gibt es hier irgendwo eine Jugendherberge?**	gipt ehss heer **eer**gerntvoa **igh**ner **yoo**gernthehrbehrger

CAMPING EQUIPMENT, see page 106

Eating out

There are many types of places where you can eat and drink in Germany, Austria and Switzerland.

Beisel (**bigh**zerl) — The Austrian equivalent to a *Gasthaus*.

Bierhalle (**beer**hahler) — Beer hall; besides beer served from huge barrels, you'll also be able to order hot dishes, sausages, salads and pretzels. The best-known beer halls are those in Munich which has a giant beer festival *(Oktoberfest)* annually in late September.

Bierstube (**beer**shtoober) — The nearest equivalent to an English pub or an American tavern though the atmosphere may be very different; usually only serves a few "dishes of the day".

Café (kah**fay**) — Coffee shop; besides coffee, you'll be able to get pastries, snacks and drinks. There's a small dance floor in a *Tanzcafé*.

Gasthaus/Gasthof (**gahs**thowss/**gahst**hoaf) — Inn, usually in the country. It offers home-cooking and a folksy atmosphere.

Gaststätte (**gahst**shtehter) — Another word for *Restaurant*.

Kaffeehaus (kah**fay**howss) — The Austrian equivalent to a *Café*.

Konditorei (kondeetoa**righ**) — A pastry shop; will often have a salon for coffee and pastries.

Milchbar (**milkh**baar) — A bar serving mainly plain and flavoured milk drinks with pastries. Also called a *Milchstübl*.

Raststätte (**rahst**shtehter) — Roadside restaurant; also called a *Rasthof* in Austria; it's usually found on a motorway (expressway). Lodging and service-station facilities are on the premises.

Ratskeller (**rahts**kehlerr) — A restaurant in the cellar of the town-hall (often a very historic, old building); food is generally excellent.

Restaurant (rehstorr**ahng**) — These are generally found only in urban areas. Menus often cater to foreign visitors as well as offering numerous local specialities.

Schnellbuffet (**shnehl**bewfay) — A snack bar; often with counter service.

Schnellimbiß (**shnehl**imbiss) — Snack bar; the English term is also seen. The principal fare is beer and sausages. A sausage stand *(Würstchenstand)* is often quite similar.

Tea-room ("tea-room") — The Swiss equivalent to a *Café*.

Weinstube (**vighn**shtoober) — A cozy type of restaurant found in wine-producing districts where you can sample new wine with simple hot dishes and snacks. In Austria, it's called a *Heuriger* and is identified by a wreath hanging over the portal.

Meal times *Essenszeiten*

Breakfast (*das Frühstück*—dahss **frew**shtewk) is served from 7 a.m. to 10 a.m. and is generally included in the hotel arrangement.

Lunch (*das Mittagessen*—dahss **mit**tahgehssern) is generally served from 11.30 a.m. until 2 p.m.

Dinner (*das Abendessen*—dahss **aa**berntehssern) is served from 6.30 to 8.30 p.m., in large restaurants to 10 or 11 p.m. After this it's usually a case of cold snacks or hot sausages only.

Eating habits *Eßgewohnheiten*

Germans start the day early with a meal that is somewhat more substantial than the typical "continental" breakfast, and they like to eat their main meal in the middle of the day. Supper is generally a slightly more copious version of breakfast—cold meat and cheese, with the addition of a salad. Most restaurants will, however, serve a three course dinner in the evening.

On weekends Germans often eat an afternoon snack. It can be either coffee or tea with pastries, or cold meat and cheese.

Fellow diners usually wish each other *"Mahlzeit"* or *"Guten Appetit"*.

German cuisine *Die deutsche Küche*

German cuisine has undergone many changes in the postwar years. Non-fattening, healthy fare has become more popular, and the influence of French, Italian, Greek, Chinese and other cuisines is remarkable. However, rich hearty dishes, mostly with pork and potatoes, are still served. Each region has its own specialities, and almost each town its own beer (or wine), but everywhere you'll find an extraordinary range of sausages, smoked ham, soused fish and many kinds of good bread. Not to mention *Sauerkraut, Schnitzel, Spätzle, Frankfurter, Frikadellen, Rollmops* ... And if you like game, Germany is the place.

Möchten Sie etwas essen?	Would you like to eat something?
Was nehmen Sie?	What would you like?
Ich empfehle Ihnen ...	I recommend ...
Was trinken Sie?	What would you like to drink?
Möchten Sie ...?	Do you want ...?
... haben wir nicht.	We haven't got ...

Hungry? *Hungrig?*

I'm hungry/I'm thirsty.	**Ich habe Hunger/ Ich habe Durst.**	ikh **haa**ber **hun**ger/ikh **haa**ber doorst
Can you recommend a good restaurant?	**Können Sie mir ein gutes Restaurant empfehlen?**	**kur**nern zee meer ighn **goo**terss rehstor**rahng** ehm**pfay**lern
Is there an inexpensive restaurant around here?	**Gibt es in der Nähe ein preiswertes Restaurant?**	gibt ehss in derr **nai**er ighn **prighs**vehrterss rehstor**rahng**

If you want to be sure of getting a table in well-known restaurants, it may be better to telephone in advance.

I'd like to reserve a table for 4.	**Ich möchte einen Tisch für 4 Personen reservieren lassen.**	ikh **murkh**ter **ighn**ern tish fewr 4 pehr**zoa**nern rehzehr**vee**rern **lah**ssern
We'll come at 8.	**Wir kommen um 8 Uhr.**	veer **kom**mern um 8 oor
Could we have a table ...?	**Können wir einen Tisch ... haben?**	**kur**nern veer **ighn**ern tish ... **haa**bern
in the corner	**in der Ecke**	in derr **eh**ker
by the window	**am Fenster**	ahm **fehn**sterr
outside	**im Freien**	im **frigh**ern
on the terrace	**auf der Terrasse**	owf derr teh**rah**sser
in a nonsmoking area	**in der Nichtraucher-ecke**	in derr **nikht**rowkherr-ehker

Asking and ordering *Fragen und Bestellen*

Waiter/Waitress!	**Herr Ober/Fräulein, bitte!**	hehr **oa**berr/**froy**lighn **bit**ter
I'd like something to eat/drink.	**Ich möchte gerne essen/etwas trinken.**	ikh **murkh**ter **gehr**ner **eh**ssern/**eht**vahss **trin**kern
May I have the menu, please?	**Kann ich bitte die Speisekarte haben?**	kahn ikh **bit**ter dee **shpigh**zerkahrter **haa**bern
Do you have a set menu/local dishes?	**Haben Sie ein Gedeck/ hiesige Gerichte?**	**haa**bern zee ighn ger**dehk**/ **hee**zigger ger**rikh**ter
What do you recommend?	**Was würden Sie mir empfehlen?**	vahss **vewr**dern zee meer ehm**pfay**lern
I'd like ...	**Ich hätte gern ...**	ikh **heh**ter gehrn
Could we have a/ an ..., please?	**Könnten wir bitte ... haben?**	**kurn**tern veer **bit**ter ... **haa**bern
ashtray	**einen Aschenbecher**	**igh**nern **ah**shernbehkherr
cup	**eine Tasse**	**igh**ner **tah**sser
fork	**eine Gabel**	**igh**ner **gaa**berl
glass	**ein Glas**	ighn glaass
knife	**ein Messer**	ighn **meh**sserr
napkin (serviette)	**eine Serviette**	**igh**ner sehr**vieh**ter
plate	**einen Teller**	**igh**nern **teh**lerr
spoon	**einen Löffel**	**igh**nern **lur**ferl
May I have some ...?	**Könnte ich etwas ... haben?**	**kurn**ter ikh **eht**vahss ... **haa**bern
bread	**Brot**	broat
butter	**Butter**	**but**terr

lemon	**Zitrone**	tsi**troa**ner
mustard	**Senf**	zehnf
pepper	**Pfeffer**	**pfeh**ferr
salt	**Salz**	zahlts
seasoning	**Würze**	**vewr**tser
sugar	**Zucker**	**tsuk**kerr

Some useful expressions for dieters and special requirements:

I'm on a diet.	**Ich muß Diät leben.**	ikh muss dee**ait lay**bern
I don't drink alcohol.	**Ich trinke keinen Alkohol.**	ikh **trin**ker kighnern **ahl**kohoal
I mustn't eat food containing ...	**Ich darf nichts essen, was ... enthält.**	ikh dahrf nikhts **eh**ssern vahss ... ehnt**hehlt**
flour/fat	**Mehl/Fett**	mayl/feht
salt/sugar	**Salz/Zucker**	zahlts/**tsuk**kerr
Do you have ... for diabetics?	**Haben Sie ... für Diabetiker?**	**haa**bern zee ... fewr deeah**bay**tikkerr
cakes	**Kuchen**	**koo**khern
fruit juice	**Fruchtsaft**	**frukht**zahft
special menu	**ein Spezialmenü**	ighn shpeh**tsiahl**maynew
Do you have vegetarian dishes?	**Haben Sie vegetarische Gerichte?**	**haa**bern zee vehgeh**taa**risher ger**rikh**ter
Could I have cheese/fruit instead of the dessert?	**Könnte ich statt der Süßspeise Käse/Obst haben?**	**kurn**ter ikh shtaht derr **zews**shpighzer **kai**zer/opst **haa**bern
Can I have an artificial sweetener?	**Kann ich Süßstoff haben?**	kahn ikh **zews**shtof **haa**bern

And ...

I'd like some more.	**Ich möchte etwas mehr.**	ikh **murkh**ter **eht**vahss mayr
Can I have more ..., please.	**Kann ich noch ... haben, bitte?**	kahn ikh nokh ... **haa**bern **bit**ter
Just a small portion.	**Nur eine kleine Portion.**	noor **igh**ner **kligh**ner por**tsioan**
Nothing more, thanks.	**Nichts mehr, danke.**	nikhts mayr **dahn**ker
Where are the toilets?	**Wo ist die Toilette?**	voa ist dee toah**leh**ter

Breakfast *Frühstück*

A German breakfast is a rather substantial meal. You may be served cold meat, cheese, a variety of breads—*Schwarzbrot, Vollkornbrot, Roggenbrot, Weißbrot* (black, wholegrain, rye, white)—and rolls *(Brötchen* or *Semmeln)* or croissants *(Hörnchen)* with butter and jam, accompanied by coffee or tea.

I'd like breakfast, please.	**Ich möchte frühstücken, bitte.**	ikh **murkh**ter **frew**-shtewkern **bit**ter
I'll have a/an/some ...	**Ich hätte gern ...**	ikh **heh**ter gehrn
bacon and eggs	**Spiegeleier mit Speck**	**shpee**gerligherr mit shpehk
boiled egg	**ein gekochtes Ei**	ighn ger**kokh**terss igh
soft/hard	**weich/hartgekocht**	vighkh/**hahrt**gerkokht
cereal	**Getreideflocken**	ger**trigh**derflokkern
cheese	**Käse**	**kai**zer
eggs	**Eier**	**igh**err
fried eggs	**Spiegeleier**	**shpee**gerligherr
scrambled eggs	**Rühreier**	**rewr**igherr
grapefruit juice	**Grapefruitsaft**	**grehp**frootzahft
ham and eggs	**Spiegeleier mit Schinken**	**shpee**gerligherr mit **shin**kern
jam	**Marmelade**	mahrmeh**laa**der
marmalade	**Apfelsinenmarmelade**	ahpferl**zee**nern-mahrmeh**laa**der
orange juice	**Orangensaft**	or**rahng**zhernzahft
toast	**Toast**	toast
May I have some ...?	**Kann ich ... haben?**	kahn ikh ... **haa**bern
bread	**Brot**	broat
butter	**Butter**	**but**terr
(hot) chocolate	**(heiße) Schokolade**	(**high**sser) shokko**llaa**der
coffee	**Kaffee**	kah**fay**
decaffeinated	**koffeinfreien Kaffee**	koffeh**een**frighern kah**fay**
black	**schwarzen Kaffee**	**shvahrt**sern kah**fay**
with milk	**Milchkaffee**	**milkh**kahfay
honey	**Honig**	**hoa**nikh
milk	**Milch**	milkh
hot/cold	**heiße/kalte**	**high**sser/**kahl**ter
rolls	**Brötchen**	**brurt**khern
tea	**Tee**	tay
with milk/lemon	**mit Milch/Zitrone**	mit milkh/tsi**troa**ner
(hot) water	**(heißes) Wasser**	(**high**sserss) **vah**sserr

What's on the menu? *Was steht auf der Speisekarte?*

Most restaurants display a menu *(Speisekarte)* outside. Besides the à la carte menu, they'll usually offer one or more set menus *(Menü* or *Gedeck)*. Value-added tax—a type of sales tax *(Mehrwertsteuer* or *Mwst)*—and a service charge *(Bedienung)* are usually included.

Under the headings below you'll find alphabetical lists of dishes that might be offered on a German menu, with their English equivalent. You can simply show the book to the waiter. If you want some cheese, for instance, let *him* point to what's available on the appropriate list. Use pages 36 and 37 for ordering in general.

Reading the menu *Die Speisekarte lesen*

Tagesgedeck	Set menu of the day
Tagesgericht	Dish of the day
Spezialität des Hauses	Speciality of the house
Unser Küchenchef empfiehlt ...	The chef recommends ...
Nach ... art	... style
Hausgemacht	Home-made
Dasselbe mit ...	The same served with ...
Nur auf Bestellung	Made to order
Alle Preise sind inklusive Bedienung und Mehrwertsteuer	Service charge and VAT (sales tax) included
... im Preis inbegriffen	... included in the price
Nach Wahl	At your choice
Extraaufschlag	Extra charge

Beilagen	**bigh**laagern	accompaniments
Eierspeisen	**igh**ershpighzern	egg dishes
Eintopfgerichte	**ighn**topfgerrikhter	stews
Eis	ighss	ice-cream
Fischgerichte	**fish**gerrikhter	fish
Fleischgerichte	**flighsh**gerrikhter	meat
Glace	**glah**sser	ice-cream
Gemüse	ger**mew**zer	vegetables
Geflügel	ger**flew**gerl	poultry
Getränke	ger**train**ker	drinks
Hauptgerichte	**howpt**gerrikhter	main course
Käse	**kai**zer	cheese
Meeresfrüchte	**may**rersfrewkhter	seafood
Nachspeisen/ Nachtisch	**naakh**shpighzern/ **naakh**tish	desserts
Obst	oapst	fruit
Reisgerichte	**righs**gerrikhter	rice
Salate	zah**laa**ter	salads
Suppen	**zup**pern	soups
Süßspeisen	**zews**shpighzern	desserts
Teigwaren	**tighk**vaarern	pasta
Vom Rost	fom roast	grilled (broiled)
Vorspeisen	**foar**shpighzern	first course
Wein	vighn	wine
Wild	vilt	game

Appetizers *Vorspeisen*

If you feel like something to whet your appetite, choose carefully, for the German appetizer can be filling. Starters may also be listed on the menu under *Kleine Gerichte* or *Kalte Platten*.

I'd like an appetizer.	**Ich hätte gern eine Vorspeise.**	ikh **heh**ter gehrn **igh**ner **foar**shpighzer
Aal (in Gelee)	aal in zher**lay**	(jellied) eel
Appetithäppchen	ahpeh**teet**hehpkhern	canapés
Artischocken	ahrti**shok**kern	artichoke
Austern	**ow**sterrn	oysters
Bündnerfleisch	**bewnd**nerrflighsh	cured, dried beef served in thin slices
Bückling	**bewk**ling	bloater, kipper
Fleischpastete	**flighsh**pahstayter	meat loaf
Froschschenkel	**frosh**shehnkerl	frog's legs
Gänseleberpastete	**gehn**zerlayberr-pahstayter	pâté, goose liver purée
Hering	**hay**ring	herring
Hummer	**hum**merr	lobster
Hummerkrabben	**hum**merrkrahbern	large prawns
Käsehäppchen	**kai**zerhehpkhern	cheese sticks
Krabben	**krah**bern	prawns, shrimps
Krebs	krayps	river crayfish
Lachs	lahks	salmon
Languste	lahng**gus**ter	spiny lobster
Makrele	mah**kray**ler	mackerel
Muscheln	**mus**herln	mussels
Pilze	**pil**tser	mushrooms
Räucheraal	**roy**kherraal	smoked eel
Räucherhering	**roy**kherrhayring	smoked herring
Rollmops	**rol**mops	soused herring
Rohschinken	**roa**shinkern	cured ham
Russische Eier	russisher **igh**err	hard-boiled eggs with mayonnaise
Sardellen	zahr**deh**lern	anchovies
Sardinen	zahr**dee**nern	sardines
Schinken	**shin**kern	ham
Schnecken	**shneh**kern	snails
Spargelspitzen	**shpaar**gerlshpitsern	asparagus tips
Thunfisch	**toon**fish	tunny, tuna
Wurst	voorst	sausage
Wurstplatte	**voorst**plahter	assorted cold cuts

Bismarckhering (**bis**mahrkhayring)	soused herring with onions
Frisch geräucherte Gänsebrust auf Toast (frish ger**roy**kherrter **gehn**zerbrust owf toast)	freshly smoked breast of goose on toast
Hoppel-Poppel (**hop**perl-**pop**perl)	scrambled eggs with diced sausages or bacon
Königinpastete (**kur**nigginpahstayter)	puff-pastry shell filled with diced meat and mushrooms
Matjeshering (**mah**tyehshayring)	salted young herring
Matjesfilet nach Hausfrauenart (**mah**tyehsfillay nahkh **hows**frowernahrt)	fillets of herring with apples and onions
Hausgemachte Rehpastete (**hows**germakhkter **ray**pahstayter)	home-made venison meatloaf
Schinkenröllchen mit Spargel (**shin**kernrurlkhern mit **shpahr**gerl)	rolled ham with asparagus filling
Strammer Max (**shtrah**merr mahkss)	slice of bread with highly spiced minced pork served with fried eggs and onions

Soups and stews *Suppen und Eintopfgerichte*

German soup can be hearty fare and particularly welcome on a cold day. *Eintopf* is a stew and will usually be a meal in itself.

I'd like some soup.	**Ich möchte gern eine Suppe.**	ikh **murkh**ter gehrn **igh**ner **zup**per
Aalsuppe	**aal**zupper	eel soup
Bauernsuppe	**bow**errnzupper	cabbage and frankfurter soup
Bohnensuppe	**boa**nernzupper	bean soup with bacon
Bouillon	bool**yong**	clear soup
Erbsensuppe	**ehrp**zernzupper	pea soup
Fischsuppe	**fish**zupper	fish soup
Fischbeuschelsuppe	**fish**boysherlzupper	fish roe and vegetable soup
Fridattensuppe	frid**dah**ternzupper	broth with pancake strips

Frühlingssuppe	**frew**lingszupper	spring vegetable soup
Grießnockerlsuppe	**grees**nokkerrlzupper	semolina-dumpling soup
Gulaschsuppe	**goo**lahshzupper	spiced soup of stewed beef
Hühnerbrühe	**hew**nerrbrewer	chicken broth
Kartoffelsuppe	**kahr**tofferlzupper	potato soup
(Semmel-) Knödelsuppe	(**zeh**merl-) **knur**derlzupper	dumpling soup
Königinsuppe	**kur**nigginzupper	soup with beef, sour cream and almonds
Kraftbrühe	**krahft**brewer	beef consommé
mit Ei	mit igh	with raw egg
mit Einlage	mit **ighn**laager	with a garnish
Leberknödelsuppe	**lay**berrknurderlzupper	liver-dumpling soup
Linsensuppe	**lin**zernzupper	lentil soup
Nudelsuppe	**noo**derlzupper	noodle soup
Ochsenschwanz-suppe	**ok**sernshvahntszupper	oxtail soup
Pichelsteiner Eintopf	**pi**kherlshtighnerr **ighn**topf	meat and vegetable stew
Schildkrötensuppe	**shilt**krurternzupper	turtle soup
Serbische Bohnensuppe	**zehr**bisher **boa**nernzupper	spiced bean soup
Tomatensuppe	tom**maa**ternzupper	tomato soup
Zwiebelsuppe	**tsvee**berlzupper	onion soup

Backerbsensuppe (**bahk**ehrpsernzupper) — broth served with pea-sized balls of pasta

Basler Mehlsuppe (**baa**slerr **mayl**zupper) — flour soup with grated cheese (Swiss)

Labskaus (**laap**skowss) — thick stew of minced and marinated meat with mashed potatoes

Fish and seafood *Fisch und Meeresfrüchte*

I'd like some fish.	**Ich hätte gern Fisch.**	ikh **heh**ter gehrn fish
What kind of seafood do you have?	**Welche Meeresfrüchte haben Sie?**	**vehl**kher **may**rersfrewkhter **haa**bern zee
Aal	aal	eel
Austern	**ow**sterrn	oysters
Barsch	bahrsh	freshwater perch
Brasse/Brachse	**brah**sser/**brahk**ser	bream

Dorsch	dorsh	cod
Egli	**eh**glee	perch
Felchen	**fehl**khern	kind of trout
Fischfrikadellen	**fish**frikkahdehlern	fish croquettes
Forelle	fo**reh**ler	trout
Flunder	**flun**derr	flounder
Garnelen	gahr**nay**lern	prawns/shrimps
Hecht	hehkht	pike
Heilbutt	**highl**but	halibut
Hering	**hay**ring	herring
Hummer	**hum**merr	lobster
Jakobsmuscheln	**yaa**kopsmusherln	scallops
Kabeljau	**kaa**berlyow	cod
Kaisergranate	**kigh**zerrgrahnahter	kind of scampi
Karpfen	**kahr**pfern	carp
Krebs	krayps	river crayfish
Lachs	lahks	salmon
Languste	lahng**goo**ster	spiny lobster
Makrele	mah**kray**ler	mackerel
Muscheln	**mu**sherln	clams/mussels
Rotbarsch	**roat**bahrsh	red sea-bass
Salm	zahlm	salmon
Schellfisch	**shehl**fish	haddock
Scholle	**shol**ler	plaice
Seebarsch	**zay**bahrsh	sea bass
Seebutt	**zay**but	brill
Seezunge	**zay**tsunger	sole
Sprotten	**shprot**tern	sprats
Steinbutt	**shtighn**but	turbot
Stint	shtint	smelt
Stör	shturr	sturgeon
Zander	**tsahn**derr	(giant) pike-perch

baked	**gebacken**	ger**bah**kern
boiled in bouillon	**blau**	blow
breaded	**paniert**	pah**neert**
fried	**gebraten**	ger**braa**tern
deep-fried	**im schwimmenden Fett gebacken**	im **shvim**merndern feht ger**bah**kern
grilled	**gegrillt**	ger**grilt**
marinated	**mariniert**	mahrin**neert**
sautéed (in butter)	**(in Butter) geschwenkt**	(in **but**terr) ger**shvehnkt**
smoked	**geräuchert**	ger**roy**khert
steamed	**gedämpft**	ger**dehmpft**

Meat *Fleisch*

Bear in mind that the Germans most often write in one word what would take us two or more. For example, *Rindszunge* is *Rinds-* (beef) and *-zunge* (tongue) or *Kalbsbrust* is breast of veal. So you may have to look under two entries in the following lists to fully understand what's on the menu.

I'd like some ...	**Ich hätte gern ...**	ikh **heh**ter gehrn
beef	**Rindfleisch**	**rint**flighsh
lamb	**Lammfleisch**	**lahm**flighsh
mutton	**Hammelfleisch**	**hah**merlflighsh
pork	**Schweinefleisch**	**shvigh**nerflighsh
veal	**Kalbfleisch**	**kahlp**flighsh

Bauernomelett	**bow**errnomleht	diced bacon and onion omelet
(deutsches) Beefsteak	(**doy**tsherss) **beef**-stayk	hamburger
Beuschel	**boy**sherl	veal offal with lemon sauce
-braten	-braatern	joint, roast
-brust	-brust	breast
Eisbein	**ighs**bighn	pickled pig's knuckle
Faschiertes	fah**sheer**terss	minced meat
Filetsteak	fil**lay**stayk	beef steak
Fleischkäse	**flighsh**kaizer	type of bologna sausage
Frikadellen	frikkah**deh**lern	meat patties
Geschnetzeltes	ger**shneh**tserlterss	chipped veal served in wine sauce
Geselchtes	ger**zehlkh**terss	smoked or salted meat usually pork
Gulasch	**goo**lahsh	gulash; chunks of beef stewed in a rich paprika gravy
Hackbraten	**hahk**braatern	meatloaf
-hachse/haxe	-hahkser	shank
-herz	-hehrts	heart
Kasseler Rippenspeer	**kah**ssehlerr **rip**pernshpayr	smoked pork chops
-klößchen	-klurskhern	meatballs
-kotelett	-kotleht	cutlet, chop
Krenfleisch	**krayn**flighsh	pork, usually brawn, served with shredded vegetables and horseradish

Kutteln	**kut**terln	tripe
Leber	**lay**berr	liver
Leberkäse	**lay**berrkaizer	type of meatloaf
Lenden-	**lehn**dern	fillet of beef (tenderloin)
Nieren	**nee**rern	kidneys
Nierenstück	**nee**rernshtewk	loin
-plätzli	-plehtslee	escalope
Pökelfleisch	**pur**kerlflighsh	marinated meat
Rippensteak	**rip**pernshtayk	rib steak
Rostbraten	**roast**braatern	rumpsteak
Rouladen	roo**laa**dern	slices of beef or veal filled, rolled and braised (in brown gravy)
Sauerbraten	**zowerr**braatern	marinated, brased beef
Schinken	**shin**kern	ham
Schlachtplatte	**shlahkht**plahter	platter of various sausages and cold meats
Schnitzel	**shnit**serl	escalope
Spanferkel	**shpaan**fehrkerl	suck(l)ing pig
Speck	shpehk	bacon
-spießchen	-shpeeskhern	skewered meat
Sülze	**zewl**tser	brawn (headcheese)
Wiener Schnitzel	**vee**nerr **shnit**serl	breaded veal escalope
-zunge	-tsunger	tongue

Here are some hearty dishes you'll certainly want to try:

Bauernschmaus (**bow**errnshmowss)	sauerkraut garnished with boiled bacon, smoked pork, sausages, dumplings, potatoes (Austrian)
Berner Platte (**behr**nerr **plah**ter)	sauerkraut (or green beans) liberally garnished with pork chops, boiled bacon and beef, sausages, tongue and ham (Swiss)
Holsteiner Schnitzel (**hol**shtighnerr **shnit**serl)	breaded veal escalope topped with fried egg, garnished with vegetables and usually accompanied by bread and butter, anchovies, mussels and smoked salmon
Kohlroulade (**koal**roolaader)	cabbage leaves stuffed with minced meat
Königsberger Klopse (**kur**nigsbehrgerr klopser)	Meatballs in white caper sauce

boiled	**gekocht**	ger**kokht**
braised	**geschmort**	ger**shmoart**
fried	**(in der Pfanne) gebraten**	(in derr **pfah**ner) ger**braa**tern
grilled (broiled)	**gegrillt**	ger**grilt**
roasted	**(im Ofen) gebraten**	(im **oa**fern) ger**braa**tern
stewed	**gedämpft**	ger**dehmpft**
stuffed	**gefüllt**	ger**fewlt**
underdone (rare)	**blutig**	**bloo**tikh
medium	**mittel**	**mit**terl
well-done	**gut durchgebraten**	goot **doorch**gerbraatern

Sausages *Würste*

Sausages are produced in dozens of different varieties. Some with more garlic or spices than others. One of the mildest is the Frankfurter.

Bierwurst	**beer**voorst	smoked, pork and beef
Blutwurst	**bloot**voorst	black pudding (blood sausage)
Bockwurst	**bok**voorst	large frankfurter
Bratwurst	**braat**voorst	fried, pork
Jagdwurst	**yaagt**voorst	smoked, with garlic and mustard
Leberwurst	**lay**berrvoorst	liver sausage
Katenrauchwurst	**kaa**ternrowkhvoorst	country-style, smoked
Nürnberger Bratwurst	**newrn**behrgerr **braat**voorst	fried, veal and pork
Regensburger	**ray**gernsburgerr	highly spiced, smoked
Rotwurst	**roat**voorst	black pudding (blood sausage)
Weißwurst	**vighs**voorst	veal and bacon with parsley and onion
Wienerli	**vee**nerrli	Vienna-style frankfurter
Zervelat(wurst)	zehrveh**laat**(voorst)	seasoned, smoked, pork, beef and bacon
Zungenwurst	**tsun**gernvoorst	blood sausage with pieces of tongue and diced fat
Zwiebelwurst	**tsvee**berlvoorst	liver and onion

Game and poultry *Wild und Geflügel*

German cuisine is often said to be unimaginative, but this certainly doesn't apply to game. The venison is usually carefully marinated till tender and served with sweet raisin or red currant sauce or a purée of chestnuts *(Maronenpüree)*.

If your meal is prepared *nach Jägerart* (in the hunter's style), it's likely sautéed with mushrooms and root vegetables and served in a wine gravy (*Weinsoße*—**vighn**zoasser).

Back-	**bahk-**	fried
Brat-	**braat-**	roast
-braten	-braatern	joint, roast
Ente	**ehn**ter	duck
Fasan	fah**zaan**	pheasant
Gans	gahns	goose
Hähnchen	**hain**khern	chicken
Hase	**haa**zer	hare
-hendl	-hehndl	chicken
gespickter Hirsch	ger**shpik**terr heersh	larded venison
Huhn	hoon	chicken
Kaninchen	kah**neen**khern	rabbit
Kapaun	kah**pown**	capon
-keule	-koyler	haunch
Masthühnchen	**mahst**hewnkhern	pullet chicken
-pfeffer	-pfehferr	jugged game
Poulet	poo**lay**	chicken
Rebhuhn	**rehp**hoon	partridge
Reh	ray	venison
-rücken	-rewkern	saddle
Schnepfe	**shneh**pfer	woodcock
Taube	**tow**ber	pigeon, squab
Truthahn	**troot**haan	turkey
Wachtel	**vahkh**terl	quail
Wildschwein	**vilt**shvighn	wild boar

Potatoes *Kartoffeln*

The Germans' favourite accompaniment *(Beilage)* is undoubtedly the potato which can be prepared in a seemingly endless variety of ways.

Bratkartoffeln	**braat**kahrtofferln	fried potatoes
Geröstete	ger**rur**sterter	hashed-brown potatoes

Kartoffel(n)	kahr**toff**erl(n)	potato(es)
-bälle	-behler	balls
-brei	-brigh	mashed
-klöße	-klursser	dumplings
-mus	-mooss	mashed
-puffer	-pufferr	fritters
-stock	-shtok	mashed
-kroketten	-kroakehtern	croquettes
Kartoffelsalat	kahr**toff**erlzahlaat	potato salad
Pellkartoffeln	**pehl**kahrtofferln	potatoes boiled in their jackets
Petersilienkartoffeln	payterr**zee**liern-kahrtofferln	parsley potatoes
Pommes frites	pom frit	chips (french fries)
Reibekuchen	**righ**berkookhern	potato pancake
Rösti	**rur**shtee	hashed-brown potatoes
Röstkartoffeln	**rurst**kahrtofferln	fried potatoes
Salzkartoffeln	**zahlts**kahrtofferln	boiled potatoes

Rice and noodles *Reis und Nudeln*

Butterreis	**but**terrighss	buttered rice
Curryreis	**kur**reerighss	curried rice
Knöpfli	**knurpf**lee	kind of gnocchi
Mehlnockerln	**mayl**nokkerrln	small dumplings
Nudeln	**noo**derln	noodles
Reis	righss	rice
Spätzle	**shpehts**ler	kind of gnocchi
Teigwaren	**tighg**vaarern	pasta

Vegetables and salads *Gemüse und Salate*

What vegetables do you recommend?	**Welches Gemüse empfehlen Sie?**	**vehl**khers ger**mew**zer ehm**pfay**lern zee
I'd prefer some salad.	**Ich nehme lieber Salat.**	ikh **nay**mer **lee**berr zah**laart**
Auberginen	oaberr**zhee**nern	aubergines (eggplant)
Blaukraut	**blow**krowt	red cabbage
Blumenkohl	**bloo**mernkoal	cauliflower
Bohnen	**boa**nern	beans
grüne	**grew**ner	French (green) beens
weiße	**vigh**sser	haricot beans, white kidney beans
Brokkoli	**brok**kollee	broccoli

Champignons	**shahm**pinyong	button mushrooms
Chicorée	sheekor**ray**	endive (Am. chicory)
Endivien	ehn**dee**viern	chicory (Am. endives)
Erbsen	**ehr**psern	peas
Essiggurken	**ehs**sikhgoorkern	gherkins (pickles)
Fenchel	**fehn**kherl	fennel
Fisolen	fee**zoa**lern	french (green) beans
Gemüse	ger**mew**zer	vegetables
gemischtes	ger**mish**terss	mixed vegetables
grüner Salat	**grew**nerr zah**laat**	green salad
Grünkohl	**grewn**koal	kale
Gurken	**goor**kern	cucumber
Häuptlsalat	**hoyptl**zahlaat	lettuce salad
Karfiol	kahrfi**oal**	cauliflower
Karotten	kah**rot**tern	carrots
Kohl	koal	cabbage
Kohlrabi	koal**raa**bee	turnips
Kopfsalat	**kopf**zahlaat	lettuce salad
Krautstiel	**krowt**shteel	white beet
Kürbis	**kewr**biss	pumpkin
Lattich	**lah**tikh	lettuce
Lauch	lowkh	leeks
Leipziger Allerlei	**lighp**tseegerr **ah**lerrligh	peas, carrots, asparagus
Mais	mighss	sweet corn
Mohrrüben	**moar**rewbern	carrots
Paradeiser	pahrah**digh**zerr	tomatoes
Pfifferlinge	**pfif**ferrlinger	chanterelle mushrooms
Pilze	**pil**tser	mushrooms
Radieschen	rah**dees**khern	radishes
Rettich	**reh**tikh	black radish
Rosenkohl	**roa**zernkoal	Brussels sprouts
rote Beete/Rüben	**roa**ter **bay**ter/**rew**bern	beetroot
Rotkohl	**roat**koal	red cabbage
Rüebli	**rew**blee	carrots
Salat	zah**laat**	salad
Sauerkraut	**zow**errkrowt	sauerkraut
Schwarzwurzeln	**shvahrts**voortserln	salsify
Sellerie	**zeh**lerree	celery
Spargel	**shpaar**gerl	asparagus
Spargelspitzen	**shpaar**gerlshpitsern	asparagus tips
Spinat	shpee**naat**	spinach
Tomaten	tom**maa**tern	tomatoes
Weißkohl	**vighs**koal	cabbage
Zwiebeln	**tsvee**berln	onions
Zucchetti	tsug**geh**tee	courgette (zucchini)

Vegetables may be served ...

oven-browned	**überbacken**	ewberr**bah**kern
boiled	**gekocht**	ger**kokht**
creamed	**-püree**	-pewray
diced	**gehackt**	ger**hahkt**
stewed	**gedämpft**	ger**dehmpft**

As for the seasoning ...

Anis	**ah**nees	aniseed
Basilikum	bah**zee**likkum	basil
Dill	dil	dill
Essig	**eh**ssikh	vinegar
Estragon	**eh**strahgon	tarragon
Gewürz	ger**vewrts**	spice
Ingwer	**ing**verr	ginger
Kapern	**kaa**perrn	capers
Knoblauch	**knop**lowkh	garlic
Kräuter	**kroy**terr	mixture of herbs
Kren	krayn	horseradish
Kresse	**kreh**sser	cress
Kümmel	**kew**merl	caraway
Lorbeer	**loar**bayr	bay leaf
Majoran	mahyo**raan**	marjoram
Meerrettich	**mayr**rehtikh	horseradish
Muskatnuß	mus**kaht**nuss	nutmeg
Nelke	**nehl**ker	clove
Öl	url	oil
Petersilie	payterr**zee**lier	parsley
Pfeffer	**pfeh**ferr	pepper
Pfefferminz	**pfeh**ferrmints	mint
Rosmarin	rosmah**reen**	rosemary
Safran	zah**fraan**	saffron
Salbei	zahl**bigh**	sage
Salz	zahlts	salt
Schnittlauch	**shnit**lowkh	chives
Senf	zehnf	mustard
Süßstoff	**zews**shtof	artificial sweetener
Thymian	**tew**miaan	thyme
Tomatenketchup	tom**maa**ternkehtshup	ketchup
Wacholder	**vahk**holderr	juniper
Würze	**vewr**tser	seasoning
Zimt	tsimt	cinnamon
Zucker	**tsuk**kerr	sugar

Cheese *Käse*

Most of the cheese produced in Germany, Austria and Switzerland is mild. You may see *Käseteller* (**kai**zertehlerr) on the menu. This means you'll get a plate of three or four varieties of cheese, doubtless including the renowned *Emmentaler* (**eh**merntaalerr), which we call simply Swiss cheese. If you are looking for curd cheese, ask for *Frischkäse*.

What sort of cheese do you have?	**Welche Käsesorten haben Sie?**	**vehl**kher **kai**zerzoartern **haa**bern zee
A piece of that one, please.	**Ein Stück von dem da, bitte.**	ighn shtewk fon daym daa **bit**ter

mild	Allgäuer Bergkäse (like Swiss cheese), Allgäuer Rahmkäse, Altenburger (made of goat's milk), Appenzeller, Greyerzer, Kümmelkäse (made with caraway seeds), Quark, Räucherkäse (smoked cheese), Schichtkäse, Sahnekäse, Tilsiter, Topfen, Weißkäse.
sharp	Handkäse, Harzer Käse, Schabzieger.

curd	**frisch**	frish
hard	**hart**	hahrt
mild	**mild**	millt
ripe	**reif**	righf
sharp	**scharf**	shahrf
soft	**weich**	vighkh

The following dish in Switzerland makes a meal in itself:

fondue (fong**dew**) — a hot, bubbly mixture of melted cheese, white wine, a drop of kirsch and a hint of garlic; each guest dips a bite-size piece of bread on a fork into the pot of cheese.

And for a cheesy snack try one of the following specialities:

Käsewähe (**kai**zervaier) — a hot cheese tart

Käseschnitte (**kai**zershnitter) — an open-faced melted cheese sandwich

Fruit and nuts *Obst und Nüsse*

Do you have (fresh) fruit?	**Haben Sie (frisches) Obst?**	**haa**bern zee (**fri**sherss) oapst
I'd like a fruit cocktail.	**Ich hätte gern einen Obstsalat.**	ikh **heh**ter gehrn **igh**nern **oapst**zahlaat

Ananas	**ah**nahnahss	pineapple
Apfel	**ah**pferl	apple
Apfelsine	ahpferl**zee**ner	orange
Aprikosen	ahprek**koa**zern	apricots
Backpflaumen	**bahk**pflowmern	prunes
Banane	bah**naa**ner	banana
Birne	**beer**ner	pear
Blaubeeren	**blow**bayrern	blueberries
Brombeeren	**brom**bayrern	blackberries
Datteln	**dah**terln	dates
Erdbeeren	**ehrt**bayrern	strawberries
Erdnüsse	**ehrd**newsser	peanuts
Feigen	**figh**gern	figs
Haselnüsse	**haa**zerlnewsser	hazelnuts
Heidelbeeren	**high**derlbayrern	blueberries
Himbeeren	**him**bayrern	raspberries
Johannisbeeren	yoh**hah**nisbayrern	currants
rote/schwarze	**roa**ter/**shvahr**tser	red/black
Kirschen	**keer**shern	cherries
Kokosnuß	**kok**kosnuss	coconut
Mandarine	mahndah**ree**ner	tangerine
Mandeln	**mahn**derln	almonds
Marillen	mah**ril**lern	apricots
Melone	may**loa**ner	melon (cantaloupe)
Mirabellen	meerah**beh**lern	a variety of plums
Nüsse	**new**sser	nuts
Pampelmuse	**pahm**perlmoozer	grapefruit
Pfirsich	**pfeer**zikh	peach
Pflaumen	**pflow**mern	plums
Preiselbeeren	**prigh**zerlbayrern	cranberries
Quitte	**kvit**ter	quince
Rhabarber	rah**bahr**berr	rhubarb
Ribisel	**ree**beezl	currants
Rosinen	ro**zee**nern	raisins
Stachelbeeren	**stah**kherlbayrern	gooseberries
Walnüsse	**vahl**newsser	walnuts
Wassermelone	**vah**sserrmayloaner	watermelon
Weintrauben	**vighn**trowbern	grapes
Zitrone	tsi**troa**ner	lemon
Zwetsch(g)en	**tsveh**tsh(g)ern	plums

Dessert–Pastries *Nachtisch–Gebäck*

Desserts may also be listed on the menu under *Nachspeisen* or *Süßspeisen*. If you want an ice-cream, look under *Eis* in Germany and Austria and under *Glace* in Switzerland. The German waiter may ask you if you want your dessert served with *Schlagsahne*, the Austrian will say *Schlagobers* or simply *Schlag* and the Swiss *Schlagrahm*. Wherever you are it means whipped cream.

I'd like a dessert, please.	**Ich hätte gern eine Nachspeise.**	ikh **heh**ter gehrn **igh**ner **naakh**shpighzer
Something light, please.	**Etwas Leichtes, bitte.**	**eht**vahss **lighkh**terss **bit**ter
Just a small portion.	**Nur eine kleine Portion.**	noor **igh**ner **kligh**ner port**sioan**
Nothing more, thanks.	**Nein danke, nichts mehr.**	nighn **dahn**ker nikhts mayr
Götterspeise	**gur**terrshpighzer	fruit jelly (Jell-O)
Kaltschale	**kahlt**shaaler	chilled fruit soup
Obstsalat	**oapst**zahlaat	fruit cocktail

Here are some basic words you'll need to know if you want to order a dessert. Remember that Germans often write in one word what would take us two. The words below may be combined with a fruit or a flavour, e.g. *Apfelauflauf, Erdbeereis*, etc.

-auflauf	-owflowf	soufflé
-creme	-kraym	pudding
-eis, -glace	-ighss -glahsser	ice-cream
-kompott	-kompot	compote
-kuchen	-kookhern	cake
-pudding	-pudding	pudding
-torte	-torter	layer cake

These flavours of ice-cream are very popular:

Erdbeer-	**ehrt**bayr-	strawberry
Karamel-	kahrah**mehl**-	caramel
Mokka-	**mok**kah-	coffee
Schokoladen-	shokkol**laa**dern-	chocolate
Vanille-	vah**nil**ler-	vanilla
Zitronen-	tsi**troa**nern-	lemon

If you'd like to try something more filling with your coffee, we'd recommend ...

Apfelstrudel (**ah**pferlshtrooderl)	paper-thin layers of pastry filled with apple slices, nuts, raisins and jam
Berliner (behr**lee**nerr)	jam doughnut
Bienenstich (**bee**nernshtikh)	honey-almond cake
Cremeschnitte (**kraym**shnitter)	millefeuille (napoleon)
Gugelhupf (**goo**gerlhupf)	a moulded cake with a hole in the centre, usually filled with raisins and almonds
Hefekranz (**hay**ferkrahnts)	ring-shaped cake of yeast dough, with almonds and sometimes candied fruit
Kaiserschmarren (**kigh**zerrshmahrern)	shredded pancake with raisins served with syrup (Austrian)
Mohrenkopf (**moa**rernkopf)	chocolate meringue with whipped-cream filling
Palatschinken (pahlah**tshin**kern)	when listed under desserts, pancakes with a jam or white cheese filling, otherwise they are a savoury dish
Schillerlocke (**shil**lerrlokker)	pastry cornet with vanilla cream filling
Schwarzwälder Kirschtorte (**shvahrts**vehlderr **keersh**torter)	chocolate layer cake filled with cream and cherries, flavoured with cherry brandy
Topfenstrudel (**top**fernshtrooderl)	flaky pastry filled with creamed, vanilla-flavoured white cheese, rolled and baked
Windbeutel (**vint**boyterl)	cream puff

Here are the names of some favourite biscuits (cookies):

Honigkuchen	**hoa**nikhkookhern	honey biscuits
Leckerli	**leh**kerrli	ginger biscuits
Makronen	mah**kroa**nern	macaroons
Printen	**prin**tern	honey biscuits
Spekulatius	shpehkoo**laa**tsiuss	almond biscuits

Beer *Bier*

Needless to say, beer is the Germans' favourite drink. Almost every town with a sizable population has at least one brewery. You'll want to try some of the local brews. However, Dortmund and Bavarian beer are found throughout the country. *Bier vom Faß* (draught or draft beer) is considered to have a better taste and is less expensive, too, than bottled beer.

I'd like a beer.	**Ich hätte gern ein Bier.**	ikh **heh**ter gehrn ighn beer
a dark beer	**ein Dunkles**	ighn **dunk**lerss
a light beer	**ein Helles**	ighn **heh**lerss
I'd like a ... of beer.	**Ich hätte gern ... Bier.**	ikh **heh**ter gehrn ... beer
bottle	**eine Flasche**	**igh**ner **flah**sher
glass	**ein Glas**	ighn glaass
a small one	**ein kleines**	ighn **kligh**nerss
a large one	**ein großes**	ighn **groa**ssers
mug (a quart)	**eine Maß**	**igh**ner maass
Waiter! Another beer, please!	**Herr Ober, noch ein Bier, bitte!**	hehr **oa**berr nokh ighn beer **bit**ter

Altbier (**ahlt**beer) — a bitter beer with a high hops content

Bockbier, Doppelbock, Märzen, Starkbier (**bok**beer, **dop**perlbok, **mehr**tsern, **shtahrk**beer) — these are beers with a high alcoholic and malt content

Malzbier (**mahlts**beer) — a dark, sweetish beer with a low alcoholic content but high in calories

Pilsener (**pil**zernerr) — has a particularly strong aroma of hops

Radlermaß (**raa**dlerrmaass) — a light beer to which a bit of lemonade is added; in north Germany it's called *Alsterwasser* (**ahl**sterrvahsserr)

Weißbier (**vighs**beer) — a light beer brewed from wheat grain; Berliners love a *Berliner Weiße mit Schuß*—*Weißbier* with a shot of raspberry juice.

Wine *Wein*

The best wine-producing regions of Germany are those round the Rhine and Moselle rivers—the northernmost wine-producing areas of Europe.

More so than French vintners to the west, German wine producers are at the mercy of the vagaries of the country's climatic conditions. One type of wine can have a quite different character from one year to the next depending upon the weather. For this reason, you'll have to learn to recognize a few basic terms on German labels which will tell you something about how you can likely expect a certain wine to taste.

In good years wine may be labeled *naturrein* or *Naturwein* which just means it's been produced under ordinary methods. In a bad year, sugar is sometimes added to increase the alcoholic content. If this is done, *verbessert* (improved) is euphemistically printed on the label.

There are four other words commonly found on German wine labels which you should know. They indicate the ripeness of the grapes when they were picked—or the degree of dryness or sweetness of the wine.

Spätlese (**spait**layzer)	gathered late after the normal harvesting; dry wine
Auslese (**ows**layzer)	selected gathering of particularly ripe bunches of grapes; slightly dry wine
Beerenauslese (**bay**rernowslayzer)	selected overripe grapes, slightly sweet wine
Trockenbeerenauslese (**trok**kernbayrern-owslayzer)	selected dried or raisin-like grapes; one drop of nectar can be squeezed out of each grape; a sweet or dessert wine is produced.

In neighbouring German-speaking Switzerland, mostly red wine is produced. Austria's Wachau region along the fabled Danube riverbanks produces white wine while Burgenland to the east of Vienna has red wine.

Type of wine	Examples	Accompanies
sweet white wine	Rheinpfalz is noted for wine in this category; bottles labeled *Trockenbeerenauslese* also fall into this section.	desserts, especially puddings and cake
dry white wine	The Rheingau region produces extraordinary white wine in good vintage years; Moselle wine can usually be counted on to be very dry; wine labelled *Spätlese* or *Auslese* can go into this category as well as those with the term *naturrein* or *Naturwein*.	cold meat or shellfish, fish, boiled meat, egg dishes, first courses, fowl, veal, dishes served with sauerkraut, sausages
rosé	Sometimes referred to as *Schillerwein*	goes with almost anything but especially cold dishes, eggs, pork, lamb
light-bodied red wine	Most local red wine fits into this category, particularly the wine of Austria's Burgenland, German-speaking Switzerland, the Ahr region (look for the names *Ahrweiler, Neuenahr* and *Walporzheim* on the label) and Baden-Württemberg.	roast chicken, turkey, veal, lamb, beef steak, ham, liver, quail, pheasant, stews, dishes served with gravy
full-bodied red wine	A difficult wine to find but a *Spätburgunder* from the Ahr Valley is a good example.	duck, goose, kidneys, most game, goulash, in short, any strong-flavoured preparations
sparkling wine	German *Sekt* comes into this category; some of it rivals French champagne in quality.	if it's dry, it goes with anything; may be drunk as an aperitif or as the climax to the dinner; goes well with shellfish, nuts and dried fruit; if it's sweet, it'll go nicely with dessert and pastry like *Strudel*

May I please have the wine list?	**Die Weinkarte, bitte.**	dee **vighn**kahrter **bit**ter
I want a bottle of white wine/red wine/ sparkling wine.	**Ich möchte eine Flasche Weißwein/ Rotwein/Schaum-wein.**	ikh **mur**khter **igh**ner **flah**sher **vighs**vighn/ **roat**vighn/**showm**vighn
I'd like a glass/ carafe of ...	**Ich hätte gern ein Glas/eine Karaffe ...**	ikh **heh**ter gehrn ighn glaass/**igh**ner **kah**rahfer
Please bring me another ...	**Bitte bringen Sie mir noch ...**	**bit**ter **brin**gern zee mir nokh
Where does this wine come from?	**Woher kommt dieser Wein?**	voa**hayr** komt **dee**zerr vighn

red/white/rosé	**rot/weiß/rosé**	roat/vighss/ro**zay**
(very) dry/sweet	**(sehr) trocken/süß**	(zayr) **trok**kern/zewss
light	**leicht**	lighkht
full-bodied	**vollmundig**	**vol**mundig

A refreshing highball for the ladies is sparkling wine and orange juice, *Damengedeck* (**daa**merngerdehk) or for the men, *Herrengedeck* (**heh**rerngerdehk), which is sparkling wine and beer. The German champagne (*Sekt*—sehkt) is also worth trying.

Other alcoholic drinks *Andere alkoholische Getränke*

I'd like a/an/some ...	**Ich hätte gern ...**	ikh **heh**ter gehrn
aperitif	**einen Aperitif**	**igh**nern ahpayrit**teef**
brandy	**einen Weinbrand**	**igh**nern **vighn**brahnt
cider	**Apfelwein**	**ah**pferlvighn
cognac	**einen Kognak**	**igh**nern **kon**yahk
liqueur	**einen Likör**	**igh**nern lik**kurr**
mulled wine	**Glühwein**	**glew**vighn
port	**Portwein**	**port**vighn
rum	**einen Rum**	**igh**nern rum
vermouth	**einen Wermut**	**igh**nern **vayr**moot
vodka	**einen Wodka**	**igh**nern **vot**kah
whisky	**einen Whisky**	**igh**nern "whisky"
neat (straight)	**pur**	poor
on the rocks	**mit Eis**	mit ighss

You'll certainly want to take the occasion to sip a liqueur or brandy after your meal. The names of some well-known wine-distilled brandies are *Asbach-Uralt, Chantré* and *Dujardin*. Here are some other after-dinner drinks:

Are there any local specialities?	**Haben Sie hiesige Spezialitäten?**	**haa**bern zee **hee**zigger shpehtsiahli**tai**tern
I'd like to try a glass of ..., please.	**Ich möchte ein Glas ... probieren.**	ikh **murkh**ter ighn glaass ... proa**bee**rern

Apfelschnaps	**ah**pferlshnahps	apple brandy
Aprikosenlikör	ahprik**koa**zernlikkurr	apricot liqueur
Birnenschnaps	**beer**nernshnahps	pear brandy
Bommerlunder	bommerr**lun**derr	caraway-flavoured brandy
Doornkaat	**dorn**kaat	German gin, juniper-berry brandy
Eierlikör	**igh**errlikkurr	eggflip, eggnog
Heidelbeergeist	**high**derlbayrgighst	blueberry brandy
Himbeergeist	**him**bayrgighst	raspberry brandy
Himbeerlikör	**him**bayrlikkurr	raspberry liqueur
Kirschlikör	**kirsh**likkurr	cherry liqueur
Kirschwasser	**kirsh**vahsserr	cherry brandy
(Doppel)Korn	(**dop**perl)korn	grain-distilled liquor, akin to whisky
Kümmel	**kew**merl	caraway-flavoured liquor
Obstler	**oapst**lerr	fruit brandy
Pflümli(wasser)	**pflewm**li(vahsserr)	plum brandy
Steinhäger	**shtighn**haigerr	juniperberry brandy, akin to gin
Träsch	traish	pear and apple brandy
Weizenkorn	**vigh**tsernkorn	wheat-distilled liquor, akin to whisky
Zwetschgenwasser	**tsvehtsh**gernvahsserr	plum brandy

ZUM WOHL/PROST!
(tsum voal/proast)
YOUR HEALTH/CHEERS!

Nonalcoholic drinks *Alkoholfreie Getränke*

I'd like a/an ...	**Ich hätte gern ...**	ikh **heh**ter gehrn
apple juice	**einen Apfelsaft**	**igh**nern **ah**pferlzahft
currant juice (red or black)	**einen Johannisbeersaft**	**igh**nern yoh**hah**nisbayrzaft
fruit juice	**einen Fruchtsaft**	**igh**nern **frukht**zahft
grape juice	**einen Traubensaft**	**igh**nern **trow**bernzahft
herb tea	**einen Kräutertee**	**igh**nern **kroy**terrtay
iced tea	**einen Eistee**	**igh**nern **ighs**tay
lemonade	**eine Limonade**	**igh**ner limmon**naa**der
(glass of) milk	**(ein Glas) Milch**	(ighn glaass) milkh
milkshake	**ein Milchmixgetränk**	ighn **milkh**miksgertrehnk
mineral water	**ein Mineralwasser**	ighn minner**raal**vahsserr
fizzy (carbonated)	**mit Kohlensäure**	mit **koa**lernzoyrer
still	**ohne Kohlensäure**	oaner **koa**lernzoyrer
orange juice	**einen Orangensaft**	**igh**nern or**rahng**zhernzahft
orangeade	**eine Orangeade**	**igh**ner orahng**zhaa**der
tomato juice	**einen Tomatensaft**	**igh**nern tom**maa**ternzahft
tonic water	**ein Tonic**	ighn **ton**nik

Hot beverages *Warme Getränke*

Perhaps you'd like a coffee after dinner. In Austria, you can't ask for just "a cup of coffee"; the varieties are endless. There, you can ask for anything from a *Nußschwarzer* (**nus**shvahrtserr) or *Neger* (**nay**gerr)—strong black coffee—to an *Einspänner* (**ighn**shpehnerr)—topped with whipped cream—or a *Melange* (may**lahng**zher)—coffee and hot milk.

I'd like a/an ...	**Ich hätte gern ...**	ikh **heh**ter gehrn
(hot) chocolate	**eine (heiße) Schokolade**	**igh**ner (**high**sser) shokkol**laa**der
coffee	**einen Kaffee**	**igh**nern kah**fay**
with cream	**mit Sahne**	mit **zaa**ner
with milk	**einen Milchkaffee**	**igh**nern **milkh**kahfay
black/decaffeinated coffee	**einen schwarzen/ koffeinfreien Kaffee**	**igh**nern **shvahr**tsern/ koffeh**een**frighern kah**fay**
espresso coffee	**einen Expresso**	**igh**nern ehks**preh**soa
mokka	**einen Mokka**	**igh**nern **mok**kah
tea	**einen Tee**	**igh**nern tay
cup of tea	**eine Tasse Tee**	**igh**ner **tah**sser tay
with milk/lemon	**mit Milch/Zitrone**	mit milkh/tsi**troa**ner

Complaints *Reklamationen*

There is a plate/glass missing.	**Es fehlt ein Teller/ ein Glas.**	ehss faylt ighn **teh**lerr/ ighn glaass
I have no knife/fork/ spoon.	**Ich habe kein Messer/ keine Gabel/keinen Löffel.**	ikh **haa**ber kighn **meh**sserr/ **kigh**ner **gaa**berl/**kigh**nern **lur**ferl
That's not what I ordered.	**Das habe ich nicht bestellt.**	dahss **haa**ber ikh nikht ber**stehlt**
I asked for ...	**Ich wollte ...**	ikh **vol**ter
There must be some mistake.	**Es muß ein Irrtum sein.**	ehss muss ighn **ir**toom zighn
May I change this?	**Können Sie mir dafür etwas anderes bringen?**	**kur**nern zee meer daa**fewr** **eht**vahss **ahn**derrerss **bring**ern
I asked for a small portion (for the child).	**Ich wollte eine kleine Portion (für das Kind).**	ikh **vol**ter **igh**ner **kligh**ner port**sioan** (fewr dahss kint)
The meat is ...	**Das Fleisch ist ...**	dahss flighsh ist
overdone	**zu stark gebraten**	tsu shtahrk ger**braa**tern
underdone (too rare)	**zu roh**	tsu roa
too tough	**zu zäh**	tsu tsai
This is too ...	**Das ist zu ...**	dahss ist tsu
bitter/sour	**bitter/sauer**	**bit**ter/**zow**err
salty/sweet	**salzig/süß**	**zahl**tsikh/zewss
I don't like this.	**Das schmeckt mir nicht.**	dahs shmehkt meer nikht
The food is cold.	**Das Essen ist kalt.**	dahss **eh**ssern ist kahlt
This isn't fresh.	**Das ist nicht frisch.**	dahss ist nikht frish
What's taking you so long?	**Weshalb dauert es so lange?**	vehs**hahlp dow**errt ehss zoa **lahn**ger
Have you forgotten our drinks?	**Haben Sie unsere Getränke vergessen?**	**haa**bern zee **un**zerrer ger**trehn**ker fehr**geh**ssern
The wine is corked.	**Der Wein schmeckt nach Korken.**	derr vighn shmehkt naakh **koar**kern
This isn't clean.	**Das ist nicht sauber.**	dahss ist nikht **zow**berr
Would you ask the head waiter to come over?	**Würden Sie bitte den Oberkellner rufen?**	**vewr**dern zee **bit**ter dayn **oa**berrkehlnerr **roo**fern

The bill (check) *Die Rechnung*

A service charge is generally included automatically in restaurant bills. Anything extra for the waiter is optional. Credit cards may be used in an increasing number of restaurants.

I'd like to pay.	**Ich möchte zahlen.**	ikh **murkh**ter **tsaa**lern
We'd like to pay separately.	**Wir möchten getrennt bezahlen.**	veer **murkh**tern geh**trehnt** ber**tsaa**lern
I think you made a mistake in this bill.	**Ich glaube, Sie haben sich verrechnet.**	ikh **glow**ber zee **haa**bern zikh fehr**rehkh**nert
What is this amount for?	**Wofür ist dieser Betrag?**	voa**fewr** ist **dee**zerr ber**traakh**
Is service included?	**Ist die Bedienung inbegriffen?**	ist dee ber**dee**nung **in**bergriffern
Do you accept traveller's cheques?	**Nehmen Sie Reiseschecks?**	**nay**mern zee **righ**zer-shehks
Can I pay with this credit card?	**Kann ich mit dieser Kreditkarte bezahlen?**	kahn ikh mit **dee**zerr kray**dit**kahrter ber**tsaa**lern
That was a very good meal.	**Das Essen war sehr gut.**	dahss **eh**ssern vaar zayr goot

BEDIENUNG INBEGRIFFEN
SERVICE INCLUDED

Snacks—Picnic *Imbiß – Picknick*

A *Café* (in Austria *Kaffeehaus*) will serve anything from simple pastries to luscious, monumental sweet delicacies and often snacks. For a fast meal the German *Schnellimbiß* (snack bar) is the place. Ordering is easy since most of the snacks are on display. And if you are in a hurry have a sausage at a *Würstchenstand.*

Give me two of these and one of those.	**Geben Sie mir davon zwei und davon eins.**	**gay**bern zee meer **daa**fon tsvigh unt **daa**fon ighns
to the left/right above/below	**links/rechts darüber/darunter**	links/rehkhts dah**rew**berr/dah**run**terr
It's to take away.	**Es ist zum Mitnehmen.**	ehss ist tsum **mit**naymern

TIPPING, see inside back-cover

I'd like a piece of cake.	**Ich hätte gern ein Stück Kuchen.**	ikh **heh**ter gehrn ighn shtewk **koo**khern
fried sausage	**eine Bratwurst**	**igh**ner **braat**voorst
omelet	**ein Omelett**	ighn om**leht**
open sandwich	**ein belegtes Brot**	ighn ber**layg**terss broat
with ham	**mit Schinken**	mit **shin**kern
with cheese	**mit Käse**	mit **kai**zer
potato salad	**Kartoffelsalat**	kahr**tof**ferlzahlaat
sandwich	**ein Sandwich**	ighn **sehnd**vitsh

Here's a basic list of food and drink that might come in useful when shopping for a picnic.

I'd like a/an/ some ...	**Ich hätte gern ...**	ikh **heh**ter gehrn
apples	**Äpfel**	**ehp**ferl
bananas	**Bananen**	bah**naa**nern
biscuits (Br.)	**Kekse**	**kayk**ser
beer	**Bier**	beer
bread	**ein Brot**	ighn broat
butter	**Butter**	**but**terr
cheese	**Käse**	**kai**zer
chips (Am.)	**Kartoffelchips**	kahr**tof**ferlcheeps
chocolate bar	**eine Tafel Schokolade**	**igh**ner **taa**ferl shokkol**laa**der
coffee	**Kaffee**	kah**fay**
cold cuts	**Aufschnitt**	**owf**shnit
cookies	**Kekse**	**kayk**ser
crisps	**Kartoffelchips**	kahr**tof**ferlcheeps
eggs	**Eier**	**igh**err
gherkins (pickles)	**Essiggurken**	**eh**ssikhgoorkern
grapes	**Trauben**	**trow**bern
ice-cream	**ein Eis**	ighn ighss
milk	**Milch**	milkh
mustard	**Senf**	zehnf
oranges	**Orangen**	or**rahng**zhern
pepper	**Pfeffer**	**pfeh**ferr
rolls	**Brötchen**	**brurt**khern
salt	**Salz**	zahlts
sausage	**eine Wurst**	**igh**ner voorst
soft drink	**ein alkoholfreies Getränk**	ighn ahlko**hoal**frigherss ger**trehnk**
sugar	**Zucker**	**tsuk**kerr
tea	**Tee**	tay
yoghurt	**Joghurt**	**yoa**goort

Travelling around

Plane *Flugzeug*

Is there a flight to Vienna?	**Gibt es einen Flug nach Wien?**	gipt ehss **igh**nern floog naakh veen
Is it a direct flight?	**Ist es ein Direktflug?**	ist ehss ighn dir**rehkt**floog
When's the next flight to Hamburg?	**Wann ist der nächste Flug nach Hamburg?**	vahn ist derr **naikh**ster **floog** nahkh **hahm**boorg
Do I have to change planes?	**Muß ich umsteigen?**	muss ikh **um**shtighgern
Can I make a connection to Cologne?	**Habe ich Anschluß nach Köln?**	**haa**berr ikh **ahn**shluss nahkh kurln
I'd like a ticket to Zurich.	**Bitte ein Flugticket nach Zürich.**	**bit**ter ighn **floog**tikkert naakh **tsew**rikh
single (one-way)	**Hinflug**	**hin**floog
return (roundtrip)	**Hin- und Rückflug**	hin unt **rewk**floog
What time does the plane take off?	**Wann ist der Abflug?**	vahn ist derr **ahp**floog
What time do I have to check in?	**Wann muß ich einchecken?**	vahn muss ikh **ighn**shehkern
Is there an airport-bus?	**Gibt es einen Flughafenbus?**	gipt ehss **igh**nern **floog**haafernbuss
What's the flight number?	**Welche Flugnummer ist es?**	**vehl**kher **floog**nummerr ist ehss
What time do we arrive?	**Wann landen wir?**	vahn **lahn**dern veer
I'd like to ... my reservation.	**Ich möchte meine Reservierung ...**	ikh **murkh**ter **migh**ner rehzer**veer**ung
cancel	**annullieren**	ahnul**lee**rern
change	**umbuchen**	**um**bookhern
confirm	**bestätigen**	ber**shtai**tiggern

ANKUNFT ARRIVAL	**FLUGSTEIG** GATE	**ABFLUG** DEPARTURE

Train *Eisenbahn*

Travel on the main railway lines is generally fast, and the trains run on time. First-class coaches are comfortable; second-class, more than adequate.

EuroCity (**oy**roa"city")	International express trains; first and second class
Intercity ("intercity")	Long distance inter-city trains; some only first, others with first and second class, with surcharge; in Switzerland the equivalent of the Austrian *Städteschnellzug*
City-D-Zug ("city"-**day**-tsoog)	Short-distance inter-city trains, with few stops at major points only; first and second class with surcharge on trips of less than 50 kilometres (Germany)
D-Zug (**day**-tsoog)	Intermediate- to long-distance trains (Germany)
Schnellzug (**shnehl**tsoog)	Fast trains, stop at big and medium towns (Austria, Switzerland)
Städteschnellzug (**shteh**tershnehltsoog)	Fast trains, connecting the biggest towns (Austria)
Expreßzug (ayk**sprehs**tsoog)	Fast trains, stop at big and medium towns (Austria)
Eilzug (**igh**ltsoog)	Medium-distance trains, not stopping at small stations (Germany, Austria)
Nahverkehrszug (**naa**fehrkayrstsoog)	Local trains, stopping at all stations; in Austria called *Personenzug* and in Switzerland *Regionalzug*
Triebwagen (**treep**vaagern)	Small diesel coach used for short runs (Austria, Germany); in Germany sometimes *Schienenbus*

Here are a few more useful terms:

Speisewagen (**shpigh**zervaagern)	Dining-car
Schlafwagen (**shlaaf**vaagern)	Sleeping-car, compartments with wash basins and 1, 2 or 3 berths
Liegewagen (**lee**gervaagern)	Coach containing berths with sheets, blankets and pillows

To the railway station *Unterwegs zum Bahnhof*

Where's the railway station?	**Wo ist der Bahnhof?**	voa ist derr **baan**hoaf
Taxi, please!	**Taxi bitte!**	**tahk**si **bit**ter
Take me to the ...	**Fahren Sie mich ...**	**faa**rern zee mikh
main railway station	**zum Hauptbahnhof**	tsum **howpt**baanhoaf
railway station	**zum Bahnhof**	tsum **baan**hoaf
What's the fare?	**Was macht das?**	vahss mahkht dahss

EINGANG	ENTRANCE
AUSGANG	EXIT
ZU DEN BAHNSTEIGEN	TO THE PLATFORMS
AUSKUNFT	INFORMATION

Where's the ...? *Wo ist ...?*

Where is/are the ...?	**Wo ist/sind ...?**	voa ist/zint
booking office	**die Platzreservierung**	dee **plahts**rehzerrveerung
currency-exchange office	**die Wechselstube**	dee **wehk**zerlshtoober
left-luggage office (baggage check)	**die Gepäckaufbewahrung**	dee ger**pehk**owfbervaarung
lost property (lost-and-found) office	**das Fundbüro**	dahss **funt**bewroa
luggage lockers	**die Schließfächer**	dee **shlees**fehkherr
newsstand	**der Zeitungsstand**	derr **tsigh**tungsshtahnt
platform 3	**Bahnsteig 3**	**baan**shtighg 3
reservations office	**die Platzreservierung**	dee **plahts**rehzerrveerung
restaurant	**das Restaurant**	dahss rehstor**rahng**
snack bar	**der Schnellimbiß**	derr **shnehl**imbiss
ticket office	**der Fahrkartenschalter**	derr **faar**kahrternshahlterr
track 7	**Gleis 7**	glighss 7
waiting room	**der Wartesaal**	derr **vahr**terzaal
Where are the toilets?	**Wo sind die Toiletten?**	voa zint dee toah**leh**tern

TAXI, see page 21

Inquiries *Auskunft*

When is the ... train to Kiel?	**Wann fährt der ... Zug nach Kiel?**	vahn fairt derr ... tsoog naakh keel
first/last/next	**erste/letzte/nächste**	**ehr**ster/**lehts**ter/**naikh**ster
What's the fare to Basle?	**Was kostet die Fahrt nach Basel?**	vahss **kos**tert dee faart naakh **baa**zerl
Is it a through train?	**Ist es ein durchgehender Zug?**	ist ehss ighn **doorkh**gayernderr tsoog
Must I pay a surcharge?	**Muß ich einen Zuschlag bezahlen?**	muss ikh **igh**nern **tsu**-shlaag ber**tsah**lern
Is there a connection to ...?	**Gibt es einen Anschluß nach ...?**	gipt ehss **igh**nern **ahn**shluss naakh
Do I have to change trains?	**Muß ich umsteigen?**	muss ikh **um**shtighgern
Is there sufficient time to change?	**Reicht die Zeit zum Umsteigen?**	righkht dee tsight tsum **um**shtighgern
Will the train leave on time?	**Fährt der Zug pünktlich ab?**	fairt derr tsoog **pewnkt**likh ahp
What time does the train arrive at Münster?	**Wann kommt der Zug in Münster an?**	vahn komt derr tsoog in **mewn**sterr ahn
Is there a dining-car/ sleeping-car on the train?	**Führt der Zug einen Speisewagen/ Schlafwagen?**	fewrt derr tsoog **igh**nern **shpigh**zervaagern/ **shlaaf**vaagern
Does the train stop at Ingolstadt?	**Hält der Zug in Ingolstadt?**	hehlt derr tsoog in **in**golshtaht
What platform does the train for Bonn leave from?	**Auf welchem Bahnsteig fährt der Zug nach Bonn ab?**	owf **vehl**kherm **baan**-shtighg fairt derr tsoog naakh bon ahp
What track does the train from Hamburg arrive at?	**Auf welchem Gleis kommt der Zug aus Hamburg an?**	owf **vehl**kherm glighss komt derr tsoog owss **hahm**boorg ahn
I'd like a time-table.	**Ich hätte gern einen Fahrplan.**	ikh **heh**ter gehrn **igh**nern **faar**plaan

ANKUNFT
ARRIVAL

ABFAHRT
DEPARTURE

Es ist ein durchgehender Zug.	It's a through train.
Sie müssen in ... umsteigen.	You have to change at ...
Steigen Sie in Heidelberg in einen Nahverkehrszug um.	Change at Heidelberg and get a local train.
Bahnsteig 7 ist ...	Platform 7 is ...
dort drüben/oben/unten links/rechts	over there/upstairs/downstairs on the left/on the right
Es gibt einen Zug nach Bonn um ...	There's a train to Bonn at ...
Ihr Zug fährt auf Gleis ... ab.	Your train will leave from track ...
Der Zug hat ... Minuten Verspätung.	There'll be a delay of ... minutes.
Erste Klasse an der Spitze/in der Mitte/ am Ende des Zuges.	First class at the front/ in the middle/at the end.

Tickets *Fahrkarten*

I want a ticket to ...	**Ich möchte eine Fahrkarte nach ...**	ikh **murkh**ter **igh**ner **faar**-kahrter naakh
single (one-way)	**einfach**	**ighn**fahkh
return (roundtrip)	**hin und zurück**	hin unt stoo**rewk**
first class	**erste Klasse**	**ehr**ster **klah**sser
second class	**zweite Klasse**	**tsvigh**ter **klah**sser
half price	**zum halben Preis**	tsum **hahl**bern prighss

Reservation *Reservierung*

I want to book a ...	**Ich möchte ... reservieren lassen.**	ikh **murkh**ter ... rehzerr**vee**rern **lah**ssern
seat (by the window)	**einen (Fenster)platz**	**igh**nern (**fehn**sterr)plahts
berth	**einen Platz im Liegewagen**	**igh**nern plahts im **lee**gervaagern
upper	**oben**	**oa**bern
middle	**in der Mitte**	in derr **mit**ter
lower	**unten**	**un**tern
berth in the sleeping car	**einen Platz im Schlafwagen**	**igh**nern plahts im **shlaaf**vaagern

NUMBERS, see page 147

All aboard *Einsteigen bitte*

Is this the right platform for the train to Vienna?	**Ist das der richtige Bahnsteig für den Zug nach Wien?**	ist dahss derr **rikh**tigger **baan**shtighg fewr dayn tsoog naakh veen
Is this the right train to Graz?	**Ist das der Zug nach Graz?**	ist dahss derr tsoog naakh graats
Excuse me. May I get by?	**Verzeihung. Kann ich vorbei?**	**fehrtsigh**ung. kahn ikh for**bigh**
Is this seat taken?	**Ist dieser Platz besetzt?**	ist **dee**zerr plahts ber**zehtst**

RAUCHER
SMOKER

NICHTRAUCHER
NONSMOKER

I think that's my seat.	**Ich glaube, das ist mein Platz.**	ikh **glow**ber dahss ist mighn plahts
Would you let me know before we get to Bamberg?	**Sagen Sie mir bitte, wenn wir in Bamberg ankommen?**	**zaa**gern zee mir **bit**ter vehn veer in **bahm**behrg **ahn**kommern
What station is this?	**Wie heißt dieser Ort?**	vee highst **dee**zerr ort
How long does the train stop here?	**Wie lange hält der Zug hier?**	vee **lahng**er hehlt derr tsoog heer
When do we get to Cologne?	**Wann kommen wir in Köln an?**	vahn **kom**mern veer in kurln ahn

Sleeping *Im Schlafwagen*

Are there any free compartments in the sleeping-car?	**Sind im Schlafwagen noch Abteile frei?**	zint im **shlaaf**vaagern nokh **ahp**tighler frigh
Where's the sleeping-car?	**Wo ist der Schlafwagen?**	voa ist derr **shlaaf**vaagern
Where's my berth?	**Wo ist mein Schlafplatz?**	voa ist mighn **shlaaf**plahts
I'd like a lower berth.	**Ich möchte unten schlafen.**	ikh **murkh**ter **un**tern **shlaa**fern

Would you make up our berths?	**Würden Sie unsere Schlafplätze machen?**	**vewr**dern zee **un**zerrer **shlaaf**plehtser **mah**khern
Would you call me at 7 o'clock?	**Würden Sie mich um 7 Uhr wecken?**	**vewr**dern zee mikh um 7 oor **veh**kern
Would you bring me coffee in the morning?	**Würden Sie mir bitte morgen früh Kaffee bringen?**	**vewr**dern zee meer **bit**ter **mor**gern frew kah**fay brin**gern

Eating *Im Speisewagen*

You can get snacks and drinks in the buffet-car and in the dining-car when it isn't being used for main meals. On some trains an attendant comes around with a cart with snacks, tea, coffee and soft drinks.

Where's the dining-car?	**Wo ist der Speisewagen?**	voa ist derr **shpigh**zer-vaagern

Baggage—Porters *Gepäck – Gepäckträger*

Porter!	**Gepäckträger!**	ger**pehk**traiger
Can you help me with my luggage?	**Können Sie mir mit meinem Gepäck helfen?**	**kur**nern zee mir mit **migh**nerm ger**pehk hehl**fern
Where are the luggage trolleys (carts)?	**Wo sind die Kofferkulis?**	voa zint dee **kof**ferr-kooliss
Where are the luggage lockers?	**Wo sind die Schließfächer?**	voa zint dee **shlees**fehkherr
Where's the left-luggage office (baggage check)?	**Wo ist die Gepäckaufbewahrung?**	voa ist dee ger**pehk**-owfbervaarung
I'd like to leave my luggage, please.	**Ich möchte mein Gepäck einstellen.**	ikh **murkh**ter mighn ger**pehk ighn**shtehlern
I'd like to register (check) my luggage.	**Ich möchte mein Gepäck aufgeben.**	ikh **murkh**ter mighn ger**pehk owf**gaybern

GEPÄCKAUFGABE
REGISTERING (CHECKING) BAGGAGE

PORTERS, see also page 18

Coach (long-distance bus) *Überlandbus*

To reach out-of-the-way places, you'll find frequent bus services available including the *Kraftpost* or *Postauto*. You'll find information on destinations and timetables at the coach terminals, usually situated near railway stations.

When's the next coach to ...?	**Wann fährt der nächste Bus nach ...?**	vahn fairt derr **naikh**ster buss naakh
Does the coach stop at ...?	**Hält der Bus in ...?**	hehlt derr buss in
How long does the journey (trip) take?	**Wie lange dauert die Fahrt?**	vee **lahn**ger **dow**errt dee faart

Note: Most of the phrases on the previous pages can be used or adapted for travelling on local transport.

Bus—Tram (streetcar) *Bus – Straßenbahn*

In most cities you'll find automatic ticket dispensers at each stop enabling you to buy your ticket in advance. In major cities it may be worthwhile to get a pass or a booklet of tickets.

I'd like a pass/booklet of tickets.	**Ich möchte eine Mehrfahrkarte/ein Fahrscheinheft.**	ikh **murkh**ter **igh**ner **mayr**-faarkahrter/ighn **faar**shighn-hehft
Which tram (streetcar) goes to the centre of town?	**Welche Straßenbahn fährt ins Stadt-zentrum?**	**vehl**kher **shtraa**ssern-baan fairt ins **shtaht**-tsehntrum
Where can I get a bus into town?	**Wo hält der Bus, der ins Stadt-zentrum fährt?**	voa hehlt derr buss derr ins **shtaht**-tsehntrum fairt
What bus do I take for ...?	**Welchen Bus muß ich nach ... nehmen?**	**vehl**khern buss muss ikh naakh ... **nay**mern
Where's the ...?	**Wo ist ...?**	voa ist
bus stop	**die Bushaltestelle**	dee **buss**hahltershtehler
terminus	**die Endstation**	dee **ehnt**shtahtsioan
When is the ... bus to ...?	**Wann fährt der ... Bus nach ...?**	vahn fairt derr ... buss naakh
first/last/next	**erste/letzte/nächste**	**ehr**ster/**lehts**ter/ **naikh**ster

How often do the buses to the airport run?	**Wie oft fahren die Busse zum Flughafen?**	vee oft **faa**rern dee **bus**ser tsum **floog**haafern
How much is the fare to ...?	**Was kostet es nach ...?**	vahss **kos**tert ehss naakh
Do I have to change buses?	**Muß ich umsteigen?**	muss ikh **um**shtighgern
How many bus stops are there to ...?	**Wie viele Haltestellen sind es bis ...?**	vee **fee**ler **hahl**tershtehlern zint ehss biss
Will you tell me when to get off?	**Können Sie mir bitte sagen, wann ich aussteigen muß?**	**kur**nern zee meer **bit**ter **zaa**gern vahn ikh **ows**shtighgern muss
I want to get off at the next stop.	**Ich möchte an der nächsten Haltestelle aussteigen.**	ikh **murkh**ter ahn derr **naikh**stern **hahl**tershtehler **ows**shtighgern

BUSHALTESTELLE	REGULAR BUS STOP
BEDARFSHALTESTELLE	STOPS ON REQUEST

Underground (subway) *U-Bahn*

The *U-Bahn* (**oo**-baan) in Berlin, Bonn, Düsseldorf, Cologne, Frankfurt, Hamburg and Munich corresponds to the London underground or the New York subway. A map showing the various lines and stations is displayed outside every station.

Where's the nearest underground station?	**Wo ist die nächste U-Bahnstation?**	voa ist dee **naikh**ster **oo**-baanshtahtsioan
Does this train go to ...?	**Fährt dieser Zug nach ...?**	fairt **dee**zerr tsoog naakh
Where do I change for ...?	**Wo muß ich nach ... umsteigen?**	voa muss ikh naakh ... **um**shtighgern
Is the next station ...?	**Ist die nächste Station ...?**	ist dee **naikh**ster shtaht**sioan**
Which line should I take for ...?	**Welche Linie fährt nach ...?**	**vehl**kher **lee**nier fairt naakh

Boat service *Auf dem Schiff*

When does a boat for ... leave?	**Wann fährt ein Schiff nach ...?**	vahn fairt ighn shif naakh
Where's the embarkation point?	**Wo ist der Anlegeplatz?**	voa ist derr **ahn**layger-plahts
When do we call at Cologne?	**Wann legen wir in Köln an?**	vahn **lay**gern veer in kurln ahn
I'd like to take a harbour roundtour.	**Ich möchte eine Hafenrundfahrt machen.**	ikh **murkh**ter **igh**ner **haa**-fernruntfaart **mah**khern
boat	**das Schiff/das Boot**	dahss shif/dahss boat
cabin	**die Kabine**	dee **kah**beener
single	**Einzelkabine**	**ighn**tserlkahbeener
double	**Zweierkabine**	**tsvigh**errkahbeener
cruise	**die Kreuzfahrt**	dee **kroyts**faart
crossing	**die Überfahrt**	dee **ew**berrfaart
deck	**das Deck**	dahss dehk
ferry	**die Fähre**	dee **fair**er
hydrofoil	**das Tragflächenboot**	dahss **traag**flehkhernboat
life belt	**der Rettungsring**	derr **reh**tungsring
life boat	**das Rettungsboot**	dahss **reh**tungsboat
port	**der Hafen**	derr **haa**fern
river cruise	**die Flußfahrt**	dee **flus**faart
ship	**das Schiff**	dahss shif
steamer	**das Dampfschiff**	dahss **dahmpf**shif

Bicycle hire *Fahrradverleih*

Many railway stations provide a bicycle-hire service.

I'd like to hire a bicycle.	**Ich möchte ein Fahrrad mieten.**	ikh **murkh**ter ighn **faar**raat **mee**tern

Other means of transport *Weitere Transportmittel*

cable car	**die Seilbahn**	dee **zighl**baan
helicopter	**der Hubschrauber**	derr **hoop**shrowberr
moped	**das Moped**	dahss **moa**peht
motorbike	**das Motorrad**	dahss **moa**torraat
scooter	**der Motorroller**	derr **moa**torrollerr

Or perhaps you prefer:

to hike	**wandern**	**vahn**derrn
to hitchhike	**trampen**	**trehm**pern
to walk	**zu Fuß gehen**	tsoo fuss **gay**ern

Car *Das Auto*

In general roads are good in Germany, Austria and Switzerland. Motorways (expressways) are free in Germany. In Austria some Alpine roads and tunnels charge tolls *(die Maut)*. If you use the motorways in Switzerland you must purchase a sticker *(die Vignette)* to be displayed on the windscreen.

A red reflector warning triangle must be carried for use in case of a breakdown, and seat-belts *(der Sicherheitsgurt)* are obligatory. In winter snow tyres or chains are compulsory on Alpine passes.

Where's the nearest filling station?	**Wo ist die nächste Tankstelle?**	voa ist dee **naikh**ster **tahnk**shtehler
Full tank, please.	**Volltanken, bitte.**	**vol**tahnkern **bit**ter
Give me ... litres of petrol (gasoline).	**Geben Sie mir ... Liter Benzin.**	**gay**bern zee mir ... **lee**terr behn**tseen**
super (premium)/ regular/lead-free/ diesel	**Super/Normal/ bleifreies Benzin/ Diesel**	**zoo**perr/nor**maal**/ **bligh**frigherss behn**tseen**/ **dee**zerl
Please check the ...	**Kontrollieren Sie bitte ...**	kontrol**leer**ern zee **bit**ter
battery	**die Batterie**	dee bahteh**ree**
brake fluid	**die Bremsflüssigkeit**	dee **brehms**flewssikhkight
oil	**das Öl**	dahss url
water	**das Wasser**	dahss **vah**sserr
Would you check the tyre pressure?	**Würden Sie bitte den Reifendruck prüfen?**	**vewr**dern zee **bit**ter dayn **righ**ferndruk **prew**fern
1.6 front, 1.8 rear.	**Vorne 1,6, hinten 1,8.**	**for**ner ighns zehks **hin**tern ighns ahkht
Please check the spare tyre, too.	**Prüfen Sie auch den Ersatzreifen, bitte.**	**prew**fern zee owkh dayn ehr**zahts**righfern **bit**ter
Can you mend this puncture (fix this flat)?	**Können Sie diesen Reifen flicken?**	**kur**nern zee **dee**zern **righ**fern **flik**kern
Would you please change the ...?	**Würden Sie bitte ... wechseln?**	**vewr**dern zee **bit**ter ... **vehk**serln
bulb	**die Glühbirne**	dee **glew**birner
fan belt	**den Keilriemen**	dayn **kighl**reemern

CAR HIRE, see page 20

spark(ing) plugs	**die Zündkerzen**	dee **tsewnt**kehrtsern
tyre	**den Reifen**	dayn **righ**fern
wipers	**die Scheibenwischer**	dee **shigh**bernvisherr
Would you clean the windscreen (windshield)?	**Würden Sie bitte die Windschutzscheibe reinigen?**	**vewr**dern zee **bit**ter dee **vint**shutsshighber **righ**niggern

Asking the way—Street directions *Nach dem Weg fragen*

Can you tell me the way to ...?	**Können Sie mir sagen, wie ich nach ... komme?**	**kur**nern zee meer **zaa**gern vee ikh naakh ... **kom**mer
How do I get to ...?	**Wie komme ich nach ...?**	vee **kom**mer ikh naakh
Are we on the right road for ...?	**Sind wir auf der richtigen Straße nach ...?**	zint veer owf derr **rikh**tiggern **shtraa**sser naakh
How far is the next village?	**Wie weit ist es bis zum nächsten Dorf?**	vee vight ist ehss biss tsum **nehkh**stern dorf
How far is it to ... from here?	**Wie weit ist es von hier nach ...?**	vee vight ist ehss fon heer naakh
Is there a motorway (expressway)?	**Gibt es eine Autobahn?**	gipt ehss **igh**ner **ow**tobbaan
Is there a road with little traffic?	**Gibt es eine wenig befahrene Straße?**	gipt ehss **igh**ner **vay**nikh ber**faa**rerner **shtraa**sser
How long does it take by car/on foot?	**Wie lange dauert es mit dem Auto/ zu Fuß?**	vee **lahn**ger **dow**errt ehss mit daym **ow**to/tsoo fuss
Can I drive to the centre of town?	**Kann ich bis ins Stadtzentrum fahren?**	kahn ikh biss ins **shtaht**tsehntrum **faa**rern
Can you tell me, where ... is?	**Können Sie mir sagen, wo ... ist?**	**kur**nern zee meer **zaa**gern voa ... ist
Where can I find this address/place?	**Wie komme ich zu dieser Adresse/ diesem Ort?**	vee **kom**mer ikh tsoo **dee**zerr ah**dreh**sser/ **dee**zerm ort
Where's this?	**Wo ist das?**	voa ist dahss
Can you show me on the map where I am?	**Können Sie mir auf der Karte zeigen, wo ich bin?**	**kur**nern zee meer owf derr **kahr**ter **tsigh**gern voa ikh bin

Sie sind auf der falschen Straße.	You're on the wrong road.
Fahren Sie geradeaus.	Go straight ahead.
Es ist dort vorne ...	It's down there on the ...
links/rechts **gegenüber/hinter ...** **neben/nach ...**	left/right opposite/behind ... next to/after ...
Nord/Süd/Ost/West	north/south/east/west
Fahren Sie bis zur ersten/ zweiten Kreuzung.	Go to the first/second crossroad (intersection).
Biegen Sie bei der Ampel links ab.	Turn left at the traffic lights.
Biegen Sie bei der nächsten Ecke rechts ab.	Turn right at the next corner.
Nehmen Sie die Straße nach ...	Take the road for ...
Sie müssen zurück nach ...	You have to go back to ...

Parking *Parken*

In town centres there are blue zones for which you need a parking disk (*eine Parkscheibe*—**igh**nerr **pahrk**shighber). You set it to show when you arrived and when you must leave. The disk can be obtained from tourist offices, petrol stations and hotels.

Where can I park?	**Wo kann ich parken?**	voa kahn ikh **pahr**kern
Is there a car park nearby?	**Gibt es einen Parkplatz hier in der Nähe?**	gipt ehss **igh**nern **pahrk**plahts heer in derr **nai**er
May I park here?	**Darf ich hier parken?**	dahrf ikh heer **pahr**kern
How long can I park here?	**Wie lange kann ich hier parken?**	vee **lahn**ger kahn ikh heer **pahr**kern
What's the charge per hour?	**Wieviel kostet es pro Stunde?**	vee**feel kos**tert ehss proa **shtun**der
Do you have some change for the parking meter?	**Haben Sie Kleingeld für die Parkuhr?**	**haa**bern zee **kligh**ngehlt fewr dee **pahrk**oor

Breakdown—Road assistance *Panne – Pannendienst*

Where's the nearest garage?	**Wo ist die nächste Reparaturwerkstatt?**	voa ist dee **naikh**ster raypahrah**toor**vehrkshtaht
Excuse me. My car has broken down.	**Entschuldigung, mein Wagen hat eine Panne.**	ehnt**shul**diggung mighn **vaa**gern haht **igh**ner **pah**ner
I've had a breakdown.	**Ich habe eine Panne.**	ikh **haa**ber **igh**ner **pah**ner
Can you send a mechanic?	**Können Sie einen Mechaniker schicken?**	**kur**nern zee **igh**nern meh**khah**nikkerr **shik**kern
My car won't start.	**Mein Auto springt nicht an.**	mighn **ow**to shpringt nikht ahn
The battery is dead.	**Die Batterie ist leer.**	dee bahteh**ree** ist layr
I've run out of petrol (gasoline).	**Ich habe eine Benzinpanne.**	ikh **haa**ber **igh**ner behnt**seen**pahner
I have a flat tyre.	**Ich habe einen Platten.**	ikh **haa**ber **igh**nern **plah**tern
The engine is overheating.	**Der Motor läuft heiß.**	derr **moa**tor loyft highss
There is something wrong with ...	**... ist/sind nicht in Ordnung.**	... ist/zint nikht in **ort**nung
brakes	**die Bremsen**	dee **brehm**zern
carburettor	**der Vergaser**	derr fehr**gaa**zerr
exhaust pipe	**der Auspuff**	derr **ows**puf
radiator	**der Kühler**	derr **kew**lerr
a wheel	**ein Rad**	ighn roat
Can you send a breakdown van (tow truck)?	**Können Sie einen Abschleppwagen schicken?**	**kur**nern zee **igh**nern **ahp**shlehpvaagern **shik**kern
How long will you be?	**Wie lange dauert es?**	vee **lah**nger **dow**errt ehss

Accident—Police *Verkehrsunfall – Polizei*

Please call the police.	**Rufen Sie bitte die Polizei.**	**roo**fern zee **bit**ter dee polli**tsigh**
There's been an accident. It's about 2 km. from ...	**Es ist ein Unfall passiert, ungefähr 2 Kilometer von ...**	ehss ist ighn **un**fahl pah**sseert un**gerfair 2 killoam**may**terr fon

Where's the nearest telephone?	**Wo ist das nächste Telefon?**	voa ist dahss **naikh**ster taylay**foan**
Call a doctor/an ambulance, quickly.	**Rufen Sie schnell einen Arzt/einen Krankenwagen.**	**roo**fern zee shnehl **igh**nern ahrtst/**igh**nern **krahn**kernvaagern
There are people injured.	**Es hat Verletzte gegeben.**	ehss haht fehr**leh**tster ger**gay**bern
Here's my driving licence.	**Hier ist mein Führerschein.**	heer ist mighn **few**rerrshighn
What's your name and address?	**Ihr Name und Ihre Anschrift, bitte?**	eer **naa**mer unt **ee**rer **ahn**shrift **bit**ter
What's your insurance company?	**Ihre Versicherungs-gesellschaft, bitte?**	**ee**rer fehr**zee**kherrungs-gerzehlshahft **bit**ter

Road signs *Verkehrszeichen*

AUSFAHRT	Exit (motorway)
DURCHGANGSVERKEHR	Through traffic
EINBAHNSTRASSE	One-way street
EINORDNEN	Get in lane
FROSTSCHÄDEN	Ice damage
FUSSGÄNGER	Pedestrians
GEFÄHRLICHES GEFÄLLE	Steep descent
GLATTEIS	Icy road
HALT, POLIZEI	Stop, police
HUPEN VERBOTEN	No honking
KURZPARKZONE	Limited parking zone
LANGSAM FAHREN	Slow down
LAWINENGEFAHR	Avalanche area
LKW	Heavy vehicles
NUR FÜR ANLIEGER	Access to residents only
PARKEN VERBOTEN	No parking
RECHTS FAHREN	Keep right
SCHLECHTE FAHRBAHN	Bad road surface
SCHULE	School
STAU	Traffic jam
STEINSCHLAG	Falling rocks
STRASSENARBEITEN	Road works ahead (men working)
UMLEITUNG	Diversion (detour)
... VERBOTEN	No ...
VORFAHRT GEWÄHREN	Give way (yield)
VORSICHT	Caution

Sightseeing

Where's the tourist office?	**Wo ist das Fremdenverkehrsbüro?**	voa ist dahss **frehm**dern-fehrkayrsbewroa
What are the main points of interest?	**Was sind die Hauptsehenswürdigkeiten?**	vahss zint dee **howpt**-zayernsvewrdikhkightern
We're here for ...	**Wir sind für ... hier.**	veer zint fewr ... heer
a few hours	**ein paar Stunden**	ighn paar **shtun**dern
a day	**einen Tag**	**igh**nern taag
a week	**eine Woche**	**igh**ner **vo**kher
Can you recommend a sightseeing tour/an excursion?	**Können Sie eine Stadtrundfahrt/einen Ausflug empfehlen?**	kurnern zee **igh**ner **shtaht**-runtfaart/**igh**nern **ows**floog ehm**pfay**lern
What's the point of departure?	**Von wo fahren wir ab?**	fon voa **fah**rern veer ahp
Will the bus pick us up at the hotel?	**Holt uns der Bus vorm Hotel ab?**	hoalt uns derr buss foarm hot**tehl** ahp
How much does the tour cost?	**Was kostet die Rundfahrt?**	vahss **ko**stert dee **runt**faart
What time does the tour start?	**Wann beginnt die Rundfahrt?**	vahn ber**gint** dee **runt**faart
Is lunch included?	**Ist das Mittagessen inbegriffen?**	ist dahss **mit**taagehssern **in**bergriffern
What time do we get back?	**Wann werden wir zurück sein?**	vahn **vayr**dern veer tsoo**rewk** zighn
Do we have free time in ...?	**Haben wir in ... Zeit zu freier Verfügung?**	**haa**bern veer in ... tsight tsoo **frigh**err fehr**few**gung
Is there an English-speaking guide?	**Gibt es einen englischsprechenden Fremdenführer?**	gipt ehss **igh**nern **ehng**lishshprehkherndern **frehm**dernfewrerr
I'd like to hire a private guide for ...	**Ich möchte einen Fremdenführer für ...**	ikh **murch**ter **igh**nern **frehm**dernfewrerr fewr
half a day	**einen halben Tag**	**igh**nern **hahl**bern taag
a full day	**einen Tag**	**igh**nern taag

Where is/Where are the ...?	**Wo ist/Wo sind ...?**	voa ist/voa zint
abbey	**die Abtei**	dee ahp**tigh**
alley	**die Gasse**	dee **gah**sser
amusement park	**der Vergnügungspark**	derr fehr**gnew**gungspahrk
art gallery	**die Kunstgalerie**	dee **kunst**gahlehree
botanical gardens	**der Botanische Garten**	derr bott**aa**nisher **gahr**tern
building	**das Gebäude**	dahss ger**boy**der
business district	**das Geschäftsviertel**	dahss ger**shehfts**feerterl
cathedral	**die Kathedrale/der Dom**	dee kahteh**draa**ler/derr doam
cave	**die Höhle**	dee **hur**ler
cemetery	**der Friedhof**	derr **free**thoaf
chapel	**die Kapelle**	dee kah**peh**ler
church	**die Kirche**	dee **keer**kher
city walls	**die Stadtmauern**	dee **shtaht**mowerrn
concert hall	**die Konzerthalle**	dee kon**tsehrt**hahler
convent	**das Kloster**	dahss **kloa**sterr
convention hall	**die Kongreßhalle**	dee kon**grehs**hahler
court house	**das Gericht**	dahss ger**rikht**
downtown area	**die Innenstadt**	dee **in**nernshtaht
exhibition	**die Ausstellung**	dee **ows**shtehlung
factory	**die Fabrik**	dee fah**brik**
fair	**die Messe**	dee **meh**sser
flea market	**der Flohmarkt**	derr **floa**mahrkt
fortress	**die Festung**	dee **feh**stung
fountain	**der Brunnen/Springbrunnen**	derr **brun**nern/**shpring**brunnern
gardens	**die Grünanlagen**	dee **grewn**ahnlaagern
harbour	**der Hafen**	derr **haa**fern
lake	**der See**	derr zay
library	**die Bibliothek**	dee biblio**tayk**
market	**der Markt**	derr mahrkt
memorial	**das Denkmal**	dahss **dehnk**maal
monastery	**das Kloster**	dahss **kloa**sterr
monument	**das Denkmal**	dahss **dehnk**maal
museum	**das Museum**	dahss mu**zay**um
old town	**die Altstadt**	dee **ahlt**shtaht
opera house	**das Opernhaus**	dahss **oa**perrnhowss
palace	**der Palast/das Schloß**	derr pah**lahst**/dahss shloss
park	**der Park**	derr pahrk
parliament building	**das Parlamentsgebäude**	dahss pahrlah**mehnts**gerboyder
ruins	**die Ruinen**	dee ru**ee**nern
shopping area	**das Geschäftsviertel**	dahss ger**shehfts**feerterl

square	**der Platz**	derr plahts
stadium	**das Stadion**	dahss **shtaa**dion
statue	**die Statue**	dee **shtaa**tuer
stock exchange	**die Börse**	dee **burr**zer
street	**die Straße**	dee **shtrah**sser
theatre	**das Theater**	dahss tay**aa**terr
tomb	**das Grab**	dahss graap
tower	**der Turm**	derr toorm
town hall	**das Rathaus**	dahss **raat**howss
university	**die Universität**	dee unnivehrzi**tait**
wall	**die Mauer**	dee **mow**err
zoo	**der Zoo**	derr tsoa

Admission *Eintritt*

Is ... open on Sundays?	**Ist ... sonntags geöffnet?**	ist ... **zon**taags ger**urf**nert
What are the opening hours?	**Welches sind die Öffnungszeiten?**	**vehl**kherss zint dee **urf**nungstsightern
When does it close?	**Wann schließt es?**	vahn shleest ehss
How much is the entrance fee?	**Was kostet der Eintritt?**	vahss **kos**tert derr **ighn**trit
Is there any reduction for ...?	**Gibt es Ermäßigung für ...?**	gipt ehss ehr**mais**siggung fewr
children	**Kinder**	**kin**derr
disabled	**Behinderte**	ber**hin**derrter
groups	**Gruppen**	**grup**pern
pensioners	**Rentner**	**rehnt**nerr
students	**Studenten**	**shtud**dehntern
Have you a guide book (in English)?	**Haben Sie einen Reiseführer (in Englisch)?**	**haa**bern zee **igh**nern **righ**zerfewrerr (in **ehng**lish)
Can I buy a catalogue?	**Kann ich einen Katalog kaufen?**	kahn ikh **igh**nern kahtah**loag kow**fern
Is it all right to take pictures?	**Darf man fotografieren?**	dahrf mahn fotto-grah**fee**rern

EINTRITT FREI	ADMISSION FREE
FOTOGRAFIEREN VERBOTEN	NO CAMERAS ALLOWED

Who—What—When? *Wer – Was – Wann?*

What's that building?	**Was für ein Gebäude ist das?**	vahss fewr ighn ger**boy**der ist dahss
Who was the ...?	**Wer war der ...?**	vayr vaar derr
architect	**Architekt**	ahrkhit**tehkt**
artist	**Künstler**	**kewnst**lerr
painter	**Maler**	**maa**lerr
sculptor	**Bildhauer**	**bilt**howerr
Who built it?	**Wer hat es gebaut?**	vayr haht ehss ger**bowt**
Who painted that picture?	**Wer hat das Bild gemalt?**	vayr haht dahss bilt ger**maalt**
When did he live?	**Wann hat er gelebt?**	vahn haht ehr ger**laybt**
When was it built?	**Wann wurde es erbaut?**	vahn **voor**der ehss ehr**bowt**
Where's the house where ... lived?	**Wo ist das Haus, in dem ... wohnte?**	voa ist dahss howss in daym ... **voan**ter
We're interested in ...	**Wir interessieren uns für ...**	veer intehreh**ssee**rern uns fewr
antiques	**Antiquitäten**	ahntikvit**tai**tern
archaeology	**Archäologie**	ahrkhehollo**gee**
art	**Kunst**	kunst
botany	**Botanik**	bot**taa**nik
ceramics	**Keramik**	kehr**raa**mik
coins	**Münzen**	**mewn**tsern
fine arts	**bildende Künste**	**bil**dernder **kewn**ster
furniture	**Möbel**	**mur**berl
geology	**Geologie**	gayollo**gee**
handicrafts	**Kunsthandwerk**	**kunst**hahntvehrk
history	**Geschichte**	ger**shikh**ter
medicine	**Medizin**	mehdi**tseen**
music	**Musik**	mu**zeek**
natural history	**Naturkunde**	nah**toor**kunder
ornithology	**Vogelkunde**	**foa**gerlkunder
painting	**Malerei**	maaleh**righ**
pottery	**Töpferei**	turpfeh**righ**
religion	**Religion**	rayli**ggioan**
sculpture	**Bildhauerei**	**bilt**howerrigh
zoology	**Zoologie**	tsoaollo**gee**
Where's the ... department?	**Wo ist die ...-Abteilung?**	voa ist dee ... **ahp**tighlung

It's ...	**Es ist ...**	ehss ist
amazing	**erstaunlich**	ehr**shtown**likh
awful	**scheußlich**	**shoyss**likh
beautiful	**schön**	shurn
gloomy	**düster**	**dew**sterr
impressive	**eindrucksvoll**	**ighn**druksfol
interesting	**interessant**	intehreh**ssahnt**
lovely	**wunderschön**	**voon**derrshurn
magnificent	**großartig**	**groass**ahrtikh
overwhelming	**überwältigend**	ewberr**vehl**tiggernt
pretty	**hübsch**	hewpsh
romantic	**romantisch**	rom**mahn**tish
sinister	**unheimlich**	**un**highmlikh
strange	**seltsam**	**zehlt**zaam
superb	**prächtig**	**prehkh**tikh
terrible	**schrecklich**	**shrehk**likh
tremendous	**außerordentlich**	owsserr**or**derntlikh
ugly	**häßlich**	**hehss**likh

Churches—Religious services *Kirchen – Gottesdienste*

Most churches and cathedrals are open to the public except, of course, when a service is being conducted.

Services are conducted in English in many towns. Ask the local tourist office for further details.

Is there a ... near here?	**Gibt es eine ... in der Nähe?**	gipt ehss **igh**ner ... in derr **nai**er
Catholic church	**katholische Kirche**	kah**toa**lisher **keer**kher
Protestant church	**evangelische/protestantische Kirche**	ehvahn**gay**lisher/protteh**shtahn**tisher **keer**kher
synagogue	**Synagoge**	zewnah**goa**ger
mosque	**Moschee**	mo**shay**
At what time is ...?	**Wann beginnt ...?**	vahn ber**gint**
mass	**die Messe**	dee **meh**sser
the service	**der Gottesdienst**	derr **got**tersdeenst
Where can I find a ... who speaks English?	**Wo finde ich einen ..., der Englisch spricht?**	voa **fin**der ikh **igh**nern ... derr **ehng**lish shprikht
priest/minister rabbi	**Priester/Pfarrer Rabbiner**	**pree**sterr/**pfah**rerr/ rah**bee**nerr
I'd like to visit the church.	**Ich möchte die Kirche besichtigen.**	ikh **murkh**ter dee **kir**kherr ber**zikh**tiggern

In the countryside *Auf dem Lande*

Is there a scenic route to ...?	**Gibt es eine landschaftlich schöne Straße nach ...?**	gipt ehss **igh**ner **lahnt**shahftlikh **shur**ner shtraasser naakh
How far is it to ...?	**Wie weit ist es bis ...?**	vee vight ist ehss biss
Can we walk?	**Können wir zu Fuß gehen?**	**kur**nern veer tsoo fooss **gay**ern
How high is that mountain?	**Wie hoch ist dieser Berg?**	vee hoakh ist **dee**zerr behrg
What kind of ... is that?	**Was für ... ist das?**	vahss fewr ... ist dahss
animal/bird	**ein Tier/ein Vogel**	ighn teer/ighn **foa**gerl
flower/tree	**eine Blume/ein Baum**	**igh**ner **bloo**mer/ighn bowm

Landmarks *Zur Orientierung*

bridge	**die Brücke**	dee **brew**ker
castle	**das Schloß/die Burg**	dahss shloss/dee boorg
farm	**der Bauernhof**	derr **bow**errnhoaf
field	**das Feld**	dahss fehlt
footpath	**der Fußweg**	derr **foos**vayg
forest	**der Wald**	derr vahlt
garden	**der Garten**	derr **gahr**tern
hill	**der Hügel**	derr **hew**gerl
house	**das Haus**	dahss howss
lake	**der See**	derr zay
meadow	**die Wiese**	dee **vee**zer
path	**der Weg**	derr vayg
mountain pass	**der Paß**	derr pahss
peak	**die Bergspitze**	dee **behrg**shpitser
pond	**der Teich**	derr tighkh
river	**der Fluß/der Strom**	derr fluss/derr shtroam
rock	**der Felsen**	derr fehlzern
road	**die Straße**	dee **shtraa**sser
sea	**die See/das Meer**	dee zay/dahss mayr
spring	**die Quelle**	dee **kveh**ler
valley	**das Tal**	dahss taal
village	**das Dorf**	dahss dorf
vineyard	**der Weinberg**	derr **vighn**behrg
waterfall	**der Wasserfall**	derr **vahsser**fahl
well	**der Brunnen**	derr **brun**nern
wood	**der Wald**	derr vahlt

ASKING THE WAY, see page 76

Relaxing

Cinema (movies)—Theatre *Kino – Theater*

Foreign films are usually dubbed into German, though some cinemas also screen them in the original, with German subtitles, at certain times on certain days. Since cinema showings are seldom continuous you can buy your tickets in advance. Theatre curtain time is about 8 p.m. Advance booking is advisable.

You can find out what's playing from newspapers and bill-boards. In most large towns you can buy a publication of the type "This Week in ...".

What's showing at the cinema tonight?	**Was gibt es heute abend im Kino zu sehen?**	vahss gipt ehss **hoy**ter **aa**bernt im **kee**no tsoo **zay**ern
What's playing at the ... theatre?	**Was wird im ...theater gegeben?**	vahss veert im ... tay**aa**terr ger**gay**bern
What sort of play is it?	**Was für ein Stück ist es?**	vahss fewr ighn shtewk ist ehss
Who's it by?	**Von wem ist es?**	fon vaym ist ehss
Can you recommend a ...?	**Können Sie mir ... empfehlen?**	**kur**nern zee meer ... ehmp**fay**lern
good film	**einen guten Film**	**igh**nern **goo**tern film
comedy	**eine Komödie**	**igh**ner kom**mur**dier
musical	**ein Musical**	ighn "musical"
Where's that new film by ... being shown?	**Wo läuft der neue Film von ...?**	voa loyft derr **noy**er film fon
Who's in it?	**Mit welchen Schau-spielern?**	mit **vehl**khern **show**-shpeelerrn
Who's playing the lead?	**Wer spielt die Hauptrolle?**	vayr shpeelt dee **howpt**roller
Who's the director?	**Wer ist der Regisseur?**	vayr ist derr rehzhi**ssurr**
At what theatre is that new play by ... being performed?	**In welchem Theater wird das neue Stück von ... gespielt?**	in **vehl**kherm tay**aa**terr veert dahss **noy**er shtewk fon ... ger**shpeelt**

What time does the show begin?	**Wann beginnt die Vorstellung?**	vahn ber**gint** dee **foar**shtehlung
What time does the performance end?	**Wann ist die Vorstellung zu Ende?**	vahn ist dee **foar**-shtehlung tsoo **ehn**der
Are there any tickets for tonight?	**Gibt es noch Karten für heute abend?**	gipt ehss nokh **kahr**tern fewr **hoy**ter **aa**bernt
How much are the tickets?	**Wie teuer sind die Karten?**	vee **toy**err zint dee **kahr**tern
I want to reserve 2 tickets for the show on Friday evening.	**Ich möchte 2 Karten für Freitag abend vorbestellen.**	ikh **murkh**ter 2 **kahr**tern fewr **frigh**taag **aa**bernt **foar**bershtehlern
Can I have a ticket for the matinée on ...?	**Kann ich eine Karte für die Nachmittagsvorstellung am ... bekommen?**	kahn ikh **igh**ner **kahr**ter fewr dee **nahkh**mittaags-foarshtehlung ahm ... ber**kom**mern
I want a seat in the stalls (orchestra).	**Ich hätte gern einen Platz im Parkett.**	ikh **heh**ter gehrn **igh**nern plahts im pahr**keht**
Not too far back.	**Nicht zu weit hinten.**	nikht tsu vight **hin**tern
Somewhere in the middle.	**Irgendwo in der Mitte.**	**eer**gerntvoa in derr **mit**ter
How much are the seats in the circle (mezzanine)?	**Wie teuer sind die Plätze im Rang?**	vee **toy**er zint dee **pleht**ser im rahng
May I please have a programme?	**Kann ich bitte ein Programm haben?**	kahn ikh **bit**ter ighn pro**grahm** **haa**bern
Where's the cloakroom?	**Wo ist die Garderobe?**	voa ist dee gahrder**roa**ber

Bedaure, es ist alles ausverkauft.	I'm sorry, we're sold out.
Es gibt nur noch ein paar Plätze im Rang.	There are only a few seats left in the circle (mezzanine).
Darf ich Ihre Eintrittskarte sehen?	May I see your ticket?
Hier ist Ihr Platz.	This is your seat.

DAYS OF THE WEEK, see page 151

Opera—Ballet—Concert *Oper - Ballett - Konzert*

Can you recommend a ...?	**Können Sie mir ... empfehlen?**	**kur**nern zee meer ehm**pfay**lern
ballet	**ein Ballett**	ighn bah**leht**
concert	**ein Konzert**	ighn kon**tsehrt**
opera	**eine Oper**	**igh**ner **oa**perr
operetta	**eine Operette**	**igh**ner oppeh**reh**ter
Where's the opera house/the concert hall?	**Wo ist das Opernhaus/die Konzerthalle?**	voa ist dahss **oa**perrnhowss/ dee kon**tsehrt**hahler
What's on at the opera tonight?	**Was wird heute abend in der Oper gegeben?**	vahss veert **hoy**ter **aa**bernt in derr **oa**perr ger**gay**bern
Who's singing/ dancing?	**Wer singt/tanzt?**	vayr zingt/tahntst
What orchestra is playing?	**Welches Orchester spielt?**	**vehl**khers or**keh**sterr shpeelt
What are they playing?	**Was wird gespielt?**	vahss veert ger**shpeelt**
Who's the conductor/ soloist?	**Wer ist der Dirigent/ der Solist?**	vayr ist derr dirrig**gehnt**/ derr sollist

Nightclubs *Nachtlokale*

Can you recommend a good nightclub?	**Können Sie mir ein gutes Nachtlokal empfehlen?**	**kur**nern zee meer ighn **goo**terss **nahkht**lokkaal ehm**pfay**lern
Is there a floor show?	**Gibt es Attraktionen?**	gipt ehss ahtrahk**tsioa**nern
Is evening dress necessary?	**Wird Abendgarderobe verlangt?**	veert **aa**berntgahrdehroaber fehr**lahngt**

Discos *Diskotheken*

Where can we go dancing?	**Wo können wir tanzen gehen?**	voa **kur**nern veer **tahn**tsern **gay**ern
Is there a discotheque in town?	**Gibt es hier eine Diskothek?**	gipt ehss heer **igh**ner diskot**tayk**
Would you like to dance?	**Möchten Sie tanzen?**	**murkh**tern zee **tahn**tsern

Sports *Sport*

You name the sport, and you'll doubtless be able to find it in Germany, Austria and Switzerland. The most popular spectator sport is by far football (soccer).

Is there a football (soccer) game anywhere this Saturday?	**Findet diesen Samstag irgendwo ein Fußballspiel statt?**	**fin**dert **dee**zern **zahms**taag **ir**gerntvoa ighn **foos**bahlshpeel shtaht
Which teams are playing?	**Welche Mannschaften spielen?**	**vehl**kher **mahn**shahftern **shpee**lern
Can you get me a ticket?	**Können Sie mir eine Karte besorgen?**	**kur**nern zee meer **igh**ner **kahr**ter ber**zor**gern

basketball	**Basketball**	**baas**kertbahl
boxing	**Boxen**	**bok**sern
car racing	**Autorennen**	**ow**torrehnern
cycling	**Radfahren**	**raat**faarern
football (soccer)	**Fußball**	**foos**bahl
horse racing	**Pferderennen**	**pfayr**derrehnern
horseback riding	**Reiten**	**righ**tern
mountaineering	**Bergsteigen**	**behrg**shtighgern
skiing	**Skifahren**	**shee**faarern
swimming	**Schwimmen**	**shvim**mern
tennis	**Tennis**	**teh**niss
volleyball	**Volleyball**	**vol**libbahl

I'd like to see a boxing match.	**Ich möchte gern einen Boxkampf sehen.**	ikh **murkh**ter gehrn **igh**nern **boks**kahmpf **zay**ern
What's the admission charge?	**Was kostet der Eintritt?**	vahss **kos**tert derr **ighn**trit
Where's the nearest golf course?	**Wo ist der nächste Golfplatz?**	voa ist derr **naikh**ster **golf**plahts
Where are the tennis courts?	**Wo sind die Tennisplätze?**	voa zint dee **teh**nisplehtser
Can I hire (rent) rackets?	**Kann ich Tennisschläger mieten?**	kahn ikh **teh**nisshlaigerr **mee**tern
What's the charge per ...?	**Wieviel kostet es pro ...**	vee**feel kos**tert ehss proa
day/round/hour	**Tag/Spiel/Stunde**	taag/shpeel/**shtun**der

DAYS OF THE WEEK, see page 151

Where's the nearest race course (track)?	**Wo ist die nächste Pferderennbahn?**	voa ist dee **naikh**ster **pfehr**derrehnbaan
Is there any good fishing around here?	**Kann man hier in der Nähe angeln?**	kahn mahn heer in derr **nai**er **ahng**erln
Do I need a permit?	**Brauche ich einen Angelschein?**	**brow**kher ikh **igh**nern **ahng**erlshighn
Where can I get one?	**Wo bekomme ich einen?**	voa ber**kom**mer ikh **igh**nern
Can one swim in the lake/river?	**Kann man im See/Fluß baden?**	kahn mahn im zay/ fluss **baa**dern
Is there a swimming pool here?	**Gibt es hier ein Schwimmbad?**	gipt ehss heer ighn **shvim**baat
Is it open-air or indoor?	**Ist es ein Freibad oder ein Hallenbad?**	ist ehss ighn **frigh**baat **oa**derr ighn **hah**lernbaat
Is it heated?	**Ist es geheizt?**	ist ehss ger**hightst**
What's the temperature of the water?	**Welche Temperatur hat das Wasser?**	**vehl**kher tehmperrah**toor** haht dahss **vah**sser
Is there a sandy beach?	**Gibt es einen Sandstrand?**	gipt ehss **igh**nern **zahnt**shtrahnt

On the beach *Am Strand*

The sea is very calm.	**Das Meer ist sehr ruhig.**	dahss mayr ist zayr **roo**ikh
There are some big waves.	**Das Meer hat hohen Wellengang.**	dahss mayr haht **hoa**ern **veh**lerngahng
Is it safe for swimming?	**Kann man hier gefahrlos schwimmen?**	kahn mahn heer ger**faar**-loass **shvim**mern
Is there a lifeguard?	**Gibt es einen Rettungsdienst?**	gipt ehss **igh**nern **reh**tungsdeenst
Is it safe for children?	**Ist es für Kinder ungefährlich?**	ist ehss fewr **kin**derr **un**gerfairlikh
Are there any dangerous currents?	**Gibt es gefährliche Strömungen?**	gipt ehss ger**fair**likher **shtrur**mungern
What time is high tide/low tide?	**Wann ist Flut/Ebbe?**	vahn ist floot/**eh**ber

I want to hire (rent) a/an/some ...	**Ich möchte ... mieten.**	ikh **murkh**ter ... **mee**tern
bathing hut (cabana)	**eine Badekabine**	**igh**ner **baa**derkahbeener
deck-chair	**einen Liegestuhl**	**igh**nern **lee**gershtool
motorboat	**ein Motorboot**	ighn **moa**torboat
rowing-boat	**ein Ruderboot**	ighn **roo**derrboat
sailboard	**einen Windsurfer**	**igh**nern **vint**surrferr
sailing-boat	**ein Segelboot**	ighn **zay**gerlboat
skin-diving equipment	**eine Taucher-ausrüstung**	**igh**ner **tow**kherr-owsrewstung
sunshade (umbrella)	**einen Sonnenschirm**	**igh**nern **zon**nernsheerm
surfboard	**ein Surfbrett**	ighn **surf**breht
water-skis	**Wasserski**	**vah**ssershee

PRIVATSTRAND	PRIVATE BEACH
BADEN VERBOTEN	NO SWIMMING

Winter sports *Wintersport*

Is there a skating-rink near here?	**Gibt es hier in der Nähe eine Eisbahn?**	gipt ehss heer in derr **nai**er **igh**ner **ighs**baan
I'd like to ski.	**Ich möchte skifahren.**	ikh **murkh**ter **shee**faarern
downhill/cross-country skiing	**Abfahrtslauf/ Langlauf**	**ahp**fahrtslowf/ **lahng**lowf
Are there any ski runs for ...?	**Gibt es Skipisten für ...?**	gipt ehss **shee**pistern fewr
beginners	**Anfänger**	**ahn**faingerr
good skiers	**Fortgeschrittene**	**fort**gershritterner
Can I take skiing lessons?	**Kann ich Ski-unterricht nehmen?**	kahn ikh **shee**unterrrikht **nay**mern
Are there ski lifts?	**Gibt es Skilifte?**	gipt ehss **shee**lifter
I want to hire a/ some ...	**Ich möchte ... mieten.**	ikh **murkh**ter ... **mee**tern
poles	**Skistöcke**	**shee**shturker
skates	**Schlittschuhe**	**shlit**shooer
ski boots	**Skischuhe**	**shee**shooer
skiing equipment	**eine Skiausrüstung**	**igh**ner **shee**owsrewstung
skis	**Skier**	**shee**err

Making friends

Introductions *Vorstellen*

May I introduce ...?	**Darf ich ... vorstellen?**	dahrf ikh ... **foar**shtehlern
John, this is ...	**John, das ist ...**	John dahss ist
My name is ...	**Ich heiße ...**	ikh **high**sser
Glad to know you.	**Sehr erfreut.**	zayr ehr**froyt**
What's your name?	**Wie heißen Sie?**	vee **high**ssern zee
How are you?	**Wie geht es Ihnen?**	vee gayt ehss **ee**nern
Fine, thanks. And you?	**Danke, gut. Und Ihnen?**	**dahn**ker goot. unt **ee**nern

Follow-up *Näheres Kennenlernen*

How long have you been here?	**Wie lange sind Sie schon hier?**	vee **lahn**ger zint zee shoan heer
We've been here a week.	**Wir sind seit einer Woche hier.**	veer zint zight **igh**nerr **vo**kher heer
Is this your first visit?	**Sind Sie zum ersten Mal hier?**	zint zee tsum **ehr**stern maal heer
No, we came here last year.	**Nein, wir waren schon letztes Jahr hier.**	nighn veer **vaa**rern shoan **lehts**terss yaar heer
Are you enjoying your stay?	**Gefällt es Ihnen hier?**	ger**fehlt** ehss **ee**nern heer
Yes, I like it very much.	**Ja, mir gefällt es sehr gut.**	yaa meer ger**fehlt** ehss zayr goot
I like the landscape a lot.	**Die Landschaft gefällt mir sehr.**	dee **lahnt**shahft ger**fehlt** meer zayr
What do you think of the country/ the city?	**Wie gefällt Ihnen das Land/die Stadt?**	vee ger**fehlt** **ee**nern dahss lahnt/dee shtaht
Where do you come from?	**Woher kommen Sie?**	voa**hayr** kommern zee
I'm from ...	**Ich bin aus ...**	ikh bin owss

COUNTRIES, see page 146

I'm ...	**Ich bin ...**	ikh bin
American British Canadian English Irish	**Amerikaner(in)** **Brite (Britin)** **Kanadier(in)** **Engländer(in)** **Ire (Irin)**	ahmehrik**kaa**nerr(in) **brit**ter (**brit**tin) kah**naa**dierr(rin) **ehng**lehnderr(in) **ee**rer (**ee**rin)
Where are you staying?	**Wo wohnen Sie?**	voa **voa**nern zee
Are you on your own?	**Sind Sie allein hier?**	zint zee ah**lighn** heer
I'm with my ...	**Ich bin mit ... hier.**	ikh bin mit ... heer
wife husband family parents boyfriend girlfriend	**meiner Frau** **meinem Mann** **meiner Familie** **meinen Eltern** **meinem Freund** **meiner Freundin**	**migh**nerr frow **migh**nerm mahn **migh**nerr fah**mee**lier **migh**nern **ehl**terrn **migh**nerm froynt **migh**nerr **froyn**din

father/mother	**der Vater/die Mutter**	derr **faa**terr/dee **mut**terr
son/daughter	**der Sohn/die Tochter**	derr zoan/dee **tokh**terr
brother/sister	**der Bruder/die Schwester**	derr **broo**derr/dee **shveh**sterr
uncle/aunt	**der Onkel/die Tante**	derr **on**kerl/dee **tahn**ter
nephew/niece	**der Neffe/die Nichte**	derr **neh**fer/dee **neekh**ter
cousin	**der Cousin/die Cousine**	derr ku**zehng**/dee ku**zee**ner

Are you married/ single?	**Sind Sie verheiratet/ ledig?**	zint zee fehr**high**raatert/ **lay**dikh
Do you have children?	**Haben Sie Kinder?**	**haar**bern zee **kin**derr
What's your occupation?	**Was machen Sie beruflich?**	vahss **mahkh**ern zee ber**roof**likh
I'm a student.	**Ich bin Student(in).**	ikh bin shtud**dehnt**(in)
What are you studying?	**Was studieren Sie?**	vahss shtud**dee**rern zee
I'm here on a business trip.	**Ich bin auf einer Geschäftsreise hier.**	ikh bin owf **igh**nerr ger**shehfts**righzer heer
Do you travel a lot?	**Reisen Sie viel?**	**righ**zern zee feel
Do you play cards/ chess?	**Spielen Sie Karten/ Schach?**	**shpee**lern zee **kahr**tern/ shahkh

The weather *Das Wetter*

What a lovely day!	**Was für ein herrlicher Tag!**	vahss fewr ighn **hehr**likherr taag
What awful weather!	**Was für ein scheußliches Wetter!**	vahss fewr ighn **shoyss**likherss **veh**terr
Isn't it cold/hot today?	**Welche Kälte/Hitze heute!**	**vehl**kher **kehl**ter/**hit**ser **hoy**ter
Is it usually as warm as this?	**Ist es immer so warm?**	ist ehss **im**merr zoa vahrm
Do you think it's going to ... tomorrow?	**Glauben Sie, es wird morgen ...?**	**glow**bern zee ehss veert **mor**gern
be a nice day	**schön sein**	shurn zighn
rain	**regnen**	**rayg**nern
snow	**schneien**	**shnig**hern
What is the weather forecast?	**Was sagt der Wetterbericht?**	vahss zahgt derr **veh**terrberrikht

cloud	**die Wolke**	dee **vol**ker
fog	**der Nebel**	derr **nay**berl
frost	**der Frost**	derr frost
ice	**das Eis**	dahss ighss
lightning	**der Blitz**	derr blits
moon	**der Mond**	derr moant
rain	**der Regen**	derr **ray**gern
sky	**der Himmel**	derr **him**merl
snow	**der Schnee**	derr shnay
star	**der Stern**	derr shtehrn
sun	**die Sonne**	dee **zon**ner
thunder	**der Donner**	derr **don**nerr
thunderstorm	**das Gewitter**	dahss ger**vit**terr
wind	**der Wind**	derr vint

Invitations *Einladungen*

Would you like to have dinner with us on ...?	**Möchten Sie am ... mit uns zu Abend essen?**	**murkh**tern zee ahm ... mit uns tsoo **aa**bernt **eh**ssern
May I invite you for lunch?	**Darf ich Sie zum Mittagessen einladen?**	dahrf ikh zee tsum **mit**taagehssern **ighn**laadern

DAYS OF THE WEEK, see page 151

Can you come over for a drink this evening?	**Kommen Sie heute abend auf ein Gläschen zu uns?**	**kom**mern zee **hoy**ter **aa**bernt owf ighn **glais**khern tsoo uns
There's a party. Are you coming?	**Es gibt eine Party. Kommen Sie auch?**	ehss gipt ighner **paar**tee. **kom**mern zee owkh
That's very kind of you.	**Das ist sehr nett von Ihnen.**	dahss ist zayr neht fon **ee**nern
Great. I'd love to come.	**Prima, ich komme sehr gerne.**	**pree**maa ikh **kom**mer zayr **gehr**ner
What time shall we come?	**Wann sollen wir da sein?**	vahn **zol**lern veer daa zighn
May I bring a friend/ a girlfriend?	**Kann ich einen Freund/eine Freundin mitbringen?**	kahn ikh **igh**nern froynt/**igh**nerr **froynd**in **mit**bringern
I'm afraid we've got to leave now.	**Leider müssen wir jetzt gehen.**	**ligh**derr **mew**ssern veer yehtst **gay**ern
Next time you must come to visit us.	**Nächstes Mal müssen Sie uns besuchen.**	**naikh**sterss maal **mew**ssern zee uns ber**zoo**khern
Thanks for the evening. It was great.	**Vielen Dank für den schönen Abend.**	feelern dahnk fewr dayn **shur**nern **aa**bernt

Dating *Verabredung*

Do you mind if I smoke?	**Stört es Sie, wenn ich rauche?**	shturt ehss zee vehn ikh **row**kher
Would you like a cigarette?	**Möchten Sie eine Zigarette?**	**murkh**tern zee **igh**ner tsiggah**reh**ter
Do you have a light, please?	**Können Sie mir bitte Feuer geben?**	**kur**nern zee meer **bit**ter **foy**err **gay**bern
Why are you laughing?	**Warum lachen Sie?**	vah**room lahkh**ern zee
Is my German that bad?	**Ist mein Deutsch so schlecht?**	ist mighn doych zoa shlehkht
Can I get you a drink?	**Möchten Sie etwas trinken?**	**murkh**tern zee **eht**vahss **trin**kern
Are you waiting for someone?	**Warten Sie auf jemanden?**	**vahr**tern zee owf **yay**mahndern
Are you free this evening?	**Sind Sie heute abend frei?**	zint zee **hoy**ter **aa**bernt frigh

Would you like to go out with me tonight?	**Möchten Sie heute abend mit mir ausgehen?**	**murkh**tern zee **hoy**ter **aa**bernt mit meer **ows**gayern
Would you like to go dancing?	**Möchten Sie gern tanzen gehen?**	**murkh**tern zee gehrn **tahn**tsern **gay**ern
I know a good discotheque.	**Ich kenne eine gute Diskothek.**	ikh **keh**ner **igh**ner **goo**ter disko**tayk**
Shall we go to the cinema (movies)?	**Wollen wir ins Kino gehen?**	**vol**lern veer ins **kee**no **gay**ern
Would you like to go for a drive?	**Wollen wir ein bißchen durch die Gegend fahren?**	**vol**lern veer ighn **biss**khern doorkh dee **gay**gernt **faa**rern
Where shall we meet?	**Wo treffen wir uns?**	voa **treh**fern veer uns
I'll pick you up at your hotel.	**Ich hole Sie in Ihrem Hotel ab.**	ikh **hoa**ler zee in **ee**rerm hot**tehl** ahp
I'll call for you at 8.	**Ich hole Sie um 8 Uhr ab.**	ikh **hoa**ler zee um 8 oor ahp
May I take you home?	**Darf ich Sie nach Hause bringen?**	dahrf ikh zee naakh **how**zer **bring**ern
Can I see you again tomorrow?	**Kann ich Sie morgen wiedersehen?**	kahn ikh zee **mor**gern **vee**derrzayern
What's your telephone number?	**Wie ist Ihre Telefonnummer?**	vee ist **ee**rer taylay**foan**-nummerr

. . . and you might answer:

I'd love to, thank you.	**Danke, sehr gern.**	**dahn**ker zayr gehrn
Thank you, but I'm busy.	**Vielen Dank, aber ich habe keine Zeit.**	**fee**lern dahnk **aa**berr ikh **haa**ber **kigh**ner tsight
No, I'm not interested, thank you.	**Nein, das interessiert mich nicht.**	nighn dahss intehreh**sseert** mikh nikht
Leave me alone, please.	**Lassen Sie mich bitte in Ruhe!**	**lah**ssern zee mikh **bit**ter in rooer
Thank you. It's been a wonderful evening.	**Danke, es war ein wunderbarer Abend.**	**dahn**ker ehss vaar ighn **voon**derrbaarerr **aa**bernt
I've enjoyed myself.	**Ich habe mich gut unterhalten.**	ikh **haa**ber mikh goot unterr**hahl**tern

Shopping guide

This shopping guide is designed to help you find what you want with ease, accuracy and speed. It features:

1. a list of all major shops, stores and services (p. 98)
2. some general expressions required when shopping to allow you to be specific and selective (p. 100)
3. full details of the shops and services most likely to concern you. Here you'll find advice, alphabetical lists of items and conversion charts listed under the headings below.

LAUNDRY, see page 29/HAIRDRESSER'S, see page 30

Shops, stores and services *Geschäfte, Läden usw.*

Shops in Germany, Austria and Switzerland usually open around 8 or 9 a.m. and close at 6 or 6.30 p.m. Some close for an hour or two at noon—but never department stores. On Saturdays shops in Germany and Austria remain open until noon or 2 p.m. (the first Saturday of the month German shops are open until 6 p.m.). In Switzerland most shops remain open until 4 or 5 p.m. on Saturdays, usually taking Monday morning off.

Where's the nearest ...?	**Wo ist der/die/das nächste ...?**	voa ist derr/dee/dahss **naikh**ster
antique shop	**das Antiquitätengeschäft**	dahss ahntikvit**tay**terngershehft
art gallery	**die Kunstgalerie**	dee **kunst**gahlehree
baker's	**die Bäckerei**	dee behkerr**igh**
bank	**die Bank**	dee bahnk
barber's	**der Friseur**	derr fri**zurr**
beauty salon	**der Kosmetiksalon**	derr kos**may**tikzahlong
bookshop	**die Buchhandlung**	dee **bukh**hahndlung
butcher's	**die Fleischerei/ Metzgerei**	dee flighsherr**igh**/ mehtsgerr**igh**
cake shop	**die Konditorei**	dee kondittorr**igh**
camera shop	**das Fotogeschäft**	dahss **foa**togershehft
chemist's	**die Apotheke**	dee ahpot**tay**ker
dairy	**die Milchhandlung**	dee **milkh**hahndlung
delicatessen	**das Delikatessengeschäft**	dahss dehlikkah**teh**sserngershehft
dentist	**der Zahnarzt**	derr **tsaan**ahrtst
department store	**das Warenhaus**	dahss **vaa**rernhowss
doctor	**der Arzt**	derr ahrtst
dress shop	**das Modengeschäft**	dahss **moa**derngershehft
drugstore	**die Apotheke**	dee ahpot**tay**ker
dry cleaner's	**die chemische Reinigung**	dee **khay**misher **righ**niggung
electrician	**der Elektriker**	derr ay**lehk**trikkerr
fishmonger's	**die Fischhandlung**	dee **fish**hahndlung
flea market	**der Flohmarkt**	derr **floa**mahrkt
florist's	**das Blumengeschäft**	dahss **bloo**merngershehft
furrier's	**das Pelzgeschäft**	dahss **pehlts**gershehft
greengrocer's	**die Gemüsehandlung**	dee ger**mew**zerhahndlung
grocery	**das Lebensmittelgeschäft**	dahss **lay**bernsmitterlgershehft

hairdresser's (ladies/men)	**der Damenfriseur/ Herrenfriseur**	derr **daa**mernfrizurr/ **heh**rernfrizurr
hardware store	**die Eisenwarenhandlung**	dee **igh**zernvaarernhahndlung
health food shop	**das Reformhaus**	dahss reh**form**howss
hospital	**das Krankenhaus**	dahss **krahn**kernhowss
ironmonger's	**die Eisenwarenhandlung**	dee **igh**zernvaarernhahndlung
jeweller's	**der Juwelier**	derr yuvveh**leer**
launderette	**der Waschsalon**	derr **vahsh**zahlong
laundry	**die Wäscherei**	dee vehsher**righ**
library	**die Bibliothek**	dee bibliot**tayk**
market	**der Markt**	derr mahrkt
newsagent's	**der Zeitungshändler**	derr **tsigh**tungshehndlerr
newsstand	**der Zeitungsstand**	derr **tsigh**tungsshtahnt
optician	**der Optiker**	derr **op**tikkerr
pastry shop	**die Konditorei**	dee kondittor**righ**
photographer	**der Fotograf**	derr foato**graaf**
police station	**die Polizeiwache**	dee polli**tsigh**vahkher
post office	**das Postamt**	dahss **post**ahmt
second-hand shop	**der Gebrauchtwarenladen**	derr ger**browkht**vaarernlaadern
shoemaker's (repairs)	**der Schuhmacher**	derr **shoo**mahkherr
shoe shop	**das Schuhgeschäft**	dahss **shoo**gershehft
shopping centre	**das Einkaufszentrum**	dahss **ighn**kowfstsehntrum
souvenir shop	**der Andenkenladen**	derr **ahn**dehnkernlaadern
sporting goods shop	**das Sportgeschäft**	dahss **shport**gershehft
stationer's	**das Schreibwarengeschäft**	dahss **shrighp**vaarerngershehft
supermarket	**der Supermarkt**	derr **zoo**perrmahrkt
tailor's	**der Schneider**	derr **shnigh**derr
telegraph office	**das Telegrafenamt**	dahss taylay**graa**fernahmt
tobacconist's	**der Tabakladen**	derr tah**bahk**laadern
toy shop	**das Spielwarengeschäft**	dahss **shpeel**vaarerngerhehft
travel agency	**das Reisebüro**	dahss **righ**zerbewroa
vegetable store	**die Gemüsehandlung**	dee ger**mew**zerhahndlung
veterinarian	**der Tierarzt**	derr **teer**ahrtst
watchmaker's	**der Uhrmacher**	derr **oor**mahkherr
wine merchant's	**die Weinhandlung**	dee **vighn**hahndlung

EINGANG	ENTRANCE
AUSGANG	EXIT
NOTAUSGANG	EMERGENCY EXIT

General expressions *Allgemeine Redewendungen*

Where? *Wo?*

Where's there a good ...?	**Wo gibt es einen guten/eine gute/ ein gutes ...?**	voa gipt ehss **igh**nern **goo**tern/**igh**ner **goo**ter/ ighn **goo**terss
Where can I find ...?	**Wo finde ich ...?**	voa **fin**der ikh
Where's the main shopping area?	**Wo ist das Geschäftsviertel?**	voa ist dahss ger**shehfts**feerterl
Is it far from here?	**Ist es weit von hier?**	ist ehss vight fon heer
How do I get there?	**Wie komme ich dorthin?**	vee **kom**mer ikh dort**hin**

Service *Bedienung*

Can you help me?	**Können Sie mir helfen?**	**kur**nern zee meer **hehl**fern
I'm just looking.	**Ich sehe mich nur um.**	ikh **zay**er mikh noor um
I want ...	**Ich möchte ...**	ikh **murkh**ter
Can you show me some ...?	**Können Sie mir einige ... zeigen?**	**kur**nern zee meer **igh**nigger ... **tsigh**gern
Do you sell ...?	**Verkaufen Sie ...?**	fehr**kow**fern zee
I'd like to buy ...	**Ich möchte ... kaufen.**	ikh **murkh**ter ... **kow**fern
Do you have any ...?	**Haben Sie ...?**	**haa**bern zee
Where's the ... department?	**Wo ist die ... -Abteilung?**	voa ist dee ... **ahp**tighlung
Where is the lift (elevator)/escalator?	**Wo ist der Fahrstuhl/ die Rolltreppe?**	voa ist derr **faar**shtool/ dee **rol**trehper

That one *Das da*

Can you show me ...?	**Können Sie mir ... zeigen?**	**kur**nern zee meer ... **tsigh**gern
that/those	**das da/die dort**	dahss daa/dee dort
the one in the window/in the display case	**das im Schaufenster/ in der Vitrine**	dahss im **show**fehnsterr/ in derr vi**tree**ner

Defining the article *Beschreibung des Artikels*

It must be ...	**Es muß ... sein.**	ehss muss ... zighn
big	**groß**	groass
cheap	**billig**	**bil**likh
dark	**dunkel**	**dun**kerl
good	**gut**	goot
heavy	**schwer**	shvayr
large	**groß**	groass
light (weight)	**leicht**	lighkht
light (colour)	**hell**	hehl
oval	**oval**	oa**vaal**
rectangular	**rechteckig**	**rehkht**ehkikh
round	**rund**	runt
small	**klein**	klighn
square	**viereckig**	**feer**ehkikh
sturdy	**robust**	rob**bust**
I don't want anything too expensive.	**Ich möchte nichts allzu Teures.**	ikh **murkh**ter nikhts **ahll**tsu **toy**rerss

Preference *Ich hätte lieber ...*

Can you show me some more?	**Können Sie mir noch andere zeigen?**	**kur**nern zee meer nokh **ahn**derrer **tsigh**gern
Haven't you anything ...?	**Haben Sie nichts ...?**	**haa**bern zee nikhts
cheaper/better	**Billigeres/Besseres**	**bil**liggerrerss/**beh**sserrerss
larger/smaller	**Größeres/Kleineres**	**grur**sserrerss/**kligh**nerrerss

How much? *Wieviel?*

How much is this?	**Wieviel kostet das?**	vee**feel kos**tert dahss
I don't understand.	**Ich verstehe nicht.**	ikh fehr**shtay**er nikht
Please write it down.	**Schreiben Sie es bitte auf.**	**shrigh**bern zee ehss **bit**ter owf
I don't want to spend more than ... marks.	**Ich möchte nicht mehr als ... Mark ausgeben.**	ikh **murkh**ter nikht mayr ahlss ... mahrk **ows**gaybern

AUSVERKAUF SALE

COLOURS, see page 113

Decision *Entscheidung*

It's not quite what I want.	**Es ist nicht ganz das, was ich möchte.**	ehss ist nikht gahnts dahss vahss ikh **murkh**ter
No, I don't like it.	**Nein, das gefällt mir nicht.**	nighn dahss ger**fehlt** meer nikht
I'll take it.	**Ich nehme es.**	ikh **nay**mer ehss

Ordering *Bestellen*

Can you order it for me?	**Können Sie es mir bestellen?**	**kur**nern zee ehss meer ber**shteh**lern
How long will it take?	**Wie lange dauert es?**	vee **lahng**er **dow**errt ehss

Delivery *Lieferung*

I'll take it with me.	**Ich nehme es mit.**	ikh **nay**mer ehss mit
Deliver it to the ... Hotel.	**Liefern Sie es bitte ins Hotel ...**	**lee**ferrn zee ehss **bit**ter ins hot**tehl**
Please send it to this address.	**Senden Sie es bitte an diese Anschrift.**	**zehn**dern zee ehss **bit**ter ahn **dee**zer **ahn**shrift
Will I have any difficulty with the customs?	**Werde ich Schwierigkeiten mit dem Zoll haben?**	**vayr**der ikh **shvee**rikh-kightern mit daym tsol **haa**bern

Paying *Bezahlen*

Where do I pay?	**Wo ist die Kasse?**	voa ist dee **kah**sser
How much is it?	**Wieviel kostet es?**	vee**feel kos**tert ehss
Can I pay with this credit card?	**Kann ich mit dieser Kreditkarte bezahlen?**	kahn ikh mit **dee**zerr kray**dit**kahrter bert**saa**lern
Do you accept ...?	**Nehmen Sie ...?**	**nay**mern zee
dollars pounds traveller's cheques	**Dollar** **Pfund** **Reiseschecks**	**dol**lahr pfunt **righ**zershehks
Do I have to pay the VAT (sales tax)?	**Muß ich die Mehrwertsteuer bezahlen?**	muss ikh dee **mayr**vayrt-shtoyerr bert**saa**lern
Haven't you made a mistake in the bill?	**Haben Sie sich nicht verrechnet?**	**haa**bern zee zikh nikht fehr**rehkh**nert

Anything else? *Sonst noch etwas?*

No, thanks, that's all.	**Nein danke, das ist alles.**	nighn **dahn**ker dahss ist **ah**lerss
Yes. I want ...	**Ja, ich möchte ...**	yaa ikh **murkh**ter
Show me ...	**Zeigen Sie mir ...**	**tsigh**gern zee meer
May I have a bag, please?	**Kann ich bitte eine Tragetasche haben?**	kahn ikh **bit**ter **igh**ner **traa**gertahsher **haa**bern

Dissatisfied *Unzufrieden*

Can you please exchange this?	**Können Sie das bitte umtauschen?**	**kur**nern zee dahss **bit**ter **um**towshern
I want to return this.	**Ich möchte das zurückgeben.**	ikh **murkh**ter dahss tsoo**rewk**gaybern
I'd like a refund. Here's the receipt.	**Ich möchte das Geld zurückerstattet haben. Hier ist die Quittung.**	ikh **murkh**ter dahss gehlt tsoo**rewk**ehrshtahtert **haa**bern. heer ist dee **kvit**tung

Kann ich Ihnen helfen?	Can I help you?
Was wünschen Sie?	What would you like?
Welche ... möchten Sie?	What ... would you like?
Farbe/Form Qualität/Menge	colour/shape quality/quantity
Es tut mir leid, das haben wir nicht.	I'm sorry, we haven't any.
Das haben wir nicht vorrätig.	We're out of stock.
Sollen wir es für Sie bestellen?	Shall we order it for you?
Nehmen Sie es mit oder sollen wir es Ihnen senden?	Will you take it with you or shall we send it?
Sonst noch etwas?	Anything else?
Das macht ... Mark, bitte.	That's ... marks, please.
Die Kasse ist dort drüben.	The cash desk is over there.

Bookshop *Buchhandlung*

In Germany, bookshops and stationers' are usually separate shops, though the latter will often sell paperbacks. Newspapers and magazines are sold at newsstands.

Where's the nearest ...?	**Wo ist der/die/ das nächste ...?**	voa ist derr/dee/dahss **naikh**ster
bookshop	**die Buchhandlung**	dee **bukh**hahndlung
stationer's	**das Schreibwarengeschäft**	dahss **shrighp**vaarern-gershehft
newsstand	**der Zeitungsstand**	derr **tsigh**tungsshtahnt
Where can I buy an English-language newspaper?	**Wo kann ich eine englische Zeitung kaufen?**	voa kahn ikh **igh**ner **ehng**lisher **tsigh**tung **kow**fern
Where's the guide-book section?	**Wo stehen die Reiseführer?**	voa **shtay**ern dee **righ**zerfewrerr
Where do you keep the English books?	**Wo stehen die englischen Bücher?**	voa **shtay**ern dee **ehng**lishern **bew**kherr
Have you any of ...'s books in English?	**Haben Sie ein Buch von ... in Englisch?**	**haa**bern zee ighn bookh fon ... in **ehng**lish
Do you have second-hand books?	**Haben Sie auch antiquarische Bücher?**	**haa**ben zee owkh ahnti-**kvaa**risher **bew**kherr
I want a/an/ some ...	**Ich möchte ...**	ikh **murkh**ter
address book	**ein Adressenbüchlein**	ighn ah**dreh**ssern-bewkhlighn
ball-point pen	**einen Kugelschreiber**	**igh**nern **koo**gerlshrighberr
book	**ein Buch**	ighn bukh
calendar	**einen Kalender**	**igh**nern kah**lehn**derr
carbon paper	**Durchschlagpapier**	**doorkh**shlaagpahpeer
cellophane tape	**Klebstreifen**	**klayp**shtrighfern
crayons	**Buntstifte**	**bunt**shtifter
dictionary	**ein Wörterbuch**	ighn **vurr**terrbookh
German-English	**deutsch-englisch**	doych-**ehng**lish
pocket dictionary	**ein Taschenwörterbuch**	ighn **tah**shernvurrterr-bookh
drawing paper	**Zeichenpapier**	**tsigh**khernpahpeer
drawing pins	**Reißzwecken**	**righs**tsvehkern
envelopes	**Briefumschläge**	**breef**umshlaiger
eraser	**einen Radiergummi**	**igh**nern rah**deer**gummi
exercise book	**ein Schreibheft**	ighn **shrighp**hehft

felt-tip pen	**einen Filzstift**	**igh**nern **filts**shtift
fountain pen	**einen Füllfederhalter**	**igh**nern **fewl**fayderrhahlterr
glue	**Leim**	lighm
grammar book	**eine Grammatik**	**igh**ner grah**mah**tik
guidebook	**einen Reiseführer**	**igh**nern **righ**zerfewrerr
ink	**Tinte**	**tin**ter
black/red/blue	**schwarz/rot/blau**	shvahrts/roat/blow
(adhesive) labels	**(selbstklebende) Etikette**	(**zehlpst**klaybernder) ehtik**keh**ter
magazine	**eine Illustrierte**	**igh**ner illu**streer**ter
map	**eine Landkarte**	**igh**ner **lahnt**kahrter
map of the town	**einen Stadtplan**	**igh**nern **shtaht**plaan
road map of ...	**eine Straßenkarte von ...**	**igh**ner **shtraa**ssernkahrter fon
mechanical pencil	**einen Drehbleistift**	**igh**nern **dray**blighshtift
newspaper	**eine Zeitung**	**igh**ner **tsigh**tung
American	**amerikanische**	ahmehrik**kaa**nisher
English	**englische**	**ehng**lisher
notebook	**ein Notizheft**	ighn not**tits**hehft
note paper	**Briefpapier**	**breef**pahpeer
paintbox	**einen Malkasten**	**igh**nern **maal**kahstern
paper	**Papier**	pah**peer**
paperback	**ein Taschenbuch**	ighn **tah**shernbookh
paperclips	**Büroklammern**	bew**roa**klahmerrn
paper napkins	**Papierservietten**	pah**peer**zehrviehtern
paste	**Klebstoff**	**klayp**shtof
pen	**eine Feder**	**igh**ner **fay**derr
pencil	**einen Bleistift**	**igh**nern **bligh**shtift
pencil sharpener	**einen Bleistiftspitzer**	**igh**nern **bligh**shtiftshpitserr
playing cards	**Spielkarten**	**shpeel**kahrtern
pocket calculator	**einen Taschenrechner**	**igh**nern **tah**shernrehkhnerr
postcard	**eine Postkarte**	**igh**ner **post**kahrter
propelling pencil	**einen Drehbleistift**	**igh**nern **dray**blighshtift
refill (for a pen)	**eine Ersatzpatrone**	**igh**ner ehr**zahts**pahtroaner
rubber	**einen Radiergummi**	**igh**nern rah**deer**gummi
ruler	**ein Lineal**	ighn linnay**aal**
staples	**Heftklammern**	**hehft**klahmerrn
string	**Bindfaden/Schnur**	**bint**faadern/shnoor
thumbtacks	**Reißzwecken**	**righs**tsvehkern
tissue paper	**Seidenpapier**	**zigh**dernpahpeer
typewriter ribbon	**ein Farbband**	ighn **fahrp**bahnt
typing paper	**Schreibmaschinenpapier**	**shrighp**mahsheenern-pahpeer
writing pad	**einen Schreibblock**	**igh**nern **shrighp**blok

Camping equipment *Campingausrüstung*

I'd like a/an/ some ...	**Ich hätte gern ...**	ikh **heh**ter gehrn
bottle-opener	**einen Flaschenöffner**	**igh**nern **flah**shernurfnerr
bucket	**einen Eimer**	**igh**nern **igh**merr
butane gas	**Butangas**	but**taan**gaass
campbed	**ein Feldbett**	ighn **fehlt**beht
can opener	**einen Büchsenöffner**	**igh**nern **bewk**sernurfnerr
candles	**Kerzen**	**kehr**tsern
chair	**einen Stuhl**	**igh**nern shtool
folding chair	**Klappstuhl**	**klahp**shtool
charcoal	**Holzkohle**	**holts**koaler
clothes pegs	**Wäscheklammern**	**veh**sherklahmerrn
compass	**einen Kompaß**	**igh**nern **kom**pahss
cool box	**eine Kühltasche**	**igh**ner **kewl**tahsher
corkscrew	**einen Korkenzieher**	**igh**nern **kor**kerntseeherr
crockery	**Geschirr**	ger**shir**
cutlery	**Besteck**	ber**shtehk**
deckchair	**einen Liegestuhl**	**igh**nern **lee**gershtool
dishwashing detergent	**Spülmittel**	**shpewl**mitterl
first-aid kit	**einen Verbandkasten**	**igh**nern fehr**bahnt**kahstern
fishing tackle	**Angelzeug**	**ahn**gerltsoyg
flashlight	**eine Taschenlampe**	**igh**ner **tah**shernlahmper
food box	**einen Proviant-behälter**	**igh**nern provvi**ahnt**-berhehlterr
frying-pan	**eine Bratpfanne**	**igh**ner **braat**pfahner
groundsheet	**einen Zeltboden**	**igh**nern **tsehlt**boadern
hammer	**einen Hammer**	**igh**nern **hah**merr
hammock	**eine Hängematte**	**igh**ner **hehn**germahter
haversack	**eine Provianttasche**	**igh**ner provvi**ahnt**tahsher
ice pack	**einen Kühlbeutel**	**igh**nern **kewl**boyterl
kerosene	**Petroleum**	pay**troa**layum
lamp	**eine Lampe**	**igh**ner **lahm**per
lantern	**eine Laterne**	**igh**ner lah**tehr**ner
matches	**Streichhölzer**	**shtrighkh**hurltserr
(air)mattress	**eine (Luft)matratze**	**igh**ner (luft)mah**trah**tser
methylated spirits	**Brennspiritus**	**brehn**shpeerittuss
mosquito net	**ein Mückennetz**	ighn **mew**kernnehts
pail	**einen Eimer**	**igh**nern **igh**merr
paper napkins	**Papierservietten**	pah**peer**zehrviehtern
paraffin	**Petroleum**	pay**troa**layum
penknife	**ein Taschenmesser**	ighn **tah**shernmehsserr
picnic basket	**einen Picknickkorb**	**igh**nern **pik**nikkorp
plastic bag	**einen Plastikbeutel**	**igh**nern **plah**stikboyterl

CAMPING, see page 32

rope	**ein Seil**	ighn zighl
rucksack	**einen Rucksack**	**igh**nern **ruk**zahk
saucepan	**einen Kochtopf**	**igh**nern **kokh**topf
scissors	**eine Schere**	**igh**ner **shay**rer
screwdriver	**einen Schrauben-zieher**	**igh**nern **shrow**bern-tseeherr
sleeping bag	**einen Schlafsack**	**igh**nern **shlaaf**zahk
stew pot	**einen Schmortopf**	**igh**nern **shmoar**topf
table	**einen Tisch**	**igh**nern tish
folding table	**Klapptisch**	**klahp**tish
tent	**ein Zelt**	ighn tsehlt
tent pegs	**Heringe**	**hay**ringer
tent pole	**eine Zeltstange**	**igh**ner **tsehlt**shtahnger
tinfoil	**Aluminiumfolie**	ahlu**mee**niumfoalier
tin opener	**einen Büchsenöffner**	**igh**nern **bewk**sernurfnerr
tongs	**eine Zange**	**igh**ner **tsahn**ger
torch	**eine Taschenlampe**	**igh**ner **tah**shernlahmper
vacuum flask	**eine Thermosflasche**	**igh**ner **tehr**mosflahsher
washing powder	**Waschpulver**	**vahsh**pulferr
washing-up liquid	**Spülmittel**	**shpewl**mitterl
water carrier	**einen Wasserkanister**	**igh**nern **vah**sserkahnisterr
water flask	**eine Feldflasche**	**igh**ner **fehlt**flahsher
wood alcohol	**Brennspiritus**	**brehn**shpeerittuss

Crockery *Geschirr*

cups	**Tassen**	**tah**ssern
mugs	**Becher**	**beh**kherr
plates	**Teller**	**teh**lerr
saucers	**Untertassen**	**un**terrtahssern
tumblers	**Wassergläser**	**vah**sserrglaizerr

Cutlery *Besteck*

forks	**Gabeln**	**gaa**berln
knives	**Messer**	**meh**sserr
dessert knives	**Dessertmesser**	deh**ssayr**mehsserr
spoons	**Löffel**	**lur**ferl
teaspoons	**Teelöffel**	**tay**lurferl
made of plastic	**aus Plastik**	owss **plah**stik
made of stainless steel	**aus rostfreiem Stahl**	owss **rost**frigherm shtaal

Chemist's (drugstore) *Apotheke*

In German, a chemist's is called *Apotheke* (ahpot**tay**ker). They don't sell cameras, books and the like. At night and on Sundays all chemists' display the address of the nearest one open. If you're looking for toiletries, household articles or film, try a *Drogerie* (drogeh**ree**). You'll also find non-prescription medicine available in a *Drogerie*.

This section has been divided into two parts:

1. Pharmaceutical—medicine, first-aid, etc.
2. Toiletry—toilet articles, cosmetics

General *Allgemeines*

Where's the nearest (all-night) chemist's?	**Wo ist die nächste Apotheke (mit Nachtdienst)?**	voa ist dee **naikh**ster ahpot**tay**ker (mit **nahkht**deenst)
What time does the chemist's open/ close?	**Um wieviel Uhr öffnet/schließt die Apotheke?**	um **vee**feel oor **urf**nert/shleest dee ahpot**tay**ker

1—Pharmaceutical *Arzneien*

I want something for ...	**Ich möchte etwas gegen ...**	ikh **murkh**ter **eht**vahss **gay**gern
a cold	**eine Erkältung**	**igh**ner ehr**kehl**tung
a cough	**Husten**	**hoo**stern
a hangover	**einen Kater**	**igh**nern **kaa**terr
hay fever	**Heuschnupfen**	**hoy**shnupfern
insect bites	**Insektenstiche**	in**zehk**ternshtikher
sunburn	**Sonnenbrand**	**zon**nernbrahnt
travel sickness	**Reisekrankheit**	**righ**zerkrahnk-hight
an upset stomach	**Magenverstimmung**	**maa**gernfehrshtimmung
Can you make up this prescription for me?	**Können Sie mir dieses Rezept machen?**	**kur**nern zee meer **dee**zerss reht**sehpt** **mah**khern
Can I get it without a prescription?	**Kann ich das ohne Rezept bekommen?**	kahn ikh dahss **oa**ner reht**sehpt** ber**kom**mern
Shall I wait?	**Soll ich warten?**	zol ikh **vahr**tern

DOCTOR, see page 137

Do you have homoeopathic remedies?	**Haben Sie homöopathische Mittel?**	**haa**bern zee hommurop**pah**tisher **mit**terl
Can I have a/an/some ...?	**Kann ich ... haben?**	kahn ikh ... **haa**bern
analgesic	**ein Schmerzmittel**	ighn **shmehrts**mitterl
antiseptic cream	**eine Wundsalbe**	**igh**ner **vunt**zahlber
aspirin	**Aspirin**	ahspi**reen**
bandage	**einen Verband**	**igh**nern fehr**bahnt**
elastic bandage	**eine elastische Binde**	**igh**ner eh**lah**stisher **bin**der
Band-Aids	**Heftpflaster**	**hehft**pflahsterr
contraceptives	**ein Verhütungsmittel**	ighn fehr**hew**tungsmitterl
corn plasters	**Hühneraugenpflaster**	**hew**nerrowgernpflahsterr
cotton wool (absorbent cotton)	**Watte**	**vah**ter
cough drops	**Hustenpastillen**	**hoo**sternpahstillern
disinfectant	**ein Desinfektionsmittel**	ighn dehsinfehk**tsioans**mitterl
ear drops	**Ohrentropfen**	**oa**rerntropfern
Elastoplast	**Heftpflaster**	**hehft**pflahsterr
eye drops	**Augentropfen**	**ow**gerntropfern
gauze	**Verbandmull**	fehr**bahnt**mul
insect repellent/spray	**einen Insektenschutz/ein Insektizid**	**igh**nern in**zehk**ternshuts/ighn inzehkti**tseet**
iodine	**Jod**	yoat
laxative	**ein Abführmittel**	ighn **ahp**fewrmitterl
mouthwash	**Mundwasser**	**munt**vahsserr
nose drops	**Nasentropfen**	**naa**zerntropfern
painkiller	**ein Schmerzmittel**	ighn **shmehrts**mitterl
sanitary towels (napkins)	**Damenbinden**	**daa**mernbindern
sleeping pills	**Schlaftabletten**	**shlaaf**tahblehtern
suppositories	**Zäpfchen**	**tsehpf**khern
tampons	**Tampons**	**tahm**pongs
thermometer	**ein Thermometer**	ighn tehrmom**may**terr
throat lozenges	**Halspastillen**	**hahls**pahstillern
tranquillizers	**Beruhigungsmittel**	ber**rooi**ggungsmitterl
vitamin pills	**Vitamintabletten**	vittah**meen**tahblehtern

GIFT	POISON
NICHT EINNEHMEN	FOR EXTERNAL USE ONLY

2—Toiletry *Toilettenartikel*

I'd like a/an/some ...	**Ich hätte gern ...**	ikh **heh**ter gehrn
acne cream	**eine Aknesalbe**	**igh**ner **ahk**nerzahlber
after-shave lotion	**ein Rasierwasser**	ighn rah**zeer**vahsserr
astringent	**ein Adstringens**	ighn ahd**stringe**hns
bath salts	**Badesalz**	**baa**derzahlts
bubble bath	**ein Schaumbad**	ighn **showm**baat
cologne	**ein Kölnischwasser**	ighn kurlnish**vah**sserr
cream	**eine Creme**	**igh**ner kraym
cleansing cream	**Reinigungscreme**	**righ**niggungskraym
for greasy/normal/dry skin	**für fettige/normale/trockene Haut**	fewr **feh**tigger/nor**mah**ler/**trok**kehner howt
foundation cream	**Grundierungscreme**	grun**dee**rungskraym
moisturizing cream	**Feuchtigkeitscreme**	**foykh**tikhkightskraym
night cream	**Nachtcreme**	**nahkht**kraym
cuticle remover	**Nagelhautentferner**	**naa**gerlhowtehntfehrnerr
deodorant	**ein Deodorant**	ighn dehoddoa**rahnt**
depilatory cream	**Haarentfernungsmittel**	**haar**ehntfehrnungsmitterl
emery board	**eine Sandpapierfeile**	**igh**ner **zahnt**pahpeerfighler
eye liner	**einen Lidstift**	**igh**nern **leed**shtift
eye pencil	**einen Augenbrauenstift**	**igh**nern **ow**gernbrowernshtift
eye shadow	**einen Lidschatten**	**igh**nern **leed**shahtern
face powder	**Gesichtspuder**	ger**zikhts**pooderr
foot cream	**Fußcreme**	**foos**kraym
foot powder	**Fußpuder**	**foos**pooderr
hand cream	**Handcreme**	**hahnt**kraym
interdental cleaners	**medizinische Zahnstocher**	maydi**tsee**nisher **tsaan**shtokherr
lipsalve	**eine Lippenpomade**	**igh**ner **lip**pernpommaader
lipstick	**einen Lippenstift**	**igh**nern **lip**pernshtift
make-up remover pads	**Abschminkwatte**	**ahp**shminkvahter
mascara	**Wimperntusche**	**vim**perrntusher
nail brush	**eine Nagelbürste**	**igh**ner **naa**gerlbewrster
nail clippers	**eine Nagelzange**	**igh**ner **naa**gerltsahnger
nail file	**eine Nagelfeile**	**igh**ner **naa**gerlfighler
nail polish	**Nagellack**	**naa**gerllahk
nail polish remover	**Nagellackentferner**	**naa**gerllahkehntfehrnerr
nail scissors	**eine Nagelschere**	**igh**ner **naa**gerlshayrer
perfume	**ein Parfüm**	ighn pahr**fewm**
powder	**Puder**	**poo**derr
razor	**einen Rasierapparat**	**igh**nern rah**zeer**ahpahraat
razor blades	**Rasierklingen**	rah**zeer**klingern

rouge	**Rouge**	roozh
safety pins	**Sicherheitsnadeln**	**zik**herrhights**naa**derln
shaving brush	**einen Rasierpinsel**	**igh**nern rah**zeer**pinzerl
shaving cream	**Rasiercreme**	rah**zeer**kraym
soap	**eine Seife**	**igh**ner **zigh**fer
sponge	**einen Schwamm**	**igh**nern shvahm
sun-tan cream	**Sonnencreme**	**zon**nernkraym
sun-tan oil	**Sonnenöl**	**zon**nernurl
talcum powder	**Körperpuder**	**kurr**perrpooderr
tissues	**Papiertücher**	pah**peer**tewkherr
toilet paper	**Toilettenpapier**	toah**leh**ternpahpeer
toilet water	**ein Toilettenwasser**	ighn toah**leh**ternvahsserr
toothbrush	**eine Zahnbürste**	**igh**ner **tsaan**bewrster
toothpaste	**Zahnpasta**	**tsaan**pahstah
towel	**ein Handtuch**	ighn **hahnt**tukh
tweezers	**eine Pinzette**	**igh**ner pin**tseh**ter

For your hair *Für Ihr Haar*

bobby pins	**Haarklemmen**	**haar**klehmern
colour shampoo	**ein Tönungsshampoo**	ighn **tur**nungsshahmpoo
comb	**einen Kamm**	**igh**nern kahm
curlers	**Lockenwickler**	**lok**kernviklerr
dry shampoo	**ein Trockenshampoo**	ighn **trok**kernshahmpoo
hairbrush	**eine Haarbürste**	**igh**ner **haar**bewrster
hair dye	**ein Haarfärbemittel**	ighn **haar**fehrbermitterl
hairgrips	**Haarklemmen**	**haar**klehmern
hair lotion	**Haarwasser**	**haar**vahsserr
hairpins	**Haarnadeln**	**haar**naaderln
hair slide	**eine Haarspange**	**igh**ner **haar**shpahnger
hair spray	**einen Haarspray**	**igh**nern **haar**shpray
setting lotion	**einen Haarfestiger**	**igh**nern **haar**fehstiggerr
shampoo	**ein Haarwaschmittel**	ighn **haar**vahshmitterl
for dry/greasy (oily) hair	**für trockenes/ fettiges Haar**	fewr **trok**kernerss/ **feh**tiggerss haar
tint	**ein Tönungsmittel**	ighn **tur**nungsmitterl
wig	**eine Perücke**	**igh**ner peh**rew**ker

For the baby *Für den Säugling*

baby food	**Säuglingsnahrung**	**zoyg**lingsnaarung
dummy (pacifier)	**einen Schnuller**	**igh**nern **shnul**lerr
feeding bottle	**eine Saugflasche**	**igh**ner **zowg**flahsher
nappies (diapers)	**Windeln**	**vin**derln

Clothing *Bekleidung*

If you want to buy something specific, prepare yourself in advance. Look at the list of clothing on page 116. Get some idea of the colour, material and size you want. They're all listed on the next few pages.

General *Allgemeines*

I'd like ...	**Ich möchte ...**	ikh **murkh**ter
I want ... for a 10-year-old boy/girl.	**Ich möchte ... für einen Jungen/ ein Mädchen von 10 Jahren.**	ikh **murkh**ter ... fewr ** igh**nern **yun**gern/ ighn **mait**khern fon 10 **yaa**rern
I want something like this.	**Ich möchte etwas in dieser Art.**	ikh **murkh**ter **eht**vahss in **dee**zerr aart
I like the one in the window.	**Das im Schaufenster gefällt mir.**	dahss im **show**fehnsterr ger**fehlt** meer
How much is that per metre?	**Wieviel kostet der Meter?**	vee**feel kos**tert derr **may**terr

1 centimetre (cm.)	= 0.39 in.	1 inch =	2.54 cm.
1 metre (m.)	= 39.37 in.	1 foot =	30.5 cm.
10 metres	= 32.81 ft.	1 yard =	0.91 m.

Colour *Farbe*

I want something in ...	**Ich möchte etwas in ...**	ikh **murkh**ter **eht**vahss in
I want a darker/ lighter shade.	**Ich möchte es etwas dunkler/heller.**	ikh **murkh**ter ehss **eht**vahss **dunk**lerr/**heh**lerr
I want something to match this.	**Ich möchte etwas hierzu Passendes.**	ikh **murkh**ter **eht**vahss **heer**tsoo **pah**sernderss
I don't like the colour.	**Die Farbe gefällt mir nicht.**	dee **fahr**ber ger**fehlt** meer nikht
Is it colour fast?	**Ist es farbecht?**	ist ehss **fahr**pehkht

NUMBERS, see page 147

beige	**beige**	bayzh
black	**schwarz**	shvahrts
blue	**blau**	blow
brown	**braun**	brown
fawn	**hellbraun**	**hehl**brown
golden	**golden**	**gol**dern
green	**grün**	grewn
grey	**grau**	grow
mauve	**lila**	**lee**lah
orange	**orange**	o**rrahng**zher
pink	**rosa**	**roa**zah
purple	**violett**	viol**leht**
red	**rot**	**roat**
scarlet	**scharlachrot**	**shahr**lahkhroat
silver	**silbern**	**zil**berrn
turquoise	**türkisfarben**	tew**rkees**fahrbern
white	**weiß**	vighss
yellow	**gelb**	gehlp
light ...	**hell ...**	hehl
dark ...	**dunkel ...**	**dun**kerl

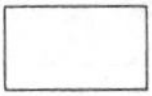

uni
(**un**ni)

gestreift
(ger**shtrighft**)

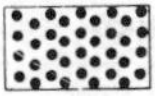

gepunktet
(ger**punk**tert)

kariert
(kah**reert**)

gemustert
(ger**mus**terrt)

Fabric *Stoff*

Do you have anything in ...?	**Haben Sie etwas in ...?**	**haa**bern zee **eht**vahss in
Is that ...?	**Ist das ...?**	ist dahss
handmade	**Handarbeit**	**hahnt**ahrbight
imported	**importiert**	impor**teert**
made here	**inländisches Fabrikat**	**in**lehndisherss fahbrik**kaat**
I want something thinner.	**Ich möchte etwas Dünneres.**	ikh **murkh**ter **eht**vahss **dew**nerrerss
Do you have any better quality?	**Haben Sie eine bessere Qualität?**	**haa**bern zee **igh**ner **behs**serrer kvahlit**tait**

cambric	**Batist**	bah**tist**
camel-hair	**Kamelhaar**	kah**mayl**haar
corduroy	**Kordsamt**	kortzahmt
cotton	**Baumwolle**	**bowm**voller
crepe	**Krepp**	krehp
denim	**Drillich**	**dril**likh
felt	**Filz**	filts
flannel	**Flanell**	flah**nehl**
gabardine	**Gabardine**	**gah**bahrdin
lace	**Spitze**	**shpit**ser
leather	**Leder**	**lay**derr
linen	**Leinen**	**ligh**nern
poplin	**Popeline**	popper**leen**
rayon	**Kunstseide**	**kunst**zighder
satin	**Satin**	zah**tehng**
silk	**Seide**	**zigh**der
suede	**Wildleder**	**vilt**layderr
towelling (terrycloth)	**Frottee**	frot**tay**
velvet	**Samt**	zahmt
velveteen	**Manchester**	mahn**sheh**sterr
wool	**Wolle**	**vol**ler
worsted	**Kammgarn**	**kahm**gahrn

Is it ...?	**Ist es ...?**	ist ehss
pure cotton	**reine Baumwolle**	**righ**ner **bowm**voller
synthetic	**synthetisch**	zewn**tay**tish
wash and wear	**bügelfrei**	**bew**gerlfrigh
crease (wrinkle) resistant	**knitterfrei**	**knit**terrfrigh
Is it hand washable/ machine washable?	**Kann man es mit der Hand/in der Maschine waschen?**	kahn mahn ehss mit derr hahnt/in derr mah**shee**ner **vah**shern
Will it shrink?	**Läuft es beim Waschen ein?**	loyft ehss bighm **vah**shern ighn

Size *Größe*

I take size 38.	**Ich habe Größe 38.**	ikh **haa**ber **grur**sser 38
Could you measure me?	**Können Sie mir Maß nehmen?**	**kur**nern zee meer maass **nay**mern
I don't know the German sizes.	**Ich kenne die deutschen Größen nicht.**	ikh **keh**ner dee **doy**chern **grur**ssern nikht

Sizes can vary somewhat from one manufacturer to another, so be sure to try on shoes and clothing before you buy.

Women *Damen*

Dresses/Suits						
American	8	10	12	14	16	18
British	10	12	14	16	18	20
Continental	36	38	40	42	44	46

Stockings						
American/British	8	8½	9	9½	10	10½
Continental	0	1	2	3	4	5

Shoes				
American	6	7	8	9
British	4½	5½	6½	7½
Continental	37	38	40	41

Men *Herren*

Suits/Overcoats						
American/British	36	38	40	42	44	46
Continental	46	48	50	52	54	56

Shirts				
American/British	15	16	17	18
Continental	38	41	43	45

Shoes									
American/British	5	6	7	8	8½	9	9½	10	11
Continental	38	39	41	42	43	43	44	44	45

A good fit? *Paßt es?*

Can I try it on?	**Kann ich es anprobieren?**	kahn ikh ehss **ahn**probbeerern
Where's the fitting room?	**Wo ist die Umkleidekabine?**	voa ist dee **um**klighderkahbeener
Is there a mirror?	**Gibt es einen Spiegel?**	gipt ehss **igh**nern **shpee**gerl
It fits very well.	**Es paßt sehr gut.**	ehss pahst zayr goot
It doesn't fit.	**Es paßt nicht.**	ehss pahst nikht

NUMBERS, see page 147

It's too ...	**Es ist zu ...**	ehss ist tsu
short/long	**kurz/lang**	koorts/lahng
tight/loose	**eng/weit**	ehng/vight
How long will it take to alter?	**Wie lange brauchen Sie, um es zu ändern?**	vee **lahng**er **brow**khern zee um ehss tsoo **ehn**derrn

Clothes and accessories *Kleidungsstücke und Zubehör*

I would like a/an/ some ...	**Ich hätte gern ...**	ikh **heh**ter gehrn
bathing cap	**eine Badekappe**	**igh**ner **baa**derkahper
bathing suit	**einen Badeanzug**	**igh**nern **baa**derahntsook
bathrobe	**einen Bademantel**	**igh**nern **baa**dermahnterl
blouse	**eine Bluse**	**igh**ner **bloo**zer
bow tie	**eine Fliege**	**igh**ner **flee**ger
bra	**einen Büstenhalter**	**igh**nern **bew**sternhahlterr
braces	**Hosenträger**	**hoa**zerntraigerr
briefs	**eine Unterhose**	**igh**ner **un**terrhoazer
cap	**eine Mütze**	**igh**ner **mewt**ser
cardigan	**eine Wolljacke**	**igh**ner **vol**yahker
coat	**einen Mantel**	**igh**nern **mahn**terl
dress	**ein Kleid**	ighn klight
dressing gown	**einen Morgenrock**	**igh**nern **mor**gernrok
evening dress (woman's)	**ein Abendkleid**	ighn **aa**berntklight
frock	**ein Kleid**	ighn klight
fur coat	**einen Pelzmantel**	**igh**nern **pehlts**mahnterl
girdle	**einen Hüfthalter**	**igh**nern **hewft**hahlterr
gloves	**Handschuhe**	**hahnt**shooer
handbag	**eine Handtasche**	**igh**ner **hahnt**tahsher
handkerchief	**ein Taschentuch**	ighn **tah**sherntookh
hat	**einen Hut**	**igh**nern hoot
jacket	**ein Jackett/eine Jacke**	ighn zhah**keht**/**igh**ner **yah**ker
jeans	**Jeans**	"jeans"
jersey	**eine Strickjacke**	**igh**ner **shtrik**yahker
jumper (Br.)	**einen Pullover**	**igh**nern pull**oa**verr
leather trousers	**eine Lederhose**	**igh**ner **lay**derrhoazer
nightdress	**ein Nachthemd**	ighn **nahkht**hehmt
pair of ...	**ein Paar ...**	ighn paar
panties	**einen Schlüpfer**	**igh**nern **shlew**pferr
pants (Am.)	**eine Hose**	**igh**ner **hoa**zer
panty girdle	**ein Strumpf-halterhöschen**	ighn **shtrumpf**hahlterr-hurskhern
panty hose	**eine Strumpfhose**	**igh**ner **shtrumpf**hoazer

pullover	**einen Pullover**	igh**nern** pull**oa**verr
roll-neck (turtle-neck)	**mit Rollkragen**	mit **rol**kraagern
round-neck	**mit rundem Ausschnitt**	mit **run**derm **ows**shnit
V-neck	**mit V-Ausschnitt**	mit **fow**owsshnit
with long/short sleeves	**mit langen/kurzen Ärmeln**	mit **lahn**gern/**koor**tsern **ehr**merln
without sleeves	**ärmellos**	**ehr**merlloass
pyjamas	**einen Schlafanzug**	**igh**nern **shlaaf**ahntsoog
raincoat	**einen Regenmantel**	**igh**nern **ray**gernmahnterl
scarf	**ein Halstuch**	ighn **hahls**tookh
shirt	**ein Hemd**	ighn hehmt
shorts	**Shorts**	"shorts"
skirt	**einen Rock**	**igh**nern rok
slip	**einen Unterrock**	**igh**nern **un**terrrok
socks	**Socken**	**zok**kern
stockings	**Strümpfe**	**shtrewm**pfer
suit (man's)	**einen Anzug**	**igh**nern **ahn**tsoog
suit (woman's)	**ein Kostüm**	ighn kos**tewm**
suspenders (Am.)	**Hosenträger**	**hoa**zerntraigerr
sweater	**einen Pullover**	**igh**nern pull**oa**verr
sweatshirt	**ein Sweatshirt**	ighn "sweatshirt"
swimming trunks	**eine Badehose**	**igh**ner **baa**derhoazer
swimsuit	**einen Badeanzug**	**igh**nern **baa**derahntsoog
T-shirt	**ein T-Shirt**	ighn "T-shirt"
tie	**eine Krawatte**	**igh**ner krah**vah**ter
tights	**eine Strumpfhose**	**igh**ner **shtrumpf**hoazer
tracksuit	**einen Trainingsanzug**	**igh**nern **trai**ningsahntsoog
trousers	**eine Hose**	**igh**ner **hoa**zer
umbrella	**einen Regenschirm**	**igh**nern **ray**gernshirm
underpants	**eine Unterhose/ einen Slip**	**igh**ner **un**terrhoazer/ **igh**nern "slip"
undershirt	**ein Unterhemd**	ighn **un**terrhehmt
vest (Am.)	**eine Weste**	**igh**ner **veh**ster
vest (Br.)	**ein Unterhemd**	ighn **un**terrhehmt
waistcoat	**eine Weste**	**igh**ner **veh**ster

belt	**der Gürtel**	derr **gewr**terl
buckle	**die Schnalle**	dee **shnah**ler
button	**der Knopf**	derr knopf
pocket	**die Tasche**	dee **tah**sher
press stud (snap fastener)	**der Druckknopf**	derr **druk**knopf
zip (zipper)	**der Reißverschluß**	derr **righs**fehrshluss

Shoes *Schuhe*

I'd like a pair of ...	**Ich möchte ein Paar ...**	ikh **murkh**ter ighn paar
boots	**Stiefel**	**shtee**ferl
moccasins	**Mokassins**	**mok**kahssins
plimsolls (sneakers)	**Turnschuhe**	**toorn**shooer
rain boots	**Gummistiefel**	**gum**mishteeferl
sandals	**Sandalen**	zahn**daa**lern
shoes	**Schuhe**	**shoo**er
flat	**flache**	**flah**kher
with a heel	**mit hohen Absätzen**	mit **hoa**ern **ahp**zehtsern
with leather soles	**mit Ledersohlen**	mit **lay**derzoalern
with rubber soles	**mit Gummisohlen**	mit **gum**mizoalern
slippers	**Hausschuhe**	**hows**shooer
These are too ...	**Diese sind zu ...**	**dee**zer zint tsu
narrow/wide	**eng/weit**	ehng/vight
large/small	**groß/klein**	groass/klighn
Do you have a larger/ smaller size?	**Haben Sie eine größere/kleinere Nummer?**	**haa**bern zee **igh**ner **grur**sserrer/**kligh**nerrer **num**merr
Do you have the same in black?	**Haben Sie die gleichen in Schwarz?**	**haa**bern zee dee **gligh**khern in shvahrts
cloth/leather	**Stoff/Leder**	shtof/**lay**derr
rubber/suede	**Gummi/Wildleder**	**gum**mi/**vilt**layderr
Is it genuine leather?	**Ist es echtes Leder?**	ist ehss **ehkh**ters **lay**derr
I need some shoe polish/shoelaces.	**Ich brauche Schuhcreme/ Schnürsenkel.**	ikh **brow**kher **shoo**kraym/ **shnewr**zehnkerl

Shoes worn out? Here's the key to getting them fixed again:

Can you repair these shoes?	**Können Sie diese Schuhe reparieren?**	**kur**nern zee **dee**zer **shoo**er rehpah**ree**rern
Can you stitch this?	**Können Sie das nähen?**	**kur**nern zee dahss **nai**ern
I want new soles and heels.	**Ich möchte neue Sohlen und Absätze.**	ikh **murkh**ter **noy**er **zoa**lern unt **ahp**zehtser
When will they be ready?	**Wann sind sie fertig?**	vahn zint zee **fehr**tikh

COLOURS, see page 113

Electrical appliances *Elektrische Geräte*

220 volt, 50-cycle A.C. is almost universal in Germany as well as in Austria and Switzerland.

What's the voltage?	**Welche Spannung haben Sie hier?**	**vehl**kher **shpah**nung **haa**bern zee heer
Do you have a battery for this?	**Haben Sie eine Batterie hierfür?**	**haa**bern zee **igh**ner bahter**ree** heer**fewr**
This is broken. Can you repair it?	**Das ist kaputt. Können Sie es reparieren?**	dahss ist kah**put**. **kur**nern zee ehss rehpah**ree**rern
Can you show me how it works?	**Können Sie mir zeigen, wie es funktioniert?**	**kur**nern zee meer **tsigh**gern vee ehss funktsion**neert**
I'd like a video cassette.	**Ich möchte eine Videokassette.**	ikh **murkh**ter **igh**ner **vee**dehokkahssehter
I'd like a/an/some ...	**Ich möchte ...**	ikh **murkh**ter
adaptor	**einen Zwischenstecker**	**igh**nern **tsvi**shern-shtehkerr
amplifier	**einen Verstärker**	**igh**nern fehr**shtair**kerr
bulb	**eine Glühbirne**	**igh**ner **glew**beerner
cassette recorder	**einen Kassettenrecorder**	**igh**nern kah**sseh**tern-rehkorderr
clock-radio	**einen Radiowecker**	**igh**nern **raa**diovehkerr
electric toothbrush	**eine elektrische Zahnbürste**	**igh**ner ay**lehk**trisher **tsaan**bewrster
extension lead (cord)	**eine Verlängerungsschnur**	**igh**ner fehr**lehng**errungs-shnoor
hair dryer	**einen Haartrockner**	**igh**nern **haar**troknerr
headphones	**einen Kopfhörer**	**igh**nern **kopf**hurrerr
(travelling) iron	**ein (Reise)bügeleisen**	ighn (**righ**zer)bewgerlighzern
lamp	**eine Lampe**	**igh**ner **lahm**per
plug	**einen Stecker**	**igh**nern **shteh**kerr
portable ...	**Koffer- ...**	**ko**fferr
radio	**ein Radio**	ighn **raa**dio
car radio	**Autoradio**	**ow**torraadio
record player	**einen Plattenspieler**	**igh**nern **plah**ternshpeelerr
shaver	**einen Rasierapparat**	**igh**nern rah**zee**rahpahraat
speakers	**Lautsprecher**	**lowt**shprehkherr
(colour) television	**einen (Farb)fernseher**	**igh**nern (**fahrp**)fehrnzayerr
transformer	**einen Transformator**	**igh**nern trahnsfor**maa**tor
video-recorder	**einen Videorecorder**	**igh**nern **vee**dehorrehkorderr

Grocery *Lebensmittelgeschäft*

I'd like some bread, please.	**Ich möchte ein Brot, bitte.**	ikh **murkh**ter ighn broat **bit**ter
What sort of cheese do you have?	**Welche Käsesorten haben Sie?**	**vehl**kher **kai**zerzortern **haa**bern zee
A piece of ...	**Ein Stück von ...**	ighn shtewk fon
this one	**diesem**	**dee**zerm
the one on the shelf	**dem auf dem Regal**	daym owf daym reh**gaal**
I'll have one of those, please.	**Ich möchte eins von denen, bitte.**	ikh **murkh**ter ighnss fon **day**nern **bit**ter
May I help myself?	**Kann ich mich selbst bedienen?**	kahn ikh mikh zehlpst ber**dee**nern
I'd like ...	**Ich möchte ...**	ikh **murkh**ter
a kilo of apples	**ein Kilo Äpfel**	ighn **kee**lo **eh**pferl
half a kilo of tomatoes	**ein halbes Kilo Tomaten**	ighn **hahl**bers **kee**lo tom**maa**tern
100 grams of butter	**100 Gramm Butter**	100 grahm **but**terr
a litre of milk	**einen Liter Milch**	**igh**nern **lee**terr milkh
half a dozen eggs	**ein halbes Dutzend Eier**	ighn **hahl**bers **dut**sernd **igh**err
4 slices of ham	**4 Scheiben Schinken**	4 **shigh**bern **shin**kern
a box of chocolate	**eine Schachtel Schokolade**	**igh**ner **shahkh**terl shokkol**laa**der
a jar of jam	**ein Glas Marmelade**	ighn glaass mahrmer**laa**der
a tin (can) of peaches	**eine Büchse Pfirsiche**	**igh**ner **bew**kser **pfeer**zikher
a tube of mustard	**eine Tube Senf**	**igh**ner **too**ber zehnf
a packet of tea	**eine Packung Tee**	**igh**ner **pah**kung tay

Weights and measures

1 kilogram or kilo (kg.) = 1000 grams (g.)

100 g. = 3.5 oz. ½ kg. = 1.1 lb.
200 g. = 7.0 oz. 1 kg. = 2.2 lb.

1 oz. = 28.35 g.
1 lb. = 453.60 g.

1 litre (l.) = 0.88 imp. quarts = 1.06 U.S. quarts

1 imp. quart = 1.14 l. 1 U.S. quart = 0.95 l.
1 imp. gallon = 4.55 l. 1 U.S. gallon = 3.8 l.

FOOD, see also page 64

Jeweller's—Watchmaker's *Juwelier – Uhrmacher*

I want a small present for ...	**Ich möchte ein kleines Geschenk für ...**	ikh **murkh**ter ighn **kligh**nerss ger**shehnk** fewr
Could I please see that?	**Könnte ich das bitte sehen?**	**kurn**ter ikh dahss **bit**ter **zay**ern
Do you have anything in gold?	**Haben Sie etwas in Gold?**	**haa**bern zee **eht**vahss in golt
How many carats is this?	**Wieviel Karat hat es?**	vee**feel** kah**raat** haht ehss
Is this real silver?	**Ist das Echtsilber?**	ist dahss **ekht**zilberr
Can you repair this watch?	**Können Sie diese Uhr reparieren?**	**kur**nern zee **dee**zer oor rehpah**ree**rern
I'd like a/an/some ...	**Ich möchte ...**	ikh **murkh**ter
alarm clock	**einen Wecker**	**igh**nern **veh**kerr
bangle	**einen Armreif**	**igh**nern **ahrm**righf
battery	**eine Batterie**	**igh**ner bahter**ree**
bracelet	**ein Armband**	ighn **ahrm**bahnt
chain bracelet	**Gliederarmband**	**glee**derrahrmbahnt
charm bracelet	**Amulettarmband**	ahmul**leht**ahrmbahnt
brooch	**eine Brosche**	**igh**ner **bro**sher
chain	**eine Kette**	**igh**ner **keh**ter
charm	**ein Amulett**	ighn ahmul**leht**
cigarette case	**ein Zigarettenetui**	ighn tsiggah**reh**ternehtvee
cigarette lighter	**ein Feuerzeug**	ighn **foy**errtsoyg
clip	**einen Klipp**	**igh**nern klip
clock	**eine Uhr**	**igh**ner oor
cross	**ein Kreuz**	ighn kroyts
cuckoo clock	**eine Kuckucksuhr**	**igh**ner **kuk**kuksoor
cuff links	**Manschettenknöpfe**	mahn**sheh**ternknurpfer
cutlery	**Tafelbesteck**	**taa**ferlbershtehk
earrings	**Ohrringe**	**oar**ringer
gem	**einen Edelstein**	**igh**nern **ay**derlshtighn
jewel box	**ein Schmuckkästchen**	ighn **shmuk**kehstkhern
music box	**eine Spieldose**	**igh**ner **shpeel**doazer
necklace	**eine Halskette**	**igh**ner **hahls**kehter
pendant	**einen Anhänger**	**igh**nern **ahn**hehngerr
pin	**eine Anstecknadel**	**igh**ner **ahn**shtehknaaderl
pocket watch	**eine Taschenuhr**	**igh**ner **tah**shernoor
powder compact	**eine Puderdose**	**igh**ner **poo**derrdoazer

ring	**einen Ring**	**igh**nern ring
engagement ring	**Verlobungsring**	fehr**loa**bungsring
signet ring	**Siegelring**	**zee**gerlring
wedding ring	**Ehering**	**ay**erring
rosary	**einen Rosenkranz**	**igh**nern **roa**zernkrahnts
silverware	**Tafelsilber**	**taa**ferlzilberr
tie clip	**einen Krawatten-klipp**	**igh**nern krah**vah**ternklip
tie pin	**eine Krawatten-nadel**	**igh**ner krah**vah**ternnaaderl
watch	**eine Uhr**	**igh**ner oor
automatic	**automatische**	owto**maa**tisher
digital	**Digital-**	diggi**taal**
quartz	**Quarz-**	kvahrts
with a second hand	**mit Sekundenzeiger**	mit zeh**kun**derntsighgerr
waterproof	**wasserdicht**	**wah**sserrdikht
watchstrap	**ein Uhrarmband**	ighn **oor**ahrmbahnt
wristwatch	**eine Armbanduhr**	**igh**ner **ahrm**bahntoor

amber	**Bernstein**	**behrn**shtighn
amethyst	**Amethyst**	ahmeh**tist**
chromium	**Chrom**	kroam
copper	**Kupfer**	**ku**pferr
coral	**Koralle**	kor**rah**ler
crystal	**Kristall**	kri**stahl**
cut glass	**geschliffenes Glas**	ger**shliff**ernerss glahss
diamond	**Diamant**	diah**mahnt**
emerald	**Smaragd**	smah**rahgt**
enamel	**Email**	eh**mahi**
gold	**Gold**	golt
gold-plated	**vergoldet**	fehr**gol**dert
ivory	**Elfenbein**	**ehl**fernbighn
jade	**Jade**	**yaa**der
onyx	**Onyx**	**oa**niks
pearl	**Perle**	**pehr**ler
pewter	**Zinn**	tsin
platinum	**Platin**	**plaa**teen
ruby	**Rubin**	ru**been**
sapphire	**Saphir**	zah**feer**
silver	**Silber**	**zil**berr
silver-plated	**versilbert**	fehr**zil**bert
stainless steel	**rostfreier Stahl**	**rost**frigherr shtaal
topaz	**Topas**	top**paass**
turquoise	**Türkis**	tewr**keess**

Optician *Optiker*

I've broken my glasses.	**Meine Brille ist zerbrochen.**	**migh**ner **bril**ler ist tsehr**bro**khern
Can you repair them for me?	**Können Sie sie reparieren?**	**kur**nern zee zee rehpah**ree**rern
When will they be ready?	**Wann ist sie fertig?**	vahn ist zee **fehr**tikh
Can you change the lenses?	**Können Sie die Gläser auswechseln?**	**kur**nern zee dee **glai**zerr **ows**vehkserln
I want tinted lenses.	**Ich möchte getönte Gläser.**	ikh **murkh**ter ger**turn**ter **glai**zerr
The frame is broken.	**Das Gestell ist zerbrochen.**	dahss ger**shtehl** ist tsehr**bro**khern
I'd like a spectacle case.	**Ich möchte ein Brillenetui.**	ikh **murkh**ter ighn **bril**lernehtvee
I'd like to have my eyesight checked.	**Ich möchte meine Augen kontrollieren lassen.**	ikh **murkh**ter **migh**ner **ow**gern kontrol**lee**rern **lah**ssern
I'm short-sighted/long-sighted.	**Ich bin kurzsichtig/weitsichtig.**	ikh bin **kurts**zikhtikh/**vight**zikhtikh
I want some contact lenses.	**Ich möchte Kontaktlinsen.**	ikh **murkh**ter kon**tahkt**linzern
I've lost one of my contact lenses.	**Ich habe eine Kontaktlinse verloren.**	ikh **haa**ber **igh**ner kon**tahkt**linzer fehr**loa**rern
Could you give me another one?	**Können Sie mir eine Ersatzlinse geben?**	**kur**nern zee meer **igh**ner err**zahts**linzer **gay**bern
I have hard/soft lenses.	**Ich habe harte/weiche Linsen.**	ikh **haa**ber **hahr**ter/**vigh**kher **lin**zern
Have you any contact-lens liquid?	**Haben Sie eine Flüssigkeit für Kontaktlinsen?**	**haa**bern zee **igh**ner **flew**ssikhkight fewr kon**tahkt**linzern
I'd like to buy a pair of sunglasses.	**Ich hätte gern eine Sonnenbrille.**	ikh **heh**ter gehrn **igh**ner **zon**nernbriller
May I look in a mirror?	**Kann ich mich im Spiegel sehen?**	kahn ikh mikh im **shpee**gerl **zay**ern
I'd like to buy a pair of binoculars.	**Ich hätte gern ein Fernglas.**	ikh **heh**ter gehrn ighn **fehrn**glaass

Photography *Fotogeschäft*

I want a(n) ... camera.	**Ich möchte einen ... Fotoapparat.**	ikh **murkh**ter **igh**nern ... **foa**toahpahraat
automatic	**automatischen**	owtom**maa**tishern
inexpensive	**billigen**	**bil**liggern
simple	**einfachen**	**ighn**fahkhern
Show me some cine (movie) cameras, please.	**Zeigen Sie mir bitte einige Filmkameras.**	**tsigh**gern zee meer **bit**ter **igh**nigger **film**kahmehraass
Show me that one in the window.	**Zeigen Sie mir die im Schaufenster.**	**tsigh**gern zee meer dee im **show**fehnsterr
I'd like to have some passport photos taken.	**Ich möchte Paßbilder machen lassen.**	ikh **murkh**ter **pahss**bilderr **mah**khern lahssern

Film *Filme*

I'd like a film for this camera.	**Ich hätte gern einen Film für diese Kamera.**	ikh **heh**ter gehrn **igh**nern film fewr **dee**zer **kah**mehraa
black and white	**Schwarzweißfilm**	shvahrts**vighs**film
colour	**Farbfilm**	**fahrp**film
colour negative	**Farbnegativfilm**	**fahrp**nehgahteeffilm
colour slide	**Film für Farbdias**	film fewr **fahrp**deeahss
cartridge	**eine Kassette**	**igh**ner kah**sseh**ter
roll film	**ein Rollfilm**	ighn **rol**film
24/36 exposures	**vierundzwanzig/ sechsunddreißig Aufnahmen**	**feer**unttsvahntsikh/ **zehks**untdrighssikh **owf**naamern
this size	**dieses Format**	**dee**zers for**maat**
this ASA/DIN number	**diese ASA/DIN-Zahl**	**dee**zer **aazaa**/deen tsaal
artificial light type	**Kunstlichtfilm**	**kunst**likhtfilm
daylight type	**Tageslichtfilm**	**taa**gerslikhtfilm
fast (high speed)	**hochempfindlich**	**hoakh**ehmpfintlikh
fine grain	**Feinkorn**	**fighn**korn

Processing *Entwickeln*

How much do you charge for developing?	**Was kostet das Entwickeln?**	vahss **kos**tert dahss ehnt**vik**kerln

NUMBERS, see page 147

I want ... prints of each negative.	**Ich möchte ... Abzüge von jedem Negativ.**	ikh **murkh**ter ... **ahp**tsewger fon **yay**derm **neh**gahteef
with a mat finish	**matt**	maht
with a glossy finish	**Hochglanz**	**hokh**glahnts
Will you please enlarge this?	**Können Sie das bitte vergrößern?**	**kur**nern zee dahss **bit**ter fehr**grurs**serrn
When will the photos be ready?	**Wann sind die Fotos fertig?**	vahn zint dee **foa**toss **fehr**tikh

Accessories and repairs *Zubehör und Reparaturen*

I want a/an/some ...	**Ich möchte ...**	ikh **murkh**ter
battery	**eine Batterie**	**igh**ner bahter**ree**
cable release	**einen Drahtauslöser**	**igh**nern **draat**owslurzer
camera case	**eine Fototasche**	**igh**ner **foa**totahsher
(electronic) flash	**einen (Elektronen) blitz**	**igh**nern (aylehk**troa**nern) blits
filter	**einen Filter**	**igh**nern **fil**terr
for black and white	**für schwarzweiß**	fewr shvahrts**vighss**
for colour	**für Farbe**	fewr **fahr**ber
lens	**ein Objektiv**	ighn obyehk**teef**
telephoto lens	**ein Teleobjektiv**	ighn **tay**lerobyehkteef
wide-angle lens	**ein Weitwinkel-objektiv**	ighn **vight**vinkerlobyehkteef
lens cap	**einen Objektivdeckel**	**igh**nern obyehk**teef**dehkerl
Can you repair this camera?	**Können Sie diesen Fotoapparat reparieren?**	**kur**nern zee **dee**zern **foa**toahpahraat rehpah**ree**rern
The film is jammed.	**Der Film klemmt.**	derr film klehmt
There's something wrong with the ...	**Mit ... stimmt etwas nicht.**	mit ... shtimt **eht**vahss nikht
exposure counter	**dem Bildzählwerk**	daym **bilt**tsailvehrk
film winder	**dem Filmtransport**	daym **film**trahnsport
flash attachment	**dem Blitzgerät**	daym **blits**gerrait
lens	**dem Objektiv**	daym obyehk**teef**
light meter	**dem Belichtungs-messer**	daym ber**likh**tungsmehsserr
rangefinder	**dem Entfernungs-messer**	daym ehnt**fehr**nungsmehsser
shutter	**dem Verschluß**	daym fehr**shluss**

Tobacconist's *Tabakladen*

Cigarettes are sold in specialized tobacco shops, at kiosks and from vending machines. In Switzerland you can also buy cigarettes in restaurants, supermarkets, etc.

A packet of cigarettes, please.	**Eine Schachtel Zigaretten, bitte.**	**igh**ner **shahkh**terl tsiggah**reh**tern **bit**ter
Do you have any American/English cigarettes?	**Haben Sie amerikanische/ englische Zigaretten?**	**haa**bern zee ahmehrik**kaa**nisher **ehng**lisher tsiggah**reh**tern
I'd like a carton.	**Ich möchte eine Stange.**	ikh **murkh**ter **igh**ner **shtahng**er
Give me a/some ..., please.	**Geben Sie mir bitte ...**	**gay**bern zee meer **bit**ter
candy	**Bonbons**	bong**bongs**
chewing gum	**Kaugummi**	**kow**gummi
chewing tobacco	**Kautabak**	**kow**tahbahk
chocolate	**Schokolade**	shokkol**laa**der
cigarette case	**ein Zigarettenetui**	ighn tsiggah**reh**ternehtvee
cigarette holder	**eine Zigarettenspitze**	**igh**ner tsiggah**reh**tern-shpitser
cigarettes	**Zigaretten**	tsiggah**reh**tern
filter-tipped	**mit Filter**	mit **fil**terr
without filter	**ohne Filter**	**oa**ner **fil**terr
light/dark tobacco	**heller/dunkler Tabak**	**heh**lerr/**dunk**lerr tah**bahk**
mild/strong	**milder/starker**	**mil**derr/**shtahr**kerr
menthol	**Menthol-**	mehn**toal**
king-size	**extra lang**	**ehks**traa lahng
cigars	**Zigarren**	tsig**gah**rern
lighter	**ein Feuerzeug**	ighn **foy**errtsoyg
lighter fluid/gas	**Benzin/Gas fürs Feuerzeug**	behn**tseen**/gaass fewrs **foy**errtsoyg
matches	**Streichhölzer**	**shtrighkh**hurltserr
pipe	**eine Pfeife**	**igh**ner **pfigh**fer
pipe cleaners	**Pfeifenreiniger**	**pfigh**fernrighniggerr
pipe tobacco	**Pfeifentabak**	**pfigh**ferntahbahk
pipe tool	**ein Pfeifenbesteck**	ighn **pfigh**fernbershtehk
postcard	**eine Postkarte**	**igh**ner **post**kahrter
snuff	**Schnupftabak**	**shnupf**tahbahk
stamps	**Briefmarken**	**breef**mahrkern
sweets	**Bonbons**	bong**bongs**
wick	**einen Docht**	**igh**nern dokht

Miscellaneous *Verschiedenes*

Souvenirs *Andenken*

Here are some suggestions for articles which you might like to bring back as a souvenir or a gift from Germany.

Bavarian peasant dress	**das Dirndl(kleid)**	dahss **deerndl**(klight)
beer stein	**der Bierkrug**	derr **beer**kroog
glassware	**die Glaswaren**	dee **glahs**vaarern
leather goods	**die Lederwaren**	dee **lay**derrvaarern
music box	**die Spieldose**	dee **shpeel**doazer
porcelain	**das Porzellan**	dahss portseh**laan**
waterproof woollen overcoat	**der Lodenmantel**	**derr loa**dernmahnterl
wood carving	**die Holzschnitzarbeit**	dee **holts**shnitsahrbight

The high quality of Austrian and Swiss winter sports equipment is well known. But petit-point embroidery and porcelain in Austria and linens and organdies in Switzerland are also good buys. Consider leather goods and *Lederhosen* (knee-length leather trousers) in Austria, and don't miss the fabulous array of watches and luscious chocolate in Switzerland.

chocolate	**die Schokolade**	dee shokkol**laa**der
cuckoo clock	**die Kuckucksuhr**	dee **kuk**kuksoor
embroidery	**die Stickerei**	dee shtikker**righ**
linen	**das Leinenzeug**	dahss **ligh**nerntsoyg
ski equipment	**die Skiausrüstung**	dee **shee**owsrewstung
Swiss army knife	**das Schweizer Armeemesser**	dahss **shvigh**tserr ahr**may**mehsserr
Tyrolean hat	**der Tirolerhut**	derr tee**roa**lerrhoot
Tyrolean pipe	**die Tiroler Pfeife**	dee tee**roa**lerr **pfigh**fer
watch	**die Uhr**	dee oor

Records—Cassettes *Schallplatten – Kassetten*

Do you have any records by ...?	**Haben Sie Schallplatten von ...?**	**haa**bern zee **shahl**plahtern fon
Can I listen to this record?	**Kann ich diese Platte hören?**	kahn ikh **dee**zer **plah**ter **hur**rern

L.P. (33 rpm)	**die Langspielplatte (33 UpM)**	dee **lahng**shpeelplahter (**drig**huntdrighssikh oo pay ehm)
E.P. (45 rpm)	**45 UpM**	**fewnf**untfeertsikh oo pay ehm
single	**die Single**	dee "single"

Have you any songs by ...?	**Haben Sie Lieder von ...?**	**haa**bern zee **lee**derr fon
I'd like a ...	**Ich hätte gern ...**	ikh **heh**ter gehrn
cassette	**eine Kassette**	**igh**ner kahs**seh**ter
video cassette	**eine Videokassette**	**igh**ner **vee**dehokkahssehter
compact disc	**eine Compact Disc**	**igh**ner "compact disc"
chamber music	**die Kammermusik**	dee **kah**merrmuzeek
classical music	**die klassische Musik**	dee **klah**ssisher mu**zeek**
folk music	**die Volksmusik**	dee **folks**muzeek
instrumental music	**die Instrumental-musik**	dee instrumehn**taal**muzeek
jazz	**der Jazz**	derr dzhaiss
light music	**die Unterhaltungs-musik**	dee unterr**hahl**tungsmuzeek
orchestral music	**die Orchestermusik**	dee or**keh**sterrmuzeek
pop music	**die Popmusik**	dee **pop**muzeek

Toys *Spielwaren*

I'd like a toy/ game ...	**Ich möchte ein Spiel-zeug/Spiel ...**	ikh **murkh**ter ighn **shpeel**-tsoyg/shpeel
for a boy	**für einen Jungen**	fewr **igh**nern **yung**ern
for a 5-year-old girl	**für ein 5-jähriges Mädchen**	fewr ighn 5**yai**riggerss **mait**khern
ball	**einen Ball**	**igh**nern bahl
bucket and spade (pail and shovel)	**Eimer und Schaufel**	**igh**merr unt **show**ferl
building blocks	**einen Baukasten**	**igh**nern **bow**kahstern
card game	**ein Kartenspiel**	ighn **kahr**ternshpeel
chess set	**ein Schachspiel**	ighn **shahkh**shpeel
doll	**eine Puppe**	**igh**ner **pup**per
electronic game	**ein elektronisches Spiel**	ighn aylek**troa**nishers shpeel
roller skates	**Rollschuhe**	**rol**shooer

NUMBERS, see page 147

Your money: banks—currency

Banking hours in Germany are usually from 8.30 a.m. to 1 p.m. and from 2.30 to 4 p.m., Monday to Friday (Thursday until 5.30 p.m.). Hours are slightly different in Austria and Switzerland. Small currency-exchange offices, indicated by the words *Geldwechsel* or *Wechselstube* are sometimes open outside regular banking hours.

The *Deutsche Mark* (abbreviated to *DM* and called *D-Mark* —**day** mahrk) is the unit of currency in Germany. It's divided into 100 *Pfennig* (**pfeh**nikh), abbreviated *Pf.*

Coins: 1, 2 and 5 marks; 1, 2, 5, 10 and 50 pfennigs.
Banknotes: 5, 10, 20, 50, 100, 500 and 1,000 marks.

In Austria, the basic unit is the *Schilling* (**shil**ling), abbreviated *S.* It's divided into 100 *Groschen* (**gro**shern), abbreviated *g.*

Coins: 1, 5, 10 and 20 schillings; 10 and 50 groschen.
Banknotes: 20, 50, 100, 500 and 1,000 schillings.

The *Franken* (**frahn**kern), usually abbreviated *Fr.,* is the Swiss unit of currency. There are 100 *Rappen* (**rah**pern), abbreviated *Rp.,* to a franc.

Coins: 1, 2 and 5 francs; 5, 10, 20 and 50 Rappen.
Banknotes: 10, 20, 50, 100, 500 and 1,000 francs.

Credit cards may be used in an increasing number of hotels, restaurants, shops, etc. Signs are posted indicating which cards are accepted.

Traveller's cheques are accepted by hotels, travel agents and many shops, although the exchange rate is invariably better at a bank. Eurocheques are also accepted.

Where's the nearest bank?	**Wo ist die nächste Bank?**	voa ist dee **naikh**ster bahnk
Where is the currency exchange office?	**Wo ist die Wechselstube?**	voa ist dee **vehk**serlshtoober

At the bank *In der Bank*

I want to change some dollars/ pounds.	**Ich möchte Dollar/ Pfund wechseln.**	ikh **murkh**ter **dol**lahr/ pfunt **vehk**serln
I want to cash a traveller's cheque.	**Ich möchte einen Reisescheck einlösen.**	ikh **murkh**ter **igh**nern **righ**zershehk **ighn**lurzern
What's the exchange rate?	**Wie ist der Wechselkurs?**	vee ist derr **vehk**serlkoorss
How much commission do you charge?	**Welche Gebühr erheben Sie?**	**vehl**kher ger**bewr** ehr**hay**bern zee
Can you telex my bank in London?	**Können Sie meiner Bank in London ein Telex schicken?**	**kur**nern zee **migh**nerr bahnk in **lon**don ighn **tay**lehks **shik**kern
I have a/an/some ...	**Ich habe ...**	ikh **haa**ber
bank card	**eine Kontokarte**	**igh**ner **kon**tokkahrter
credit card	**eine Kreditkarte**	**igh**ner kray**dit**kahrter
Eurocheques	**Eurocheques**	**oy**roshehks
introduction from ...	**einen Empfehlungsbrief von ...**	**igh**nern ehm**pfay**lungsbreef fon
letter of credit	**einen Kreditbrief**	**igh**nern kray**dit**breef
I'm expecting some money from New York. Has it arrived yet?	**Ich erwarte Geld aus New York. Ist es schon angekommen?**	ikh ehr**vahr**ter gehlt owss "New York". ist ehss shoan **ahn**gerkommern
Please give me ... notes (bills) and some small change.	**Geben Sie mir bitte ... Scheine und etwas Kleingeld.**	**gay**bern zee meer **bit**ter ... **shigh**ner unt **eht**vahss **klighn**gehlt
Give me ... large notes and the rest in small notes.	**Geben Sie mir ... große Scheine und den Rest in kleinen Scheinen.**	**gay**bern zee meer ... **groa**sser **shigh**ner unt dayn rehst in **kligh**nern **shigh**nern

Depositing—Withdrawing *Einzahlen – Abheben*

I want to ...	**Ich möchte ...**	ikh **murkh**ter
open an account	**ein Konto eröffnen**	ighn **kon**to ehr**urf**nern
withdraw ...	**... abheben**	... **ahp**haybern
Where should I sign?	**Wo muß ich unterschreiben?**	voa muss ikh unterr**shrigh**bern

NUMBERS, see page 147

I want to deposit this in my account.	**Ich möchte das auf mein Konto einzahlen.**	ikh **murkh**ter dahss owf mighn **kon**to **ighn**tsaalern

Business terms *Geschäftsausdrücke*

My name is ...	**Ich heiße ...**	ikh **high**sser
Here's my card.	**Hier ist meine Karte.**	heer ist **migh**ner **kahr**ter
I have an appointment with Mr./Mrs. ...	**Ich bin mit Herrn/ Frau ... verabredet.**	ikh bin mit hehrn/frow ... fehr**ahp**raydert
Can you give me an estimate of the cost?	**Können Sie mir einen Kostenvoranschlag machen?**	**kur**nern zee meer **igh**nern **ko**sternfoarahnshlaak **mah**khern
What's the rate of inflation?	**Wie hoch ist die Inflationsrate?**	vee hoakh ist dee inflah**tsioans**raater
Can you provide me with an interpreter/ a secretary?	**Können Sie mir einen Dolmetscher/eine Sekretärin besorgen?**	**kur**nern zee meer **igh**nern **dol**mehtsherr/**igh**ner zaykray**tai**rin ber**zoar**gern
Where can I make photocopies?	**Wo kann ich Fotokopien machen?**	voa kahn ikh foato-kop**ee**ern **mah**khern

amount	**der Betrag**	derr ber**traag**
balance	**die Bilanz**	dee bil**lahnts**
capital	**das Kapital**	dahss kahpit**taal**
cheque book	**das Scheckbuch**	dahss **shehk**bookh
contract	**der Vertrag**	derr fehr**traag**
expenses	**die Unkosten**	dee **oon**kostern
interest	**die Zinsen**	dee **tsin**zern
investment	**die Kapitalanlage**	dee kahpit**taal**ahnlaager
invoice	**die Rechnung**	dee **rehkh**nung
loss	**der Verlust**	derr fehr**lust**
mortgage	**die Hypothek**	dee hippo**tayk**
payment	**die Zahlung**	dee **tsaa**lung
percentage	**der Prozentsatz**	derr prot**sehnt**zahts
profit	**der Gewinn**	derr ger**vin**
purchase	**der Kauf**	derr kowf
sale	**der Verkauf**	derr fehr**kowf**
share	**die Aktie**	dee **ahk**tsier
transfer	**die Überweisung**	dee ewberr**vigh**zung
value	**der Wert**	derr vayrt

At the post office

The offices of Germany's *Bundespost* are open from 8 a.m. to 6 p.m. They close at noon on Saturdays. Swiss post offices are open from 7.30 a.m. to midday and from 1.30 to 6.30 p.m. (8 to 11 a.m. on Saturdays). In Austria, post offices are open from 8 a.m. to midday and from 2 to 5 p.m. (8 to 10 or noon on Saturdays). Letter boxes (mailboxes) are painted yellow in Germany and Switzerland and yellow or blue in Austria. In principal cities, some post offices are open outside the normal hours. Remember that for telephoning and cables you should go to the post office—there are no separate telephone or cable offices.

Where's the nearest post office?	**Wo ist das nächste Postamt?**	voa ist dahss **naikh**ster **post**ahmt
What time does the post office open/ close?	**Wann öffnet/schließt das Postamt?**	vahn **urf**nert/shleest dahss **post**ahmt
A stamp for this letter/postcard, please.	**Eine Briefmarke für diesen Brief/diese Postkarte, bitte.**	**igh**ner **breef**maarker fewr **dee**zern breef/**dee**zer **post**kaarter **bit**ter
A ...-pfennig stamp, please.	**Eine Briefmarke zu ... Pfennig, bitte.**	**igh**ner **breef**maarker tsoo ... **pfeh**nikh **bit**ter
What's the postage for a letter to London?	**Was kostet ein Brief nach London?**	vahss **kos**tert ighn breef naakh **lon**don
What's the postage for a postcard to Los Angeles?	**Was kostet eine Postkarte nach Los Angeles?**	vahss **kos**tert **igh**ner **post**kaarter naakh los **ehnd**zehrlerss
Where's the letter box (mailbox)?	**Wo ist der Brief-kasten?**	voa ist derr **breef**kahstern
I want to send this by ...	**Ich möchte dies ... senden.**	ikh **murkh**ter deess ... **zehn**dern
airmail	**per Luftpost**	pehr **luft**post
express (special delivery)	**per Expreß**	pehr ehks**prehss**
registered mail	**per Einschreiben**	pehr **ighn**shrighbern

I want to send this parcel.	**Ich möchte dieses Paket schicken.**	ikh **murkh**ter **dee**zers pah**kayt** **shik**kern
At which counter can I cash an international money order?	**An welchem Schalter kann ich eine internationale Postanweisung einlösen?**	ahn **vehl**kherm **shahl**terr kahn ikh **igh**ner interrnahtsioa**naa**ler **post**ahnvighzung **ighn**lurzern
Where's the poste restante (general delivery)?	**Wo ist der Schalter für postlagernde Sendungen?**	voa ist derr **shahl**terr fewr **post**laagerrnder **zehn**dungern
Is there any mail for me? My name is ...	**Ist Post für mich da? Ich heiße ...**	ist post fewr mikh daa? ikh **high**sser

BRIEFMARKEN	STAMPS
PAKETE	PARCELS
POSTANWEISUNGEN	MONEY ORDERS

Telegrams *Telegramme*

For telegrams you should go to the post-office—there are no separate cable offices.

I want to send a telegram/telex. May I please have a form?	**Ich möchte ein Telegramm/Telex aufgeben. Kann ich bitte ein Formular haben?**	ikh **murkh**ter ighn taylay**grahm**/**tay**lehks **owf**gaybern. kahn ikh **bit**ter ighn formul**laar** **haa**bern
How much is it per word?	**Was kostet es pro Wort?**	vahss **ko**stert ehss proa vort
How long will a cable to Chicago take?	**Wie lange braucht ein Telegramm nach Chicago?**	vee **lahn**ger browkht ighn taylay**grahm** naakh tshik**kaa**go

Telephoning *Telefonieren*

The telephone networks of Germany, Austria and Switzerland are almost entirely automated. Coin-operated booths are to be found on the street, with instructions posted inside, often in English.

International calls can be made from almost all public telephones in Germany and in Switzerland. In Austria, only some are equipped for long-distance calls. If you need assistance in placing the call, go to the post office or ask at your hotel.

Phone numbers are given in pairs. Note that, in telephoning, *zwei* becomes *zwo* (tsvoa).

Where's the telephone?	**Wo ist das Telefon?**	voa ist dahss taylay**foan**
Where's the nearest telephone booth?	**Wo ist die nächste Telefonzelle?**	voa ist dee **naikh**ster taylay**foan**tsehler
May I use your phone?	**Darf ich Ihr Telefon benutzen?**	dahrf ikh eer taylay**foan** ber**nut**sern
Do you have a telephone directory for Bonn?	**Haben Sie ein Telefonbuch von Bonn?**	**haa**bern zee ighn taylay**foan**bukh fon bon
What's the dialling (area) code for ...?	**Wie ist die Vorwählnummer von ...?**	vee ist dee **foar**vailnummerr fon
How do I get the international operator?	**Welche Nummer hat die (internationale) Vermittlung?**	**vehl**kher **num**merr haht dee (interrnahtsion**naa**ler) fehr**mit**lung

Operator *Vermittlung*

Good morning, I want Hamburg 12 34 56.	**Guten Morgen. Ich möchte Hamburg 12 34 56.**	**goo**tern **mor**gern. ikh **murkh**ter **hahm**boorg 12 34 56
Can you help me get this number?	**Können Sie mir helfen, diese Nummer zu bekommen?**	**kur**nern zee meer **hehl**fern **dee**zer **num**merr tsoo ber**kom**mern
I want to place a personal (person-to-person) call.	**Ich möchte ein Gespräch mit Voranmeldung.**	ikh **murkh**ter ighn ger**shpraikh** mit **foar**ahnmehldung
I want to reverse the charges (call collect).	**Ich möchte ein R-Gespräch anmelden.**	ikh **murkh**ter ighn **ehr**-gershpraikh **ahn**mehldern

NUMBERS, see page 147

Speaking *Am Apparat*

Hello. This is ... speaking.	**Hallo. Hier spricht ...**	**hah**loa. heer shprikht
I want to speak to ...	**Ich möchte ... sprechen.**	ikh **murkh**ter ... **shpreh**khern
I want extension ...	**Ich möchte Nebenanschluß ...**	ikh **murkh**ter **nay**bern-ahnshluss
Speak louder/more slowly, please.	**Sprechen Sie bitte etwas lauter/langsamer.**	**shpreh**khern zee **bit**ter **eht**vahss **low**terr/**lahng**-zaamerr

Bad luck *Pech gehabt*

Would you please try again later?	**Würden Sie es bitte später noch einmal versuchen?**	**vewr**dern zee ehss **bit**ter **shpai**terr nokh **ighn**maal fehr**zoo**khern
Operator, you gave me the wrong number.	**Fräulein, Sie haben mich falsch verbunden.**	**froy**lighn zee **haa**bern mikh fahlsh fehr**bun**dern
We were cut off.	**Wir sind unterbrochen worden.**	veer zint unterr**bro**khern **vor**dern

Telephone alphabet *Buchstabiertabelle*

A	**Anton**	**ahn**toan	O	**Otto**	otto
Ä	**Ärger**	**ehr**gerr	Ö	**Ökonom**	urkon**noam**
B	**Berta**	**behr**tah	P	**Paula**	**pow**lah
C	**Caesar**	**tsai**zahr	Q	**Quelle**	**kveh**ler
CH	**Charlotte**	shahr**lot**ter	R	**Richard**	**rik**hahrt
D	**Dora**	**doa**rah	S	**Samuel**	**zaa**muehl
E	**Emil**	ay**meel**	SCH	**Schule**	**shoo**ler
F	**Friedrich**	**freed**rikh	T	**Theodor**	**tay**oddoar
G	**Gustav**	**gus**tahf	U	**Ulrich**	**ul**rikh
H	**Heinrich**	**highn**rikh	Ü	**Übel**	**ew**berl
I	**Ida**	**ee**dah	V	**Viktor**	**vik**tor
J	**Julius**	**yoo**liuss	W	**Wilhelm**	**vil**hehlm
K	**Kaufmann**	**kowf**mahn	X	**Xanthippe**	ksahn**tip**per
L	**Ludwig**	**lood**vikh	Y	**Ypsilon**	**ewp**seelon
M	**Martha**	**mahr**tah	Z	**Zacharias**	tsahkhah**ree**ahss
N	**Nordpol**	**nort**poal			

Not there *Nicht da*

When will he/she be back?	**Wann ist er/sie zurück?**	vahn ist ehr/zee tsoo**rewk**
Will you tell him/her I called?	**Würden Sie ihm/ihr sagen, daß ich angerufen habe?**	**vewr**dern zee eem/eer **zaa**gern dahss ikh **ahn**gerroofern **haa**ber?
My name's ...	**Mein Name ist ...**	mighn **naa**mer ist
Would you ask him/her to call me?	**Würden Sie ihn/sie bitten, mich anzurufen?**	**vewr**dern zee een/zee **bit**tern mikh **ahn**tsooroofern
Would you please take a message?	**Würden Sie bitte etwas ausrichten?**	**vewr**dern zee **bit**ter **eht**vahss **ows**rikhtern

Charges *Gebühren*

What was the cost of that call?	**Was hat das Gespräch gekostet?**	vahss haht dahss ger**shpraikh** ger**kos**tert
I want to pay for the call.	**Ich möchte das Gespräch bezahlen.**	ikh **murkh**ter dahss ger**shpraikh** bert**saa**lern

Ein Anruf für Sie.	There's a telephone call for you.
Welche Nummer haben Sie gewählt?	What number are you calling?
Die Linie ist besetzt.	The line's engaged.
Es meldet sich niemand.	There's no answer.
Sie sind falsch verbunden.	You've got the wrong number.
Das Telefon funktioniert nicht.	The phone is out of order.
Einen Augenblick, bitte.	Just a moment.
Bitte bleiben Sie am Apparat.	Hold on, please.
Er/Sie ist im Augenblick nicht da.	He's/She's out at the moment.

Doctor

To be at ease, make sure your health insurance policy covers any illness or accident while on holiday. If not, ask your insurance representative, automobile association or travel agent for details of special health insurance.

General *Allgemeines*

Can you get me a doctor?	**Können Sie einen Arzt holen?**	**kur**nern zee **igh**nern ahrtst **hoa**lern
Is there a doctor here?	**Gibt es hier einen Arzt?**	gipt ehss heer **igh**nern ahrtst
I need a doctor quickly.	**Ich brauche schnell einen Arzt.**	ikh **brow**kher shnehl **igh**nern ahrtst
Where's there a doctor who speaks English?	**Wo gibt es einen Arzt, der Englisch spricht?**	voa gipt ehss **igh**nern ahrtst derr **ehng**lish shprikht
Where's the surgery (doctor's office)?	**Wo ist die Arztpraxis?**	voa ist dee **ahrtst**prahksiss
What are the surgery (office) hours?	**Wann sind die Sprechstunden?**	vahn zint dee **shprekh**shtundern
Could the doctor come to see me here?	**Könnte der Arzt mich hier behandeln?**	**kurn**ter derr ahrtst mikh heer ber**hahn**derln
What time can the doctor come?	**Wann kann der Arzt kommen?**	vahn kahn derr ahrtst **kom**mern
Can you recommend a/an ...?	**Können Sie mir ... angeben?**	**kur**nern zee meer ... **ahn**gaybern
general practitioner	**einen praktischen Arzt**	**igh**nern **prahk**tishern ahrtst
children's doctor	**einen Kinderarzt**	**igh**nern **kin**derrahrtst
eye specialist	**einen Augenarzt**	**igh**nern **ow**gernahrtst
gynaecologist	**einen Frauenarzt**	**igh**nern **frow**ernahrtst
Can I have an appointment ...?	**Kann ich ... einen Termin haben?**	kahn ikh ... **igh**nern tehr**meen haa**bern
tomorrow	**morgen**	**mor**gern
as soon as possible	**so bald wie möglich**	zo bahlt vee **murg**likh

CHEMIST'S, see page 108

Parts of the body *Körperteile*

appendix	**der Blinddarm**	derr **blint**dahrm
arm	**der Arm**	derr ahrm
artery	**die Arterie**	dee ahr**tay**rier
back	**der Rücken**	derr **rew**kern
bladder	**die Blase**	dee **blaa**zer
bone	**der Knochen**	derr **kno**khern
bowel	**der Darm**	derr dahrm
breast	**die Brust**	dee brust
chest	**der Brustkorb**	derr **brust**korp
ear	**das Ohr**	dahss oar
eye	**das Auge**	dahss **ow**ger
face	**das Gesicht**	dahss ger**zikht**
finger	**der Finger**	derr **fing**err
foot	**der Fuß**	derr fooss
gland	**die Drüse**	dee **drew**zer
hand	**die Hand**	dee hahnt
head	**der Kopf**	derr kopf
heart	**das Herz**	dahss hehrts
jaw	**der Kiefer**	derr **kee**ferr
joint	**das Gelenk**	dahss ger**lehnk**
kidney	**die Niere**	dee **nee**rer
knee	**das Knie**	dahss knee
leg	**das Bein**	dahss bighn
lip	**die Lippe**	dee **lip**per
liver	**die Leber**	dee **lay**berr
lung	**die Lunge**	dee **lun**ger
mouth	**der Mund**	derr munt
muscle	**der Muskel**	derr **mus**kerl
neck	**der Hals**	derr hahls
nerve	**der Nerv**	derr nehrf
nervous system	**das Nervensystem**	dahss **nehr**fernzewstaym
nose	**die Nase**	dee **naa**zer
rib	**die Rippe**	dee **rip**per
shoulder	**die Schulter**	dee **shul**terr
skin	**die Haut**	dee howt
spine	**die Wirbelsäule**	dee **veer**berlzoyler
stomach	**der Magen**	derr **maa**gern
tendon	**die Sehne**	dee **zay**ner
thigh	**der Schenkel**	derr **shehn**kerl
throat	**der Hals**	derr hahls
thumb	**der Daumen**	derr **dow**mern
toe	**die Zehe**	dee **tsay**er
tongue	**die Zunge**	dee **tsun**ger
tonsils	**die Mandeln**	dee **mahn**derln
vein	**die Vene**	dee **vay**ner

Accident—Injury *Unfall – Verletzung*

There has been an accident.	**Es ist ein Unfall passiert.**	ehss ist ighn **un**fahl pah**sseert**
My child has had a fall.	**Mein Kind ist hingefallen.**	mighn kint ist **hin**gerfahlern
He/She has hurt his/her head.	**Er/Sie ist am Kopf verletzt.**	ehr/zee ist ahm kopf fehr**lehtst**
He's/She's unconscious.	**Er/Sie ist bewußtlos.**	ehr/zee ist ber**vust**loass
He's/She's bleeding (heavily).	**Er/Sie blutet (stark).**	ehr/zee **bloo**tert (shtahrk)
He's/She's (seriously) injured.	**Er/Sie ist (schwer) verletzt.**	ehr/zee ist (shvayr) fehr**lehtst**
His/Her arm is broken.	**Sein/Ihr Arm ist gebrochen.**	zighn/eer ahrm ist ger**bro**khern
His/Her ankle is swollen.	**Sein/Ihr Knöchel ist geschwollen.**	zighn/eer **knur**kherl ist ger**shvol**lern
I've been stung.	**Ich bin gestochen worden.**	ikh bin ger**shto**khern **voar**dern
I've got something in my eye.	**Ich habe etwas im Auge.**	ikh **haa**ber **eht**vahss im **ow**ger
I've got a/an ...	**Ich habe ...**	ikh **haa**ber
blister	**eine Blase**	**igh**ner **blaa**zer
boil	**einen Furunkel**	**igh**nern foo**run**kerl
bruise	**eine Quetschung**	**igh**ner **kveht**shung
burn	**eine Brandwunde**	**igh**ner **brahnt**vunder
cut	**eine Schnittwunde**	**igh**ner **shnit**vunder
graze	**eine Abschürfung**	**igh**ner **ahp**shewrfung
insect bite	**einen Insektenstich**	**igh**nern in**zehk**ternshtikh
lump	**eine Beule**	**igh**ner **boy**ler
rash	**einen Ausschlag**	**igh**nern **ows**shlaag
sting	**einen Stich**	**igh**nern shtikh
strained muscle	**eine Muskelzerrung**	**igh**nern **mus**kerltsehrrung
swelling	**eine Schwellung**	**igh**ner **shveh**lung
wound	**eine Wunde**	**igh**ner **vun**der
Could you have a look at it?	**Sehen Sie es bitte mal an.**	**zay**ern zee ehss **bit**ter maal ahn
I can't move my ... It hurts.	**Ich kann den/die/das ... nicht bewegen. Es tut weh.**	ikh kahn dayn/dee/dahss ... nikht ber**vay**gern. ehss toot vay

Wo haben Sie Schmerzen?	Where does it hurt?
Was für Schmerzen haben Sie?	What kind of pain is it?
dumpfe/stechende **pulsierende/anhaltende** **unregelmäßig auftretende**	dull/sharp throbbing/constant on and off
Es ist ...	It's ...
gebrochen/verstaucht **verrenkt/gerissen**	broken/sprained dislocated/torn
Sie müssen geröntgt werden.	I want you to have an X-ray taken.
Sie bekommen einen Gipsverband.	You'll get a plaster.
Es ist infiziert.	It is infected.
Sind Sie gegen Wundstarrkrampf geimpft?	Have you been vaccinated against tetanus?
Ich gebe Ihnen ein Antiseptikum/Schmerzmittel.	I'll give you an antiseptic/ a painkiller.
In ... Tagen möchte ich Sie wiedersehen.	I'd like you to come back in ... days.

Illness *Krankheit*

I'm not feeling well.	**Ich fühle mich nicht wohl.**	ikh **few**ler mikh nikht voal
I'm ill.	**Ich bin krank.**	ikh bin krahnk
I feel dizzy/ sick.	**Mir ist schwindlig/ übel.**	meer ist **shvind**likh/ **ew**berl
I've got a fever.	**Ich habe Fieber.**	ikh **haa**ber **fee**berr
My temperature is 38 degrees.	**Ich habe 38° Fieber.**	ikh **haa**ber 38 graat **fee**berr
I've been vomiting.	**Ich habe mich übergeben.**	ikh **haa**ber mikh ewberr**gay**bern
I'm constipated.	**Ich habe Verstopfung.**	ikh **haa**ber fehr**shto**pfung
I've got diarrhoea.	**Ich habe Durchfall.**	ikh **haa**ber **doorkh**fahl
My ... hurts.	**Mein ... tut weh.**	mighn ... toot vay

I've got (a/an) ...	**Ich habe ...**	ikh **haa**ber
asthma	**Asthma**	**ahst**mah
backache	**Rückenschmerzen**	**rew**kernshmehrtsern
cold	**eine Erkältung**	**igh**ner ehr**kehl**tung
cough	**Husten**	**hoo**stern
cramps	**Krämpfe**	**krehm**pfer
earache	**Ohrenschmerzen**	**oa**rernshmehrtsern
headache	**Kopfschmerzen**	**kopf**shmehrtsern
indigestion	**eine Verdauungsstörung**	**igh**ner fehr**dow**ungs-shturrung
nosebleed	**Nasenbluten**	**naa**zernblootern
palpitations	**Herzklopfen**	**hehrts**klopfern
rheumatism	**Rheumatismus**	roymah**tis**muss
sore throat	**Halsschmerzen**	**hahls**shmehrtsern
stiff neck	**einen steifen Nacken**	**igh**nern **shtigh**fern **nah**kern
stomach ache	**Magenschmerzen**	**maa**gernshmehrtsern
sunstroke	**einen Sonnenstich**	**igh**nern **zon**nernshtikh
I have difficulties breathing.	**Ich habe Atembeschwerden.**	ikh **haa**ber **aa**term-bershvayrdern
I have a pain in my chest.	**Ich habe Schmerzen in der Brust.**	ikh **haa**ber **shmehr**tsern in derr brust
I had a heart attack ... years ago.	**Ich hatte vor ... Jahren einen Herzanfall.**	ikh **hah**ter for ... **yaa**rern **igh**nern **hehrts**-ahnfahl
My blood pressure is too high/too low.	**Mein Blutdruck ist zu hoch/zu niedrig.**	mighn **bloot**druk ist tsu hoakh/tsu **nee**drikh
I'm allergic to ...	**Ich bin gegen ... allergisch.**	ikh bin **gay**gern ... ah**lehr**gish
I'm a diabetic.	**Ich bin Diabetiker.**	ikh bin diah**bay**tikkerr

At the gynaecologist's *Beim Frauenarzt*

I have period pains.	**Ich habe Menstruationsbeschwerden.**	ikh **haa**ber mehnstruah-**tsioans**bershvayrdern
I have a vaginal infection.	**Ich habe eine Scheidenentzündung.**	ikh **haa**ber **igh**ner **shigh**dernehntsewndung
I'm on the pill.	**Ich nehme die Pille.**	ikh **nay**mer dee **pil**ler
I haven't had my period for 2 months.	**Ich habe seit zwei Monaten meine Periode nicht mehr gehabt.**	ikh **haa**ber zight tsvigh **moa**nahtern **migh**ner peh**rioa**der nikht mayr ger**hahpt**
I'm pregnant.	**Ich bin schwanger.**	ikh bin **shvahn**gerr

Wie lange fühlen Sie sich schon so?	How long have you been feeling like this?
Haben Sie das zum ersten Mal?	Is it the first time you've had this?
Ich werde Ihre Temperatur/ Ihren Blutdruck messen.	I'll take your temperature/ blood pressure.
Streifen Sie bitte den Ärmel hoch.	Roll up your sleeve, please.
Bitte machen Sie den Oberkörper frei.	Please undress down to the waist.
Legen Sie sich bitte hierhin.	Please lie down over here.
Machen Sie den Mund auf.	Open your mouth.
Tief atmen, bitte.	Breathe deeply.
Husten Sie bitte.	Cough, please.
Wo haben Sie Schmerzen?	Where do you feel the pain?
Sie haben ...	You've got (a/an) ...
Blasenentzündung	cystitis
Blinddarmentzündung	appendicitis
...entzündung	inflammation of ...
Gelbsucht	jaundice
eine Geschlechtskrankheit	venereal disease
Grippe	flu
Lebensmittelvergiftung	food poisoning
Lungenentzündung	pneumonia
Magenschleimhautentzündung	gastritis
Masern	measles
Ich gebe Ihnen eine Spritze.	I'll give you an injection.
Ich brauche eine Blutprobe/ Stuhlprobe/Urinprobe.	I want a specimen of your blood/stools/urine.
Sie müssen ... Tage im Bett bleiben.	You must stay in bed for ... days.
Sie sollten einen Spezialisten aufsuchen.	I want you to see a specialist.
Sie müssen zu einer General-untersuchung ins Krankenhaus.	I want you to go to the hos-pital for a general check-up.

Prescription—Treatment *Rezept – Behandlung*

This is my usual medicine.	**Gewöhnlich nehme ich dieses Medikament.**	ger**vurn**likh **nay**mer ikh **dee**zerss maydikah**mehnt**
Can you give me a prescription for this?	**Können Sie mir dafür ein Rezept geben?**	**kur**nern zee meer dah**fewr** ighn reh**tsehpt gay**bern
Can you prescribe some sleeping pills/ an antidepressant?	**Können Sie mir Schlaftabletten/ein Mittel gegen Depressionen verschreiben?**	**kur**nern zee mir **shlaaf**tahblehtern/ighn **mit**terl **gay**gern daypreh**ssioa**nern fehr**shrigh**bern
I'm allergic to antibiotics/penicillin.	**Ich bin allergisch gegen Antibiotika/ Penizillin.**	ikh bin ah**lehr**gish **gay**gern ahntibbi**oa**tikkah/ pehnitsil**lin**
I don't want anything too strong.	**Ich möchte kein zu starkes Mittel.**	ikh **murkh**ter kighn tsu **shtahr**kers **mit**terl
How many times a day should I take it?	**Wie oft täglich soll ich es nehmen?**	vee oft **taig**likh zol ikh ehss **nay**mern
Must I swallow them whole?	**Muß ich sie ganz schlucken?**	muss ikh zee gahnts **shluk**kern

Wie werden Sie behandelt?	What treatment are you having?
Welches Medikament nehmen Sie?	What medicine are you taking?
Als Spritze oder Tabletten?	By injection or orally?
Nehmen Sie von dieser Medizin ... Teelöffel ...	Take ... teaspoons of this medicine ...
Nehmen Sie eine Tablette mit einem Glas Wasser ...	Take one pill with a glass of water ...
alle ... Stunden	every ... hours
... mal täglich	... times a day
vor/nach jeder Mahlzeit	before/after each meal
morgens/abends	in the morning/at night
wenn Sie Schmerzen haben	if there is any pain
während ... Tagen	for ... days

CHEMIST'S, see page 108

Fee *Honorar*

How much do I owe you?	**Wieviel bin ich Ihnen schuldig?**	**vee**feel bin ikh **ee**nern **shul**dikh
May I have a receipt for my health insurance?	**Kann ich bitte eine Quittung für meine Krankenkasse haben?**	kahn ikh **bit**ter **igh**ner **kvit**tung fewr **migh**ner **krahn**kernkahsser **haa**bern
Can I have a medical certificate?	**Können Sie mir ein ärztliches Zeugnis ausstellen?**	**kur**nern zee meer ighn **ehrtst**likhers **tsoyg**niss **ows**shtehlern
Would you fill in this health insurance form, please?	**Würden Sie bitte dieses Krankenkassen-Formular ausfüllen?**	**vewr**dern zee **bit**ter **dee**zers **krahn**kernkahssern-formullaar **ows**fewlern

Hospital *Krankenhaus*

Please notify my family.	**Benachrichtigen Sie bitte meine Familie.**	ber**nahkh**rikhtiggern zee **bit**ter **migh**ner fah**mee**lier
What are the visiting hours?	**Wann ist Besuchszeit?**	vahn ist ber**zookhs**tsight
When can I get up?	**Wann darf ich aufstehen?**	vahn dahrf ikh **owf**-shtayern
When will the doctor come?	**Wann kommt der Arzt?**	vahn komt derr ahrtst
I'm in pain.	**Ich habe Schmerzen.**	ikh **haa**ber **shmehrt**sern
I can't eat/sleep.	**Ich kann nicht essen/ schlafen.**	ikh kahn nikht **eh**ssern/ **shlaa**fern
Where is the bell?	**Wo ist die Klingel?**	voa ist dee **kling**erl

nurse	**die Krankenschwester**	dee **krahn**kernshvehsterr
patient	**der Patient/die Patientin**	derr paht**siehnt**/dee paht**siehn**tin
anaesthesia	**die Narkose**	dee nahr**koa**zer
blood transfusion	**die Bluttransfusion**	dee **bloot**trahnsfuzioan
injection	**die Spritze**	dee **shprit**ser
operation	**die Operation**	dee oppehraht**sioan**
bed	**das Bett**	dahss beht
bedpan	**die Bettpfanne**	dee **beht**pfahner
thermometer	**das Thermometer**	dahss tehrmom**may**terr

Dentist *Zahnarzt*

Can you recommend a good dentist?	**Können Sie mir einen guten Zahnarzt empfehlen?**	**kur**nern zee meer **igh**nern **goo**tern **tsaan**ahrtst ehm**pfay**lern
Can I make an (urgent) appointment to see Dr ...?	**Kann ich einen (dringenden) Termin bei Herrn/Frau Dr. ... haben?**	kahn ikh **igh**nern (**dring**erndern) tehr**meen** bigh hehrn/frow **dok**tor ... **haa**bern
Can't you possibly make it earlier than that?	**Geht es wirklich nicht eher?**	gayt ehss **virk**likh nikht **ay**er
I have toothache.	**Ich habe Zahnschmerzen.**	ikh **haa**ber **tsaan**shmehrtsern
Is it an abscess/ infection?	**Ist es ein Abszeß/ eine Infektion?**	ist ehss ighn ahps**tsehss**/ **igh**ner infehk**tsioan**
This tooth hurts.	**Dieser Zahn schmerzt.**	**dee**zerr tsaan shmehrtst
at the top	**oben**	**oa**bern
at the bottom	**unten**	**un**tern
in the front	**vorne**	**for**ner
at the back	**hinten**	**hin**tern
Can you fix it temporarily?	**Können Sie ihn provisorisch behandeln?**	**kur**nern zee een provvi**zoa**rish ber**hahn**derln
I don't want it extracted.	**Ich möchte ihn nicht ziehen lassen.**	ikh **murkh**ter een nikht **tsee**ern **lah**ssern
Could you give me an anaesthetic?	**Können Sie mir eine Spritze geben?**	**kur**nern zee meer **igh**ner **shprit**ser **gay**bern
I've lost a filling.	**Ich habe eine Plombe verloren.**	ikh **haa**ber **igh**ner **plom**ber fehr**loa**rern
The gum ...	**Das Zahnfleisch ...**	dahss **tsahn**flighsh
is very sore	**ist wund**	ist vunt
is bleeding	**blutet**	**bloo**tert
I've broken this denture.	**Mein Gebiß ist zerbrochen.**	mighn ger**biss** ist tsehr**bro**khern
Can you repair this denture?	**Können Sie das Gebiß reparieren?**	**kur**nern zee dahss ger**biss** rehpah**ree**rern
When will it be ready?	**Wann ist es fertig?**	vahn ist ehss **fehr**tikh

Reference section

Where do you come from? *Woher kommen Sie?*

I'm from ...	**Ich komme aus ...**	ikh **kom**mer ows
Africa	**Afrika**	**ah**frikkah
Asia	**Asien**	**aa**ziern
Australia	**Australien**	ow**straa**liern
Europe	**Europa**	oy**roa**pah
North America	**Nordamerika**	**nort**ahmayrikkah
South America	**Südamerika**	**zewd**ahmayrikkah
Austria	**Österreich**	**urs**terrighkh
Belgium	**Belgien**	**behl**giern
Canada	**Kanada**	**kah**nahdah
Czechoslovakia	**der Tschechoslowakei**	derr chehkhoslovvah**kigh**
China	**China**	**khee**nah
Denmark	**Dänemark**	**dai**nermahrk
England	**England**	**ehng**lahnt
Finland	**Finnland**	**fin**lahnt
France	**Frankreich**	**frahnk**righkh
Germany	**Deutschland**	**doych**lahnt
East Germany	**der DDR**	derr day day ehr
West Germany	**der Bundesrepublik**	derr **bun**dersrehpublik
Great Britain	**Großbritannien**	**groas**brittahniern
Greece	**Griechenland**	**gree**khernlahnt
Ireland	**Irland**	**eer**lahnt
Israel	**Israel**	**iz**rahayl
Italy	**Italien**	**itaa**liern
Japan	**Japan**	**yaa**pahn
Liechtenstein	**Liechtenstein**	**likh**ternshtighn
Luxembourg	**Luxemburg**	**luks**ermboorg
Netherlands	**den Niederlanden**	dayn **nee**derrlahndern
Norway	**Norwegen**	**nor**vaygern
Poland	**Polen**	**poa**lern
Portugal	**Portugal**	**por**tuggahl
Scotland	**Schottland**	**shot**lahnt
South Africa	**Südafrika**	**zewd**ahfrikkah
Soviet Union	**der Sowjetunion**	derr zov**yeht**unnioan
Spain	**Spanien**	**shpaa**niern
Sweden	**Schweden**	**shvay**dern
Switzerland	**der Schweiz**	derr shvights
United States	**den Vereinigten Staaten**	dayn fehr**igh**nigtern **shtaa**tern
Wales	**Wales**	"Wales"

Numbers *Zahlen*

0	**null**	nul
1	**eins**	ighns
2	**zwei**	tsvigh
3	**drei**	drigh
4	**vier**	feer
5	**fünf**	fewnf
6	**sechs**	zehks
7	**sieben**	**zee**bern
8	**acht**	ahkht
9	**neun**	noyn
10	**zehn**	tsayn
11	**elf**	ehlf
12	**zwölf**	tsvurlf
13	**dreizehn**	**drigh**tsayn
14	**vierzehn**	**feer**tsayn
15	**fünfzehn**	**fewnf**tsayn
16	**sechzehn**	**zehkh**tsayn
17	**siebzehn**	**zeep**tsayn
18	**achtzehn**	**ahkh**tsayn
19	**neunzehn**	**noyn**tsayn
20	**zwanzig**	**tsvahn**tsikh
21	**einundzwanzig**	**ighn**unttsvahntsikh
22	**zweiundzwanzig**	**tsvigh**unttsvahntsikh
23	**dreiundzwanzig**	**drigh**unttsvahntsikh
24	**vierundzwanzig**	**feer**unttsvahntsikh
25	**fünfundzwanzig**	**fewnf**unttsvahntsikh
26	**sechsundzwandzig**	**zehks**unttsvahntsikh
27	**siebenundzwanzig**	**zee**bernunttsvahntsikh
28	**achtundzwanzig**	**ahkht**unttsvahntsikh
29	**neunundzwanzig**	**noyn**unttsvahntsikh
30	**dreißig**	**drigh**ssikh
31	**einunddreißig**	**ighn**untdrighssikh
32	**zweiunddreißig**	**tsvigh**untdrighssikh
33	**dreiunddreißig**	**drigh**untdrighssikh
40	**vierzig**	**feer**tsikh
50	**fünfzig**	**fewnf**tsikh
60	**sechzig**	**zehkh**tsikh
70	**siebzig**	**zeep**tsikh
80	**achtzig**	**ahkh**tsikh
90	**neunzig**	**noyn**tsikh
100	**(ein)hundert**	**(ighn)hun**derrt
101	**hunderteins**	hunderrt**ighnss**
102	**hundertzwei**	hunderrt**tsvigh**
110	**hundertzehn**	hunderrt**tsayn**
120	**hundertzwanzig**	hunderrt**tsvahn**tsikh

200	**zweihundert**	**tsvigh**hunderrt
300	**dreihundert**	**drigh**hunderrt
400	**vierhundert**	**feer**hunderrt
500	**fünfhundert**	**fewnf**hunderrt
600	**sechshundert**	**zehks**hunderrt
700	**siebenhundert**	**zee**bernhunderrt
800	**achthundert**	**ahkht**hunderrt
900	**neunhundert**	**noyn**hunderrt
1000	**(ein)tausend**	**(ighn)tow**zernt
1100	**tausendeinhundert**	towzern**tighn**hunderrt
1200	**tausendzweihundert**	towzernt**tsvigh**hunderrt
2000	**zweitausend**	**tsvigh**towzernt
10,000	**zehntausend**	**tsayn**towzernt
50,000	**fünfzigtausend**	**fewnf**tsikhtowzernt
100,000	**hunderttausend**	**hun**derrttowzernt
1,000,000	**eine Million**	**igh**ner mill**ioan**
1,000,000,000	**eine Milliarde**	**igh**ner milli**ahr**der

first	**erste**	**ehr**ster
second	**zweite**	**tsvigh**ter
third	**dritte**	**drit**ter
fourth	**vierte**	**feer**ter
fifth	**fünfte**	**fewnf**ter
sixth	**sechste**	**zehk**ster
seventh	**siebte**	**zeeb**ter
eighth	**achte**	**ahkh**ter
ninth	**neunte**	**noyn**ter
tenth	**zehnte**	**tsayn**ter
once	**einmal**	**ighn**maal
twice	**zweimal**	**tsvigh**maal
three times	**dreimal**	**drigh**maal
a half	**eine Hälfte**	**igh**ner **hehlf**ter
half a ...	**ein halber ...**	ighn **hahl**berr
half of ...	**die Hälfte von ...**	dee **hehlf**ter fon
half (adj.)	**halb**	hahlp
a quarter	**ein Viertel**	ighn **feer**terl
one third	**ein Drittel**	ighn **drit**terl
a pair of	**ein Paar**	ighn paar
a dozen	**ein Dutzend**	ighn **dut**sernd
3.4%	**3,4 Prozent**	drigh **kom**mah feer pro**tsehnt**
1981	**neunzehnhundert-einundachtzig**	noyntsaynhunderrt-**igh**nuntahkhtsikh
1992	**neunzehnhundert-zweiundneunzig**	noyntsaynhunderrt-**tsvigh**undnoyntsikh
2003	**zweitausenddrei**	tsvightowzernt**drigh**

Year and age *Jahre und Alter*

year	**das Jahr**	dahss yaar
leap year	**das Schaltjahr**	dahss **shahlt**yaar
decade	**das Jahrzehnt**	dahss yaar**tsaynt**
century	**das Jahrhundert**	dahss yaar**hun**dert
this year	**dieses Jahr**	**dee**zers yaar
last year	**letztes Jahr**	**lehts**ters yaar
next year	**nächstes Jahr**	**naikh**sters yaar
each year	**jedes Jahr**	**yay**ders yaar
2 years ago	**vor 2 Jahren**	foar tsvigh **yaa**rern
in one year	**in einem Jahr**	in **igh**nerm yaar
in the eighties	**in den achtziger Jahren**	in dayn **ahkh**tsiggerr **yaa**rern
from the 19th century	**vom 19. Jahrhundert**	fom **noyn**tsayntern yaar**hun**derrt
in the 20th century	**im 20. Jahrhundert**	im **tsvahn**tsikhstern yaar**hun**derrt
old/young	**alt/jung**	ahlt/yung
old/new	**alt/neu**	ahlt/noy
How old are you?	**Wie alt sind Sie?**	vee ahlt zint zee
I'm 30 years old.	**Ich bin 30 Jahre alt.**	ikh bin **drigh**ssikh **yaa**rer ahlt
He/She was born in 1960.	**Er/Sie ist 1960 geboren.**	ehr/zee ist noyntsaynhun-derrt**zehkh**tsikh ger**boa**rern
What is his/her age?	**Wie alt ist er/sie?**	vee ahlt ist ehr/zee
Children under 16 are not admitted.	**Kindern unter 16 Jahren ist der Zutritt verboten.**	**kin**derrn **un**terr **zehkh**tsayn **yaa**rern ist derr **tsu**trit fehr**boa**tern

Seasons *Jahreszeiten*

spring	**der Frühling**	derr **frew**ling
summer	**der Sommer**	derr **zom**merr
autumn	**der Herbst**	derr hehrpst
winter	**der Winter**	derr **vin**terr
in spring	**im Frühling**	im **frew**ling
during the summer	**während des Sommers**	**vai**rernt dehss **zom**merrs
high season	**die Hauptsaison**	dee **howpt**zehzong
low season (before/ after season)	**die Vorsaison/ die Nachsaison**	dee **foar**zehzong/ dee **nahkh**zehzong

Months *Monate*

January	**Januar**	**yah**nuaar
February	**Februar**	**fay**bruaar
March	**März**	mehrts
April	**April**	ah**pril**
May	**Mai**	migh
June	**Juni**	**yoo**ni
July	**Juli**	**yoo**li
August	**August**	ow**gust**
September	**September**	sehp**tehm**berr
October	**Oktober**	ok**toa**berr
November	**November**	nov**vehm**berr
December	**Dezember**	day**tsehm**berr
after June	**nach Juni**	nahkh **yoo**ni
before July	**vor Juli**	foar **yoo**li
during the month of August	**während des Monats August**	**vai**rernt dehss **moa**nahts ow**gust**
in September	**im September**	im zehp**tehm**berr
until October	**bis Oktober**	biss ok**toa**berr
not until November	**nicht vor November**	nikht foar no**vehm**berr
since December	**seit Dezember**	zight deh**tsehm**berr
last month	**im letzten Monat**	im **leht**stern **moa**naht
next month	**im nächsten Monat**	im **naikh**stern **moa**naht
the month before	**der vorhergehende Monat**	derr foar**hayr**gayernder **moa**naht
the month after	**der folgende Monat**	derr **fol**gernder **moa**naht
the beginning of January	**Anfang Januar**	**ahn**fahnk **yah**nuaar
the middle of February	**Mitte Februar**	**mi**terr **fay**bruaar
the end of March	**Ende März**	**ehn**der mehrts

Days and date *Tage – Datum*

What day is it today?	**Welchen Tag haben wir heute?**	**vehl**khern taag **haa**bern veer **hoy**ter
Sunday	**Sonntag**	**zon**taag
Monday	**Montag**	**moan**taag
Tuesday	**Dienstag**	**deens**taag
Wednesday	**Mittwoch**	**mit**vokh
Thursday	**Donnerstag**	**don**nerrstaag
Friday	**Freitag**	**fright**taag
Saturday	**Samstag/Sonnabend**	**zahms**taag/**zon**naabernt

What's the date today?	**Den wievielten haben wir heute?**	dayn **vee**feeltern **haa**bern veer **hoy**ter
It's ...	**Es ist ...**	ehss ist
July 1	**der 1. Juli**	derr **ehr**ster **yoo**li
March 10	**der 10. März**	derr **tsayn**ter mehrts
When's your birthday?	**Wann haben Sie Geburtstag?**	vahn **haa**bern zee ger**burts**taag
August 2nd.	**Am 2. August.**	ahm **tsvigh**tern ow**gust**
in the morning	**am Morgen**	ahm **mor**gern
during the day	**tagsüber**	**taags**ewberr
in the afternoon	**am Nachmittag**	ahm **nahkh**mittaag
in the evening	**am Abend**	ahm **aa**bernt
at night	**nachts**	nahkhts
the day before yesterday	**vorgestern**	**foar**gehsterrn
yesterday	**gestern**	**geh**sterrn
today	**heute**	**hoy**ter
tomorrow	**morgen**	**mor**gern
the day after tomorrow	**übermorgen**	**ew**berrmorgern
the day before	**der vorhergehende Tag**	derr foar**hayr**gayernder taag
the next day	**der Tag danach**	derr taag dah**naakh**
two days ago	**vor zwei Tagen**	foar tsvigh **taa**gern
in three days' time	**in drei Tagen**	in drigh **taa**gern
last week	**letzte Woche**	**leht**ster **vo**kher
next week	**nächste Woche**	**naikh**ster **vo**kher
for a fortnight (two weeks)	**zwei Wochen lang**	tsvigh **vo**khern lahng
day off	**der freie Tag**	derr **frigh**er taag
holiday	**der Feiertag**	derr **figh**errtaag
holidays (vacation)	**die Ferien/der Urlaub**	dee **fay**riern/derr **oor**lowp
week	**die Woche**	dee **vo**kher
weekend	**das Wochenende**	dahss **vo**khernehnder
working day	**der Werktag**	derr **vehrk**taag

Greetings and wishes *Grüße und Wünsche*

Merry Christmas!	**Fröhliche Weihnachten!**	**frur**likher **vigh**nahkhtern
Happy New Year!	**Glückliches Neues Jahr!**	**glew**klikhers **noy**ers yaar

Happy Easter!	**Frohe Ostern!**	**froa**er **oa**sterrn
Happy birthday!	**Alles Gute zum Geburtstag!**	**ah**lerss **goo**ter tsum ger**burts**taag
Best wishes!	**Alles Gute!**	**ah**lers **goo**ter
Congratulations!	**Herzlichen Glückwunsch!**	**hehrts**likhern **glewk**vunsh
Good luck/All the best!	**Viel Glück!**	feel glewk
Have a good trip!	**Gute Reise!**	**goo**ter **righ**zer
Have a good holiday!	**Schöne Ferien!**	**shur**ner **fay**riern
Best regards from ...	**Herzliche Grüße von ...**	**hehrts**likher **grew**sser fon
My regards to ...	**Beste Grüße an ...**	**beh**ster **grew**sser ahn

Public holidays *Feiertage*

Only national holidays in Germany (D), Austria (A) or Switzerland (CH) are cited below.

Jan. 1	**Neujahr**	New Year's Day	D A CH
Jan. 2			CH*
Jan. 6	**Dreikönigstag**	Epiphany	A
May 1	**Tag der Arbeit**	Labour Day	D A
June 17	**Tag der Deutschen Einheit**	National Unity Day	D
Aug. 1	**Nationalfeiertag**	National Day	CH*
Aug. 15	**Mariä Himmelfahrt**	Assumption Day	A
Oct. 26	**Nationalfeiertag**	National Day	A
Nov. 1	**Allerheiligen**	All Saints' Day	A
Dec. 8	**Mariä Empfängnis**	Immaculate Conception	A
Dec. 25	**1. Weihnachtstag**	Christmas Day	D A CH
Dec. 26	**2. Weihnachtstag**	St. Stephen's Day	D A CH*
Movable dates:	**Karfreitag**	Good Friday	D CH*
	Ostermontag	Easter Monday	D A CH*
	Christi Himmelfahrt	Ascension	D A CH
	Pfingstmontag	Whit Monday	D A CH*
	Fronleichnam	Corpus Christi	A

*Most cantons

What time is it? *Wie spät ist es?*

Excuse me. Can you tell me the time?	**Verzeihung. Können Sie mir bitte sagen, wie spät es ist?**	fehr**tsigh**ung. **kur**nern zee meer **bit**ter **zaa**gern vee shpait ehss ist
It's ...	**Es ist ...**	ehss ist
five past one	**fünf nach eins***	fewnf nakh ighns
ten past two	**zehn nach zwei**	tsayn nakh tsvigh
a quarter past three	**viertel nach drei**	**feer**terl nahkh drigh
twenty past four	**zwanzig nach vier**	**tsvahn**tsikh nahkh feer
twenty-five past five	**fünf vor halb sechs**	fewnf foar hahlp zehks
half past six	**halb sieben**	hahlp **zee**bern
twenty-five to seven	**fünf nach halb sieben**	fewnf nakh hahlp **zee**bern
twenty to eight	**zwanzig vor acht**	**tsvahn**tsikh foar ahkht
a quarter to nine	**viertel vor neun**	**feer**terl foar noyn
ten to ten	**zehn vor zehn**	tsayn foar tsayn
five to eleven	**fünf vor elf**	fewnf foar ehlf
twelve o'clock (noon/midnight)	**zwölf Uhr (Mittag/Mitternacht)**	tsvurlf oor (**mit**taag/**mit**terrnahkht)
in the morning	**morgens**	**mor**gerns
in the afternoon	**nachmittags**	**nahkh**mittaags
in the evening	**abends**	**aa**bernds
The train leaves at ...	**Der Zug fährt um ...**	derr tsoog fairt um
13.04 (1.04 p.m.)	**dreizehn Uhr vier**	**drigh**tsayn oor feer
0.40 (0.40 a.m.)	**null Uhr vierzig**	nul oor **feer**tsikh
in five minutes	**in fünf Minuten**	in fewnf min**noo**tern
in a quarter of an hour	**in einer Viertelstunde**	in **igh**nerr **feer**terlshtunder
half an hour ago	**vor einer halben Stunde**	foar **igh**nerr **hahl**bern **shtun**der
about two hours	**ungefähr zwei Stunden**	**un**gerfair tsvigh **shtun**dern
more than 10 minutes	**über 10 Minuten**	**ew**berr tsayn min**noo**tern
less than 30 seconds	**weniger als 30 Sekunden**	**vay**niggerr ahlss **drigh**ssikh zeh**kun**dern
The clock is fast/slow.	**Die Uhr geht vor/nach.**	dee oor gayt foar/nahkh

* In ordinary conversation, time is expressed as shown here. However, official time uses a 24-hour clock which means that after noon hours are counted from 13 to 24.

Common abbreviations *Gebräuchliche Abkürzungen*

ACS	**Automobil-Club der Schweiz**	Automobile Association of Switzerland
ADAC	**Allgemeiner Deutscher Automobil-Club**	General Automobile Association of Germany
a.M.	**am Main**	on the river Main
a.Rh.	**am Rhein**	on the river Rhine
AvD	**Automobil-Club von Deutschland**	Automobile Club of Germany
Bhf	**Bahnhof**	railway station
BRD	**Bundesrepublik Deutschland**	Federal Republic of Germany (West Germany)
DB	**Deutsche Bundesbahn**	Federal German Railway
DDR	**Deutsche Demokratische Republik**	German Democratic Republic (East Germany)
d.h.	**das heißt**	i.e. (that is)
DIN	**Deutsche Industrie-Norm**	German Industrial Standard
Frl.	**Fräulein**	Miss
G.	**Gasse**	lane
Hbf.	**Hauptbahnhof**	main railway station
Hr.	**Herr**	Mr.
LKW	**Lastkraftwagen**	lorry/truck
MEZ	**Mitteleuropäische Zeit**	Central European Time
Mio.	**Million**	million
Mrd.	**Milliarde**	1000 millions (billion)
n.Chr.	**nach Christus**	A.D.
ÖAMTC	**Österreichischer Automobil-Motorrad- und Touring-Club**	Austrian Automobile, Motorcycle and Touring Association
ÖBB	**Österreichische Bundesbahnen**	Austrian Federal Railways
PKW	**Personenkraftwagen**	motor car
Pl.	**Platz**	square
PS	**Pferdestärke**	horsepower
PTT	**Post, Telephon, Telegraph**	Post, Telephone and Telegraph Office
SBB	**Schweizerische Bundesbahnen**	Swiss Federal Railways
St.	**Stock**	floor
Str.	**Straße**	street
TCS	**Touring-Club der Schweiz**	Swiss Touring Club
usw.	**und so weiter**	etc.
v.Chr.	**vor Christus**	B.C.
z.B.	**zum Beispiel**	e.g. (for example)
z.Z.	**zur Zeit**	at present

Signs and notices *Aufschriften und Hinweise*

Achtung	Caution
Aufzug	Lift (elevator)
Ausgang	Exit
Auskunft	Information
Außer Betrieb	Out of order
Ausverkauf	Sale
Ausverkauft	Sold out
Belegt	Full/No vacancies
Besetzt	Occupied
Bitte klingeln	Please ring
Bitte nicht stören	Do not disturb
Damen	Ladies
Drücken	Push
Eingang	Entrance
Eintreten ohne zu klopfen	Enter without knocking
Eintritt frei	No admission charge
Frei	Vacant
Frisch gestrichen	Wet paint
Für Unbefugte verboten	No trespassing
Gefahr	Danger
Geschlossen	Closed
Heiß	Hot
Herren	Men
Kalt	Cold
Kasse	Cash desk
Kein Zutritt	No entrance
Lebensgefahr	Danger of death
Lift	Lift (elevator)
Nicht berühren	Do not touch
Notausgang	Emergency exit
Notruf	Emergency
Nur für Anlieger	Residents only
Privatweg	Private road
Radweg	Cycle path
Rauchen verboten	No smoking
Reserviert	Reserved
Unbefugtes Betreten verboten	No trespassing
... verboten	... forbidden/prohibited
Vorsicht	Caution
Vorsicht, bissiger Hund	Beware of the dog
Ziehen	Pull
Zimmer frei	Vacancies
Zu verkaufen	For sale
Zu vermieten	To let (for hire)

Emergency *Notfall*

Call the police	**Rufen Sie die Polizei**	**roo**fern zee dee pol**litsigh**
DANGER	**GEFAHR**	ger**faar**
FIRE	**FEUER**	**foy**err
Gas	**Gas**	gaass
Get a doctor	**Holen Sie einen Arzt**	**hoa**lern zee **igh**nern ahrtst
Go away	**Gehen Sie weg**	**gay**ern zee vehk
HELP	**HILFE**	**hil**fer
Get help	**Holen Sie Hilfe**	**hoa**lern zee **hil**fer
I'm ill	**Ich bin krank**	ikh bin krahnk
I'm lost	**Ich habe mich verirrt**	ikh **haa**ber mikh fehr**eert**
LOOK OUT	**VORSICHT**	**foar**zikht
POLICE	**POLIZEI**	polli**tsigh**
Quick	**Schnell**	shnehl
STOP	**HALT**	hahlt
Stop that man/woman	**Haltet den Mann/die Frau**	**hahl**tert dayn mahn/dee frow
STOP THIEF	**HALTET DEN DIEB**	**hahl**tert dayn deep

Emergency telephone numbers *Notrufnummern*

	Austria	Germany	Switzerland
Fire	122	112	118
Ambulance	144	112	
Police	133	110	117

Lost property—Theft *Fundsachen – Diebstahl*

Where's the ...?	**Wo ist ...?**	voa ist
lost-property (lost and found) office	**das Fundbüro**	dahss **funt**bewroa
police station	**die Polizeiwache**	dee polli**tsigh**vahkher
I want to report a theft.	**Ich möchte einen Diebstahl anzeigen.**	ikh **murkh**ter **igh**nern **deep**shtaal **ahn**tsighgern
My ... has been stolen.	**Mein(e) ... ist mir gestohlen worden.**	mighn(er) ... ist meer ger**shtoa**lern **voa**rdern
I've lost my wallet.	**Ich habe meine Brieftasche verloren.**	ikh **haa**ber **migh**ner **breef**tahsher fehr**loa**rern

CAR ACCIDENTS, see page 78

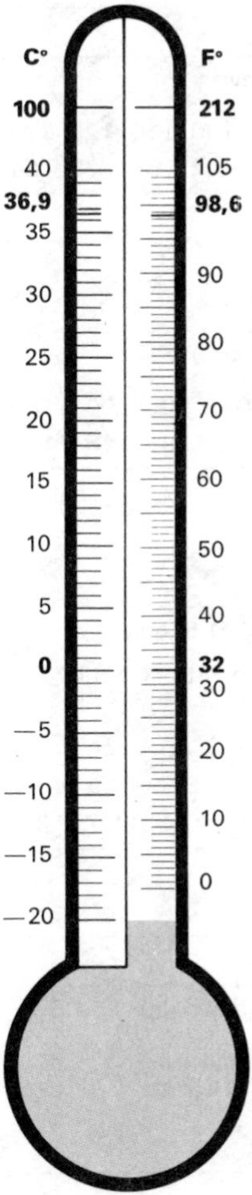

Conversion tables

Centimetres and inches

To change centimetres into inches, multiply by .39.

To change inches into centimetres, multiply by 2.54.

	in.	feet	yards
1 mm.	0.039	0.003	0.001
1 cm.	0.39	0.03	0.01
1 dm.	3.94	0.32	0.10
1 m.	39.40	3.28	1.09

	mm.	cm.	m.
1 in.	25.4	2.54	0.025
1 ft.	304.8	30.48	0.305
1 yd.	914.4	91.44	0.914

(32 metres = 35 yards)

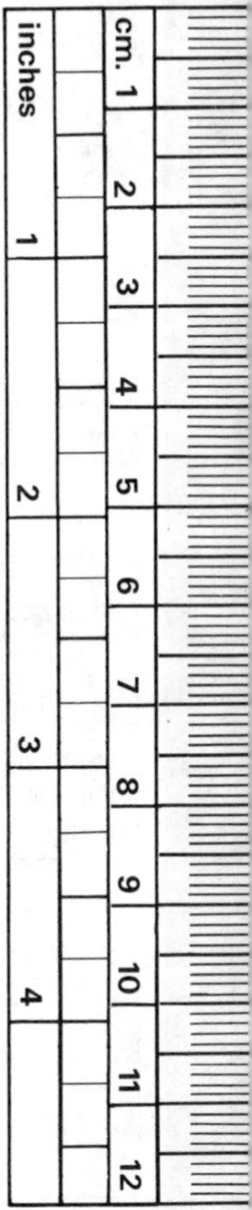

Temperature

To convert centigrade into degrees Fahrenheit, multiply centigrade by 1.8 and add 32.

To convert degrees Fahrenheit into centigrade, subtract 32 from Fahrenheit and divide by 1.8.

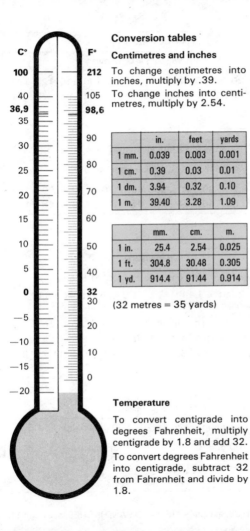

Kilometres into miles

1 kilometre (km.) = 0.62 miles

km.	10	20	30	40	50	60	70	80	90	100	110	120	130
miles	6	12	19	25	31	37	44	50	56	62	68	75	81

Miles into kilometres

1 mile = 1.609 kilometres (km.)

miles	10	20	30	40	50	60	70	80	90	100
km.	16	32	48	64	80	97	113	129	145	161

Fluid measures

1 litre (l.) = 0.88 imp. quart or 1.06 U.S. quart

1 imp. quart = 1.14 l.
1 imp. gallon = 4.55 l.

1 U.S. quart = 0.95 l.
1 U.S. gallon = 3.8 l.

litres	5	10	15	20	25	30	35	40	45	50
imp. gal.	1.1	2.2	3.3	4.4	5.5	6.6	7.7	8.8	9.9	11.0
U.S. gal.	1.3	2.6	3.9	5.2	6.5	7.8	9.1	10.4	11.7	13.0

Weights and measures

1 kilogram or kilo (kg.) = 1000 grams (g.)

100 g. = 3.5 oz.
200 g. = 7.0 oz.

½ kg. = 1.1 lb.
1 kg. = 2.2 lb.

1 oz. = 28.35 g.
1 lb. = 453.60 g.

CLOTHING SIZES, see page 115/YARDS AND INCHES, see page 112

Basic Grammar

Here is a brief outline of some essential features of German grammar.

Articles

All nouns in German are either masculine, feminine or neuter, and they are classified by the article which precedes them.

1. **Definite article** (the):

			Plural:
masc.	*der* **Mann**	the man	*die* **Männer**
fem.	*die* **Frau**	the woman	*die* **Frauen**
neut.	*das* **Kind**	the child	*die* **Kinder**

2. **Indefinite article** (a/an):

masc.	*ein* **Zug**	a train
fem.	*eine* **Reise**	a trip
neut.	*ein* **Flugzeug**	a plane

Nouns and adjectives

1. All nouns are written with a capital letter. The rules for constructing the plural are very complex.

2. **Declension:** According to their use in the sentence, German articles, nouns and modifying adjectives undergo related changes. The tables below show the declension of all three parts of speech.

	masc. sing.	masc. plur.
subject	**der reiche Mann**	**die reichen Männer**
direct object	**den reichen Mann**	**die reichen Männer**
possessive	**des reichen Mannes**	**der reichen Männer**
indirect object	**dem reichen Mann**	**den reichen Männern**

	fem. sing.	fem. plur.
subject	**die schöne Frau**	**die schönen Frauen**
direct object	**die schöne Frau**	**die schönen Frauen**
possessive	**der schönen Frau**	**der schönen Frauen**
indirect object	**der schönen Frau**	**den schönen Frauen**

	neuter sing.	neuter plur.
subject	**das kleine Kind**	**die kleinen Kinder**
direct object	**das kleine Kind**	**die kleinen Kinder**
possessive	**des kleinen Kindes**	**der kleinen Kinder**
indirect object	**dem kleinen Kind**	**den kleinen Kindern**

The indefinite article is declined in a slightly different way, as is the modifying adjective.

	masc.	fem.
subject	**ein reicher Mann**	**eine schöne Frau**
direct object	**einen reichen Mann**	**eine schöne Frau**
possessive	**eines reichen Mannes**	**einer schönen Frau**
indirect object	**einem reichen Mann**	**einer schönen Frau**

	neuter	plur.
subject	**ein kleines Kind**	**keine* großen Leute**
direct object	**ein kleines Kind**	**keine großen Leute**
possessive	**eines kleinen Kindes**	**keiner großen Leute**
indirect object	**einem kleinen Kind**	**keinen großen Leuten**

If declined without an article the adjectives take the endings of the definite article, except in the possessive, which you'll hardly use: **guter Wein** (good wine), **kalte Milch** (cold milk), **warmes Wasser** (hot water).

3. **Demonstrative adjectives:** In spoken German "that" is usually expressed by the definite article, but contrary to the

* **ein** has no plural, but the negative **kein** (declined in singular like **ein**) does.

article, it is stressed. "This" **dieser, diese, dieses** and plural **diese** is declined like the definite article.

das Buch (that book)

dieser Platz (this seat)

4. **Possessive adjectives:** These agree in number and gender with the noun they modify, i.e., with the thing possessed and not the possessor. In singular they are declined like the indefinite article, and in plural like the definite. Note that **Ihr** meaning "your" in the polite form is capitalized.

	masc. or neut.	fem. or plur.
my	**mein**	**meine**
your	**dein**	**deine**
his/its	**sein**	**seine**
her	**ihr**	**ihre**
our	**unser**	**unsere**
your	**euer**	**eure**
their	**ihr**	**ihre**
your (pol.)	**Ihr**	**Ihre**

5. **Comparatives and superlatives:** These are formed by adding **-er (-r)** and **-est (-st)** respectively, very often together with an umlaut.

alt (old)
älter (older)
ältest (oldest)

kurz (short)
kürzer (shorter)
kürzest (shortest)

Adverbs

Many adjectives are used in their undeclined form as adverbs.

schnell	quick, quickly
gut	good, well

There are a few irregularities:

glücklich – glücklicherweise	happy—happily
anders	differently
besonders	especially
gleichfalls	as well, (the) same

Viel indicates quantity and **sehr** intensity:

Er arbeitet viel. He works a lot.
Er ist sehr müde. He's very tired.

Personal pronouns

	subject	direct object	indirect object
I	**ich**	**mich**	**mir**
you	**du**	**dich**	**dir**
he	**er**	**ihn**	**ihm**
she	**sie**	**sie**	**ihr**
it	**es**	**es**	**ihm**
we	**wir**	**uns**	**uns**
you	**ihr**	**euch**	**euch**
they	**sie**	**sie**	**ihnen**
you	**Sie**	**Sie**	**Ihnen**

Note: There are two forms for "you" in German: **du** and **Sie; du** (plur.: **ihr)** is used when talking to relatives, close friends and children (and between young people); **Sie** (both sing. and plur.) in all other cases. **Sie** is written with a capital **S.** The verb has the same form as that of the 3rd person plural.

Verbs

Here we are concerned only with the infinitive, the present tense, and the imperative.

Learn these two important **auxiliary verbs:**

sein (to be)

ich bin (I am)
du bist (you are)
er, sie, es ist (he, she, it is)
wir sind (we are)
ihr seid (you are)
sie sind (they are)
Sie sind (you are)

haben (to have)

ich habe (I have)
du hast (you have)
er, sie, es hat (he, she, it has)
wir haben (we have)
ihr habt (you have)
sie haben (they have)
Sie haben (you have)

The infinitive of practically all verbs ends in **-en.** Here are the endings for the present tense:

ich lieb*e*	I love
du lieb*st*	you love
er, sie, es lieb*t*	he, she, it loves
wir lieb*en*	we love
ihr lieb*t*	you love
sie, Sie lieb*en*	they, you love

Here are four useful irregular verbs in the present tense:

	können (to be able)	**gehen** (to go)	**sehen** (to see)	**tun** (to do)
ich	**kann**	**gehe**	**sehe**	**tue**
du	**kannst**	**gehst**	**siehst**	**tust**
er/sie/es	**kann**	**geht**	**sieht**	**tut**
wir	**können**	**gehen**	**sehen**	**tun**
ihr	**könnt**	**geht**	**seht**	**tut**
sie/Sie	**können**	**gehen**	**sehen**	**tun**

For both regular and irregular verbs, the **imperative** is formed by reversing the order of the verb and the personal pronoun.

Gehen wir!	Let's go!
Gehen Sie!	Go!

Negatives

Negatives are formed with **nicht.**

Er ist nicht hier. He is not here.

Questions

These are formed by inverting the subject and the verb (putting the verb first, the subject second).

Sprechen Sie English? Do you speak English?

Dictionary
and alphabetical index

English–German

f feminine *m* masculine *nt* neuter *pl* plural

a ein(e) 159
abbey Abtei *f* 81
abbreviation Abkürzung *f* 154
able, to be können 163
about *(approximately)* ungefähr 78, 153
above oben 14
abscess Abszeß *m* 145
absorbent cotton Watte *f* 109
accept, to (an)nehmen 63, 102
accessories Zubehör *nt* 116, 125
accident Unfall *m* 78, 139
accommodation Unterkunft *f* 22
account Konto *nt* 130, 131
ache Schmerz *m* 141
adaptor Zwischenstecker *m* 119
address Adresse *f* 21, 31, 76; Anschrift *f* 79, 102
adhesive selbstklebend 105
admission Eintritt *m* 82, 89, 155
Africa Afrika *(nt)* 146
after nach 14, 77
afternoon Nachmittag *m* 151, 153
after-shave lotion Rasierwasser *nt* 110
against gegen 140
age Alter *nt* 149
ago vor 149, 151
air conditioner Klimaanlage *f* 23, 28
airmail per Luftpost 132
air mattress Luftmatratze *f* 106
airplane Flugzeug *nt* 65
airport Flughafen *m* 16, 21, 65
alarm clock Wecker *m* 121
alcohol Alkohol *m* 37
alcoholic alkoholisch 59
all alles 103
allergic allergisch 141, 143
alley Gasse *f* 81
almond Mandel *f* 53
alphabet Alphabet *nt* 15
also auch 15
alter, to ändern 116
amazing erstaunlich 84
amber Bernstein *m* 122
ambulance Krankenwagen *m* 79, 156
American Amerikaner(in) *m/f* 93
American amerikanisch 105, 126
American plan Vollpension *f* 24
amount Betrag *m* 63, 131
amplifier Verstärker *m* 119
amusement park Vergnügungspark *m* 81
anaesthesia Narkose *f* 144
analgesic Schmerzmittel *nt* 109
anchovy Sardelle *f* 41
and und 15
animal Tier *nt* 85
aniseed Anis *m* 51
ankle Knöchel *m* 139
anorak Anorak *m* 116
answer Antwort *f* 136
antibiotic Antibiotikum *nt* 143
antidepressant Mittel gegen Depressionen *nt* 143
antiques Antiquitäten *f/pl* 83
antique shop Antiquitätengeschäft *nt* 98
antiseptic Antiseptikum *nt* 140
any etwas, einige 14
anyone (irgend) jemand 11
anything (irgend) etwas 17, 25, 113

anywhere irgendwo
apartment *(flat)* Wohnung *f* 22
aperitif Aperitif *m* 59
appendicitis Blinddarmentzündung *f* 142
appendix Blinddarm *m* 138
appetizer Vorspeise *f* 41
apple Apfel *m* 53, 64, 120
apple juice Apfelsaft *m* 61
appliance Gerät *nt* 119
appointment Verabredung *f* 131; Termin *m* 137, 145
apricot Aprikose *f* 53
April April *m* 150
archaeology Archäologie *f* 83
architect Architekt *m* 83
area code Vorwählnummer *f* 134
arm Arm *m* 138, 139
arrangement *(set price)* Pauschale *f* 20
arrival Ankunft *f* 16, 65, 68
arrive, to ankommen 68, 130
art Kunst *f* 83
artery Arterie *f* 138
art gallery Kunstgalerie *f* 81, 98
artichoke Artischocke *f* 41
artificial künstlich 124
artist Künstler(in) *m/f* 83
ashtray Aschenbecher *m* 27, 36
Asia Asien *(nt)* 146
ask, to fragen 36, 76; bitten 136
asparagus Spargel *m* 41, 50
aspirin Aspirin *nt* 109
asthma Asthma *nt* 141
at an, bei 14
at least mindestens 26
at once sofort 31
aubergine Aubergine *f* 49
August August *m* 150
aunt Tante *f* 93
Australia Australien *(nt)* 146
Austria Österreich *(nt)* 146
Austrian österreichisch 18
automatic automatisch 122, 124; mit Automatik 20
autumn Herbst *m* 149
avalanche Lawine *f* 79
awful scheußlich 84, 94

B

baby Baby *nt* 24; Säugling *m* 111
baby food Säuglingsnahrung *f* 111
babysitter Babysitter *m* 27
back Rücken *m* 138
backache Rückenschmerzen *m/pl* 141
bacon Speck *m* 38, 46
bad schlecht 14, 95
bag Tasche *f* 17, 18; Tragetasche *f* 103
baggage Gepäck *nt* 17, 18, 26, 31, 71
baggage cart Kofferkuli *m* 18, 71
baggage check Gepäckaufbewahrung *f* 67, 71
baggage locker Schließfach *nt* 18, 67, 71
baked gebacken 44, 47
baker's Bäckerei *f* 98
balance *(account)* Bilanz *f* 131
balcony Balkon *m* 23
ball *(inflated)* Ball *m* 128
ballet Ballett *nt* 88
ball-point pen Kugelschreiber *m* 104
banana Banane *f* 53, 64
bandage Verband *m* 109
Band-Aid Heftpflaster *nt* 109
bangle Armreif *m* 121
bank *(finance)* Bank *f* 98, 129, 130
bank card Kontokarte *f* 130
banknote Schein *m* 130
bar *(chocolate)* Tafel *f* 64
barber's Friseur *m* 30, 98
bass *(fish)* Barsch *m* 44
bath *(hotel)* Bad *nt* 23, 24, 27
bathing cap Badekappe *f* 116
bathing suit Badeanzug *m* 116
bathrobe Bademantel *m* 116
bathroom Bad *nt* 27
bath towel Badetuch *nt* 27
battery Batterie *f* 75, 78, 119, 121, 125
bay leaf Lorbeer *m* 50
be, to sein 10, 162
beach Strand *m* 90
bean Bohne *f* 49
beard Bart *m* 31
beautiful schön 13, 84
beauty salon Kosmetiksalon *m* 30, 98
be back, to zurück sein 21, 136
bed Bett *nt* 24, 142, 144
bed and breakfast Übernachtung mit Frühstück *f* 24
bedpan Bettpfanne *f* 144
beef Rindfleisch *nt* 45
beer Bier *nt* 56, 64
beer stein Bierkrug *m* 127
beet(root) rote Beete *f* 50
before vor 14
begin, to beginnen 80, 87, 88

beginner Anfänger(in) *m/f* 91
beginning Anfang *m* 150
behind hinter 15, 77
beige beige 113
Belgium Belgien *(nt)* 146
bell *(electric)* Klingel *f* 144
bellboy Page *m* 26
below unten 15
belt Gürtel *m* 117
berth Schlafplatz *m* 69, 70, 71
best beste 152
better besser 13, 25, 101, 113
between zwischen 15
beverage Getränk *nt* 61
bicycle Fahrrad *nt* 74
big groß 13, 25
bilberry Blaubeere *f*, Heidelbeere *f* 54
bill Rechnung *f* 31, 63
billion *(Am.)* Milliarde *f* 148
binoculars Fernglas *nt* 123
bird Vogel *m* 85
birth Geburt *f* 25
birthday Geburtstag *m* 151, 152
biscuit *(Br.)* Keks *m* 64
bitter bitter 62
black schwarz 38, 105, 113
blackberry Brombeere *f* 53
blackcurrant schwarze Johannisbeere *f* 53
bladder Blase *f* 138
blade Klinge *f* 110
blanket Decke *f* 27
bleach Aufhellung *f* 30
bleed, to bluten 139, 145
blind *(window)* Rollo *nt* 29
blister Blase *f* 139
block, to verstopfen 28
blood Blut *nt* 142
blood pressure Blutdruck *m* 141, 142
blood transfusion Bluttransfusion *f* 144
blouse Bluse *f* 116
blow-dry Fönen *nt* 30
blue blau 113
blueberry Blaubeere *f*, Heidelbeere *f* 53
boar *(wild)* Wildschwein *nt* 48
boarding house Pension *f* 19, 22
boat Schiff *nt*, Boot *nt* 74
bobby pin Haarklemme *f* 111
body Körper *m* 138
boil Furunkel *m* 139
boiled gekocht 47, 51
bone Knochen *m* 138
book Buch *nt* 11, 104
book, to reservieren (lassen) 69
booking office Reservierungsschalter *m* 19; Platzreservierung *f* 67
booklet *(of tickets)* Fahrscheinheft *nt* 72
bookshop Buchhandlung *f* 98, 104
boot Stiefel *m* 118
born geboren 149
botanical gardens Botanischer Garten *m* 81
botany Botanik *f* 83
bottle Flasche *f* 17, 56, 59
bottle-opener Flaschenöffner *m* 106
bowel Darm *m* 138
bow tie Fliege *f* 116
box Schachtel *f* 120
boxing Boxen *nt* 89
boy Junge *m* 112, 128
boyfriend Freund *m* 93
bra Büstenhalter *m* 116
bracelet Armband *nt* 121
braces *(suspenders)* Hosenträger *m/pl* 116
braised geschmort 47
brake Bremse *f* 78
brake fluid Bremsflüssigkeit *f* 75
brandy Weinbrand *m*, Kognak *m* 59
bread Brot *nt* 36, 38, 64, 120
breaded paniert 44
break, to zerbrechen 123, 145; (sich) brechen 139
breakdown van Abschleppwagen *m* 78
breakfast Frühstück *nt* 24, 34, 38
breast Brust *f* 138
breathe, to atmen 141, 142
bridge Brücke *f* 85
briefs Unterhose *f* 116
bring, to bringen 12, 71
bring down, to herunterbringen 31
British Brite (Britin) *m/f* 93
broiled vom Rost 40; gegrillt 47
broken kaputt 29, 119; gebrochen 140
brooch Brosche *f* 121
brother Bruder *m* 93
brown braun 113
bruise Quetschung *f* 139
brush Bürste *f* 111
Brussels sprouts Rosenkohl *m* 50
bubble bath Schaumbad *nt* 110
bucket Eimer *m* 106, 128
buckle Schnalle *f* 117
build, to (er)bauen 83

building Gebäude *nt* 81, 82, 83
building blocks/bricks Baukasten *m* 128
bulb (Glüh)birne *f* 28, 75, 119
burn Brandwunde *f* 139
bus Bus *m* 18, 19, 65, 72, 73, 80
business Geschäft *nt* 131
business trip Geschäftsreise *f* 93
bus stop Bushaltestelle *f* 72, 73
busy beschäftigt 96
but aber 15
butane gas Butangas *nt* 32, 106
butcher's Fleischerei *f*, Metzgerei *f* 98
butter Butter *f* 36, 38, 64
button Knopf *m* 29, 117
buy, to kaufen 82, 100

C

cabbage Kohl *m* 50
cabin *(ship)* Kabine *f* 74
cable Telegramm *nt* 133
cable car Seilbahn *f* 74
café Café *nt* 33
cake Kuchen *m* 37, 54, 64
cake shop Konditorei *f* 33, 98
calculator Rechner *m* 105
calendar Kalender *m* 104
call *(phone)* (Telefon)gespräch *nt* 135, 136; Anruf *m* 136
call, to *(give name)* heißen 10; *(summon)* rufen 78, 79, 156; *(phone)* anrufen 136; *(wake)* wecken 71
call at, to *(boat)* anlegen 74
calm ruhig 90
camel-hair Kamelhaar *nt* 114
camera Fotoapparat *m* 124, 125
camera case Fototasche *f* 125
camera shop Fotogeschäft *nt* 98
camp, to zelten 32
campbed Feldbett *nt* 106
camping Camping *nt* 32
camping equipment Campingausrüstung *f* 106
camp site Campingplatz *m* 32
can *(of peaches)* Büchse *f* 120
can *(to be able)* können 11, 12, 163
Canada Kanada *(nt)* 146
Canadian Kanadier(in) *m/f* 93
cancel, to annullieren 65
candle Kerze *f* 106
candy Bonbon *nt* 126
can opener Büchsenöffner *m* 106
cap Mütze *f* 116
caper Kaper *f* 51
capital *(finance)* Kapital *nt* 131
car Auto *nt*, Wagen *m* 19, 20, 26, 32, 75, 76, 78
carat Karat *nt* 121
caravan Wohnwagen *m* 32
caraway Kümmel *m* 51
carbon paper Durchschlagpapier *nt* 104
carbonated mit Kohlensäure 61
carburetor Vergaser *m* 78
card Karte *f* 93, 131
card game Kartenspiel *nt* 128
cardigan Wolljacke *f* 116
car hire Autoverleih *m* 19, 20
car number Kraftfahrzeugnummer *f* 25
car park Parkplatz *m* 77
car racing Autorennen *nt* 89
car radio Autoradio *nt* 119
car rental Autoverleih *m* 19, 20
carrot Karotte *f* 50
carry, to tragen 21
carton *(of cigarettes)* Stange (Zigaretten) *f* 17, 126
cartridge *(camera)* Kassette *f* 124
case *(cigarettes, glasses)* Etui *nt* 121, 123
cash, to einlösen 130, 133
cash desk Kasse *f* 103, 155
cassette Kassette *f* 119, 127, 128
castle Schloß *nt*, Burg *f* 85
catalogue Katalog *m* 82
cathedral Kathedrale *f*, Dom *m* 81
Catholic katholisch 84
cauliflower Blumenkohl *m* 49
caution Vorsicht *f* 79, 155; Achtung *f* 155
cave Höhle *f* 81
celery Sellerie *m* 50
cellophane tape Klebstreifen *m* 104
cemetery Friedhof *m* 81
centimetre Zentimeter *m* 112
centre Zentrum *nt* 19, 21, 76
century Jahrhundert *nt* 149
ceramics Keramik *f* 83
cereal Getreideflocken *f/pl* 38
certificate Zeugnis *nt* 144
chain *(jewellery)* Kette *f* 121
chair Stuhl *m* 106
chamber music Kammermusik *f* 128
champagne *(German)* Sekt *m* 59
change *(money)* Kleingeld *nt* 77, 130

change, to wechseln 18, 123, 130; *(train)* umsteigen 65, 68, 73; *(reservation)* umbuchen 65
chapel Kapelle *f* 81
charcoal Holzkohle *f* 106
charge Gebühr *f* 32, 136; Rechnung *f* 28
charge, to berechnen 24; *(commission)* erheben 130
cheap billig 14, 24, 25, 101
check Scheck *m* 130; *(restaurant)* Rechnung *f* 63
check, to kontrollieren 75, 123; prüfen 75; *(luggage)* aufgeben 71
check book Scheckbuch *nt* 131
check in, to *(airport)* einchecken 65
check out, to abreisen 31
checkup *(medical)* Untersuchung *f* 142
cheers! Prost! 60
cheese Käse *m* 37, 38, 52, 64
chef Küchenchef *m* 40
chemist's Apotheke *f* 98, 108
cheque Scheck *m* 130
cheque book Scheckbuch *nt* 131
cherry Kirsche *f* 53
chess Schach *nt* 93
chess set Schachspiel *nt* 128
chest Brust(korb) *m* 138, 141
chewing gum Kaugummi *m* 126
chicken Huhn *nt* 48
chicory Endivie *f*; *(Am.)* Chicorée *f* 49
child Kind *nt* 24, 62, 82, 93, 139, 149, 159
children's doctor Kinderarzt *m* 137
China China *(nt)* 146
chips Pommes frites *f/pl* 49; *(Am.)* Kartoffelchips *m/pl* 64
chives Schnittlauch *m* 51
chocolate Schokolade *f* 38, 61, 64, 120, 126, 127
choice Wahl *f* 40
chop Kotelett *nt* 46
Christmas Weihnachten *nt* 151
church Kirche *f* 81, 84
cider Apfelwein *m* 59
cigar Zigarre *f* 126
cigarette Zigarette *f* 17, 95, 126
cigarette lighter Feuerzeug *nt* 121
cine camera Filmkamera *f* 124
cinema Kino *nt* 86, 96
cinnamon Zimt *m* 51
circle *(theatre)* Rang *m* 87
city Stadt *f* 81, 92
clam Muschel *f* 44
classical klassisch 128
clean sauber 62
clean, to reinigen 29, 76
cleansing cream Reinigungscreme *f* 110
cloakroom Garderobe *f* 87
clock Uhr *f* 119, 121, 153
clock-radio Radiowecker *m* 119
close *(near)* nahe 78, 98
close, to schließen 10, 82, 108, 132, 155
closed geschlossen 155
cloth Stoff *m* 118
clothes Kleider *nt/pl* 29, 116
clothes peg Wäscheklammer *f* 106
clothing Bekleidung *f* 112
cloud Wolke *f* 94
clove Nelke *f* 50
coach *(bus)* Bus *m* 72
coat Mantel *m* 116
coconut Kokosnuß *f* 54
cod Kabeljau *m*, Dorsch *m* 44
coffee Kaffee *m* 38, 61, 64
cognac Kognak *m* 59
coin Münze *f* 83
cold kalt 13, 24, 38, 62, 155
cold *(illness)* Erkältung *f* 108, 141
cold cuts Aufschnitt *m* 64
collect call R-Gespräch *nt* 134
cologne Kölnischwasser *nt* 110
colour Farbe *f* 103, 112, 124, 125
colour chart Farbtabelle *f* 30
colour fast farbecht 112
colour film Farbfilm *m* 124
colour negative Farbnegativ *nt* 124
colour shampoo Tönungsshampoo *nt* 111
colour slide Farbdia *nt* 124
colour television *(set)* Farbfernseher *m* 119
comb Kamm *m* 111
come, to kommen 36, 59, 92, 95, 137, 144, 146
comedy Komödie *f* 86
commission Gebühr *f* 86
common *(frequent)* gebräuchlich 154
compact disc Compact Disc *f* 127
compartment Abteil *nt* 70
compass Kompaß *m* 106
complaint Reklamation *f* 62
concert Konzert *nt* 88
concert hall Konzerthalle *f* 81, 88
conductor *(orchestra)* Dirigent *m* 88

confirm, to bestätigen 65
confirmation Bestätigung *f* 23
congratulation Glückwunsch *m* 152
connection *(train)* Anschluß *m* 65, 68
constipation Verstopfung *f* 140
contact lens Kontaktlinse *f* 123
contain, to enthalten 37
contraceptive Verhütungsmittel *nt* 109
contract Vertrag *m* 131
control Kontrolle *f* 16
convent Kloster *nt* 81
convention hall Kongreßhalle *f* 81
conversion Umrechnung *f* 157
cookie Keks *m* 64
cool box Kühltasche *f* 106
copper Kupfer *nt* 122
corduroy Kordsamt *m* 114
cork Korken *m* 62
corkscrew Korkenzieher *m* 106
corn *(Am.)* Mais *m* 50; *(foot)* Hühnerauge *nt* 109
corner Ecke *f* 21, 36, 77
corn plaster Hühneraugenpflaster *nt* 109
cost Kosten *pl* 131
cost, to kosten 10, 20, 80, 133
cotton Baumwolle *f* 114
cotton wool Watte *f* 109
cough Husten *m* 108, 141
cough, to husten 142
cough drops Hustenpastillen *f/pl* 109
counter Schalter *m* 133
country Land *nt* 93
countryside Landschaft *f*, Land *nt* 85
court house Gericht(sgebäude) *nt* 81
cousin Cousin(e) *m/f* 93
cramp Krampf *m* 141
cranberry Preiselbeere *f* 53
crayfish *(river)* Krebs *m* 41, 44
crayon Buntstift *m* 104
cream Sahne *f* 54, 61; *(toiletry)* Creme *f* 110
credit Kredit *m* 130
credit card Kreditkarte *f* 20, 31, 63, 102, 130
cress Kresse *f* 51
crisps Kartoffelchips *m/pl* 64
crockery Geschirr *nt* 106, 107
croissant Hörnchen *nt* 38
cross Kreuz *nt* 121
cross-country skiing Langlauf *m* 91
crossing *(by sea)* Überfahrt *f* 74
crossroads Kreuzung *f* 77
cruise Kreuzfahrt *f* 74
crystal Kristall *m* 122
cuckoo clock Kuckucksuhr *f* 121, 127
cucumber Gurke *f* 50
cuff link Manschettenknopf *m* 121
cuisine Küche *f* 35
cup Tasse *f* 36, 61, 107
curler Lockenwickler *m* 111
currency Währung *f* 129
currency exchange office Wechselstube *f* 18, 67, 129
current Strömung *f* 90
curtain Vorhang *m* 28
customs Zoll *m* 16, 102
cut *(wound)* Schnittwunde *f* 139
cut, to schneiden 30
cut off, to *(phone)* unterbrechen 135
cut glass geschliffenes Glas *nt* 122
cutlery Besteck *nt* 106, 107; Tafelbesteck *nt* 121
cutlet Kotelett *nt* 45
cycling Radfahren *nt* 89
cystitis Blasenentzündung *f* 142
Czechoslovakia Tschechoslowakei *f* 146

D

dairy Milchhandlung *f* 98
dance, to tanzen 88, 96
danger Gefahr *f* 155, 156
dangerous gefährlich 90
dark dunkel 24, 56, 101, 112, 113
date *(day)* Datum *nt* 25, 150; *(appointment)* Verabredung *f* 95; *(fruit)* Dattel *f* 53
daughter Tochter *f* 93
day Tag *m* 16, 20, 26, 32, 80, 150, 151
daylight Tageslicht *nt* 124
day off freier Tag *m* 151
decade Jahrzehnt *nt* 149
decaffeinated koffeinfrei 38, 61
December Dezember *m* 150
decision Entscheidung *f* 24, 102
deck *(ship)* Deck *nt* 74
deck-chair Liegestuhl *m* 91, 106
declare, to *(customs)* verzollen 17
deep tief 142
delay Verspätung *f* 69
delicatessen Delikatessengeschäft *nt* 98
deliver, to liefern 102
delivery Lieferung *f* 102
Denmark Dänemark *(nt)* 146

dentist Zahnarzt *m* 98, 145
denture Gebiß *nt* 145
deodorant Deodorant *nt* 110
department Abteilung *f* 83, 100
department store Warenhaus *nt* 98
departure Abflug *m* 65; Abfahrt *f* 69
depilatory cream Haarentfernungsmittel *nt* 110
deposit, to *(bank)* einzahlen 130, 131; *(car hire)* hinterlegen 20
dessert Nachtisch *m*, Nachspeise *f*, Süßspeise *f* 37, 40, 54
detour *(traffic)* Umleitung *f* 79
develop, to entwickeln 124
diabetic Diabetiker(in) *m/f* 37, 41
dialling code Vorwählnummer *f* 134
diamond Diamant *m* 122
diaper Windel *f* 111
diarrhoea Durchfall *m* 140
dictionary Wörterbuch *nt* 104
diesel Diesel(öl) *nt* 75
diet Diät *f* 37
difficult schwierig 13
difficulty Schwierigkeit *f* 28, 102, 141
digital Digital- 122
dill Dill *m* 51
dining-car Speisewagen *m* 66, 68, 71
dining-room Speisesaal *m* 27
dinner Abendessen *nt* 34, 94
direct direkt 65
direct to, to den Weg zeigen 12
direction Richtung *f* 76
director *(film)* Regisseur *m* 86
directory *(phone)* Telefonbuch *nt* 134
disabled Behinderte *m/f* 82
discotheque Diskothek *f* 88, 96
disease Krankheit *f* 142
dish Gericht *nt* 36, 37, 40
dishwashing detergent Spülmittel *nt* 106
disinfectant Desinfektionsmittel *nt* 109
dislocate, to verrenken 140
display case Vitrine *f* 100
dissatisfied unzufrieden 103
district *(town)* Viertel *nt* 81
disturb, to stören 155
diversion *(traffic)* Umleitung *f* 79
dizzy schwindlig 140
do, to tun 163
doctor Arzt *m*, Ärztin *f* 79, 98, 137; Herr(Frau) Doktor *m/f* 145
doctor's office Arztpraxis *f* 137
dog Hund *m* 155
doll Puppe *f* 128
dollar Dollar *m* 18, 102, 130
door Tür(e) *f* 28
double bed Doppelbett *nt* 23
double cabin Zweierkabine *f* 74
double room Doppelzimmer *nt* 19, 23
down hinunter 15
downhill skiing Abfahrtslauf *m* 91
downstairs unten 69
downtown Innenstadt *f* 81
dozen Dutzend *nt* 120, 149
draught beer Bier vom Faß *nt* 56
drawing paper Zeichenpapier *nt* 104
drawing pin Reißzwecke *f* 104
dress Kleid *nt* 116
dress shop Modengeschäft *nt* 99
dressing gown Morgenrock *m* 116
drink Getränk *nt* 40, 59, 61, 62
drink, to trinken 35, 36
drinking water Trinkwasser *nt* 32
drip, to *(tap)* tropfen 28
drive, to fahren 21, 76
driving licence Führerschein *m* 20, 79
drop *(liquid)* Tropfen *m* 109
drugstore Apotheke *f* 98, 108
dry trocken 30, 59, 110, 111
dry cleaner's chemische Reinigung *f* 29, 98
dry shampoo Trockenshampoo *nt* 111
duck Ente *f* 48
dummy Schnuller *m* 111
during während 14, 150
duty *(customs)* Zoll *m* 17
duty-free shop Duty-free-Shop *m* 19
dye, to färben 30

E

each jede(r/s) 125, 143, 149
ear Ohr *nt* 138
earache Ohrenschmerzen *m/pl* 141
ear drops Ohrentropfen *m/pl* 109
early früh 14, 31
earring Ohrring *m* 121
east Ost(en) *m* 77
Easter Ostern *nt* 152
East Germany DDR *f* 146
easy leicht 14
eat, to essen 36, 37, 144
eel Aal *m* 41, 43
egg Ei *nt* 38, 40, 64
eggplant Aubergine *f* 49
eight acht 147

eighteen achtzehn 147
eighth achte 148
eighty achtzig 147
elastic elastisch 109
elastic bandage elastische Binde *f* 109
Elastoplast Heftpflaster *nt* 109
electric(al) elektrisch 119
electrician Elektriker *m* 98
electricity *(facilities)* Stromanschluß *m* 32
electronic elektronisch 125, 128
elevator Fahrstuhl *m* 27, 100; Aufzug *m* 155
eleven elf 147
embarkation point Anlegeplatz *m* 74
embroidery Stickerei *f* 127
emerald Smaragd *m* 122
emergency Notfall *m* 156; *(phone)* Notruf *m* 155, 156
emergency exit Notausgang *m* 27, 99, 155
emery board Sandpapierfeile *f* 110
empty leer 13
enamel Email *nt* 122
end Ende *nt* 69, 150
endive Chicorée *f*; *(Am.)* Endivie *f* 49
engaged *(phone)* besetzt 136
engagement ring Verlobungsring *m* 122
engine *(car)* Motor *m* 78
England England *(nt)* 146
English englisch 104, 126
English Englisch *nt* 11, 16, 84, 137
English Engländer(in) *m/f* 93
enjoyable angenehm 31
enjoy oneself, to sich gut unterhalten 96
enlarge, to vergrößern 125
enough genug 14
enquiry Auskunft *f* 68
entrance Eingang *m* 67, 99; Zutritt *m* 155
entrance fee Eintritt *m* 82
envelope Briefumschlag *m* 27, 104
equipment Ausrüstung *f* 91, 106
eraser Radiergummi *m* 105
escalator Rolltreppe *f* 100
especially besonders 161
estimate *(cost)* Kostenvoranschlag *m* 131
Europe Europa *(nt)* 146
evening Abend *m* 9, 87, 95, 96, 151, 153
evening dress Abendgarderobe *f* 88; *(woman)* Abendkleid *nt* 116
everything alles 31
exchange, to umtauschen 103
exchange rate Wechselkurs *m* 18, 130
excursion Ausflug *m* 80
excuse me Entschuldigung 26, 78; Verzeihung 70, 153
exercise book Schreibheft *nt* 104
exhaust pipe Auspuff *m* 78
exhibition Ausstellung *f* 81
exit Ausgang *m* 67, 99, 155; *(motorway)* Ausfahrt *f* 79
expect, to erwarten 130
expenses Unkosten *pl* 131
expensive teuer 13, 19, 24, 101
exposure *(photography)* Aufnahme *f* 124
express per Expreß 132
expression Ausdruck *m* 9; Redewendung *f* 100
expressway Autobahn *f* 76
extension *(phone)* Nebenanschluß *m* 135
extension cord/lead Verlängerungsschnur *f* 119
extra zusätzlich 24
extract, to *(tooth)* ziehen 145
eye Auge *nt* 123, 138, 139
eye drops Augentropfen *m/pl* 109
eye liner Lidstift *m* 110
eye pencil Augenbrauenstift *m* 110
eye shadow Lidschatten *m* 110
eye specialist Augenarzt *m* 137

F

fabric Stoff *m* 113
face Gesicht *nt* 138
face-pack Gesichtsmaske *f* 30
face powder Gesichtspuder *m* 110
factory Fabrik *f* 81
fair Messe *f* 81
fall *(autumn)* Herbst *m* 149
family Familie *f* 93, 144
fan Ventilator *m* 28
fan belt Keilriemen *m* 75
far weit 14, 21, 100
fare Fahrpreis *m* 21, 68, 73
farm Bauernhof *m* 85
fat Fett *nt* 37
father Vater *m* 93
faucet Wasserhahn *m* 28
February Februar *m* 150

fee *(doctor)* Honorar *nt* 144
feeding bottle Saugflasche *f* 111
feel, to *(physical state)* sich fühlen 140, 142
felt Filz *m* 114
felt-tip pen Filzstift *m* 105
fennel Fenchel *m* 50
ferry Fähre *f* 74
fever Fieber *nt* 140
few wenige 14; *(a)* einige 14
field Feld *nt* 85
fifteen fünfzehn 147
fifth fünfte 148
fifty fünfzig 147
fig Feige *f* 53
file *(tool)* Feile *f* 110
fill in, to ausfüllen 26, 144
filling *(tooth)* Plombe *f* 145
filling station Tankstelle *f* 75
film Film *m* 86, 124, 125
film winder Filmtransport *m* 125
filter Filter *m* 125, 126
filter-tipped mit Filter 126
find, to finden 10, 11, 84, 100
fine *(OK)* gut 24
fine arts bildende Künste *f/pl* 83
fine grain *(film)* Feinkorn 124
finger Finger *m* 138
fire Feuer *nt* 156
first erste 68, 72, 148
first-aid kit Verbandkasten *m* 106
first class erste Klasse *f* 69
first name Vorname *m* 25
fish Fisch *m* 43
fish, to angeln 90
fishing permit Angelschein *m* 90
fishing tackle Angelzeug *nt* 106
fishmonger's Fischhandlung *f* 98
fit, to passen 115
fitting room Umkleidekabine *f* 115
five fünf 147
fix, to flicken 75, 145
fizzy *(mineral water)* mit Kohlensäure 61
flannel Flanell *m* 114
flash *(photography)* Blitzlicht *nt* 125
flash attachment Blitzgerät *nt* 125
flashlight Taschenlampe *f* 106
flat flach 118
flat *(apartment)* Wohnung *f* 22
flat tyre Reifenpanne *f* 75; Platter *m* 78
flea market Flohmarkt *m* 81
flight Flug *m* 65
flight number Flugnummer *f* 65
floor Etage *f* 27; Stock *m* 154
florist's Blumengeschäft *nt* 98
flounder Flunder *f* 44
flour Mehl *nt* 37
flower Blume *f* 85
flu Grippe *f* 142
fluid Flüssigkeit *f* 75
fog Nebel *m* 94
folding chair Klappstuhl *m* 106
folding table Klapptisch *m* 107
folk music Volksmusik *f* 128
food Essen *nt* 37, 62; Nahrung *f* 111
food box Proviantbehälter *m* 106
food poisoning Lebensmittelvergiftung *f* 142
foot Fuß *m* 138
football Fußball *m* 89
foot cream Fußcreme *f* 110
footpath Fußweg *m* 85
foot powder Fußpuder *m* 110
for für 14; während 143
forbid, to verbieten 155
forest Wald *m* 85
fork Gabel *f* 36, 62, 107
form *(document)* Formular *nt* 133; Schein *m* 25, 26
fortnight zwei Wochen *f/pl* 151
fortress Festung *f* 81
forty vierzig 147
forwarding address Nachsendeadresse *f* 31
fountain Brunnen *m*, Springbrunnen *m* 81
fountain pen Füllfederhalter *m* 105
four vier 147
fourteen vierzehn 147
fourth vierte 148
fowl Geflügel *nt* 48
frame *(glasses)* Gestell *nt* 123
France Frankreich *(nt)* 146
free frei 13, 70, 82, 95, 155
french fries Pommes frites *f/pl* 49
fresh frisch 53, 62
Friday Freitag *m* 150
fried gebraten 44, 47
fried egg Spiegelei *nt* 38
friend Freund(in) *m/f* 93, 95
fringe Ponyfransen *f/pl* 30
frock Kleid *nt* 116
frog Frosch *m* 41
from von 14
front vorne, Vorder- 75
frost Frost *m* 94

fruit Obst *nt* 37, 53
fruit cocktail Obstsalat *m* 53, 54
fruit juice Fruchtsaft *m* 37, 61
frying-pan Bratpfanne *f* 106
full voll 13; belegt 155
full board Vollpension *f* 24
full insurance Vollkaskoversicherung *f* 20
fur coat Pelzmantel *m* 116
furniture Möbel *nt/pl* 83
furrier's Pelzgeschäft *nt* 98

G

gallery Galerie *f* 81
game Spiel *nt* 128; *(food)* Wild *nt* 40
garage *(parking)* Garage *f* 26; *(repairs)* Reparaturwerkstatt *f* 78
garden Garten *m* 85
gardens Grünanlage *f* 81
garlic Knoblauch *m* 51
gas Gas *nt* 156
gasoline Benzin *nt* 75, 78
gastritis Magenschleimhautentzündung *f* 142
gauze Verbandmull *m* 109
gem Edelstein *m* 121
general allgemein 26, 100
general delivery postlagernd 133
general practitioner praktischer Arzt *m* 137
gentleman Herr *m* 155
genuine echt 118
geology Geologie *f* 83
German deutsch 114
German Deutsch *nt* 11, 95
Germany Deutschland *(nt)* 146
get, to *(find)* finden 19, 21; *(obtain)* bekommen 10, 32, 90, 108, 134; *(taxi)* bestellen 31; *(fetch)* holen 137, 156
get back, to zurück sein 80
get off, to aussteigen 73
get to, to kommen nach/zu 19, 100; ankommen in 70
get up, to aufstehen 144
gherkin Essiggurke *f* 50, 64
gift *(present)* Geschenk *nt* 17
ginger Ingwer *m* 51
girdle Hüfthalter *m* 116
girl Mädchen *nt* 112, 128
girlfriend Freundin *f* 93, 95
give, to geben 12, 13, 123, 126
give way *(traffic)* Vorfahrt gewähren 79
glad *(to know you)* sehr erfreut 92
gland Drüse *f* 138
glass Glas *nt* 36, 56, 59, 60, 62, 143
glasses Brille *f* 123
glassware Glaswaren *f/pl* 127
gloomy düster 84
glove Handschuh *m* 116
glue Leim *m* 105
go, to gehen 96, 163
go away, to weggehen 156
go out, to ausgehen 96
gold Gold *nt* 121, 122
golden golden 113
gold-plated vergoldet 122
golf Golf *nt* 89
golf course Golfplatz *m* 89
good gut 13, 101
good-bye auf Wiedersehen 9
Good Friday Karfreitag *m* 152
goods Waren *f/pl* 16
goose Gans *f* 48
gooseberry Stachelbeere *f* 53
gram Gramm *nt* 120
grammar book Grammatik *f* 105
grape (Wein)traube *f* 53, 64
grape juice Traubensaft *m* 61
grapefruit Grapefruit *f*, Pampelmuse *f* 53
grapefruit juice Grapefruitsaft *m* 38
gravy Soße *f* 48
gray grau 113
graze Abschürfung *f* 139
greasy fettig 30, 110, 111
great *(excellent)* prima 95
Great Britain Großbritannien *(nt)* 146
Greece Griechenland *(nt)* 146
green grün 113
green bean grüne Bohne *f* 49
greengrocer's Gemüsehandlung *f* 98
green salad grüner Salat *m* 50
greeting Begrüßung *f* 9; Gruß *m* 151
grey grau 113
grilled gegrillt 44, 47; vom Rost 40
grocery Lebensmittelgeschäft *nt* 98, 120
groundsheet Zeltboden *m* 106
group Gruppe *f* 82
guide Fremdenführer(in) *m/f* 80
guidebook (Reise)führer *m* 82, 104, 105
gum *(teeth)* Zahnfleisch *nt* 145
gynaecologist Frauenarzt *m* 137, 141

H

habit Gewohnheit *f* 34
haddock Schellfisch *m* 44
hair Haar *nt* 30, 111
hairbrush Haarbürste *f* 111
haircut Haarschnitt *m* 30
hairdresser's Friseur *m* 27, 30, 99
hair dryer Haartrockner *m* 119
hair dye Haarfärbemittel *nt* 111
hairgrip Haarklemme *f* 111
hair lotion Haarwasser *nt* 111
half Hälfte *f* 148
half a dozen halbes Dutzend *nt* 120
half an hour halbe Stunde *f* 153
half board Halbpension *f* 24
half price *(ticket)* zum halben Preis 69
halibut Heilbutt *m* 44
hall *(large room)* Halle *f* 81, 88
ham Schinken *m* 38, 41, 46, 64
hammer Hammer *m* 106
hand Hand *f* 138
handbag Handtasche *f* 116
hand cream Handcreme *f* 110
handicrafts Kunsthandwerk *nt* 83
handkerchief Taschentuch *nt* 116
handmade Handarbeit *f* 113
hanger Kleiderbügel *m* 27
hangover Kater *m* 108
happy glücklich, froh 151, 152
harbour Hafen *m* 74, 81
hard hart 52, 123
hard-boiled *(egg)* hartgekocht 38
hardware shop Eisenwarenhandlung *f* 98
hare Hase *m* 48
hat Hut *m* 116, 127
have, to haben 162
hay fever Heufieber *nt* 108
hazelnut Haselnuß *f* 53
he er 162
head Kopf *m* 138, 139
headache Kopfschmerzen *m/pl* 141
headphones Kopfhörer *m* 119
head waiter Oberkellner *m* 62
health food shop Reformhaus *nt* 98
health insurance Krankenkasse *f* 144
health insurance form Krankenkassenformular *nt* 144
heart Herz *nt* 138
heart attack Herzanfall *m* 141
heat, to heizen 90
heating Heizung *f* 28
heavy schwer 13, 101
heel Absatz *m* 118
helicopter Hubschrauber *m* 74
hello! *(phone)* Hallo! 135
help Hilfe *f* 156
help, to helfen 12, 21, 71, 100, 134; *(oneself)* sich bedienen 120
her ihr 161
herb Kraut *nt* 51
herb tea Kräutertee *m* 60
here hier 15
herring Hering *m* 41, 44
high hoch 85, 141
high season Hauptsaison *f* 149
high-speed *(photo)* hochempfindlich 124
high tide Flut *f* 90
hike, to wandern 74
hill Hügel *m* 85
hire Verleih *m* 20, 74
hire, to mieten 19, 20, 74, 89, 91; vermieten 155
his sein 161
history Geschichte *f* 83
hitchhike, to trampen 74
hole Loch *nt* 29
holiday Feiertag *m* 151
holidays Ferien *pl*, Urlaub *m* 151
home address Wohnort *m* 25; Wohnadresse *f* 31
home-made hausgemacht 40
homeopathic homöopathisch 109
honey Honig *m* 38
horse racing Pferderennen *nt* 89
horseback riding Reiten *nt* 89
horseradish Meerrettich *m* 51
hospital Krankenhaus *nt* 142, 144
hot heiß 14, 24, 38, 61, 155
hotel Hotel *nt* 19, 21, 22, 80
hotel guide Hotelverzeichnis *nt* 19, 22
hotel reservation Hotelreservierung *f* 20
hot water warmes Wasser *nt* 23, 28
hot-water bottle Wärmflasche *f* 27
hour Stunde *f* 153
house Haus *nt* 83, 85
how wie 10
how far wie weit 10, 76, 85
how long wie lange 10, 24
how many wie viele 10
how much wieviel 10, 24
hundred (ein)hundert 147
hungry hungrig 35; *(to be)* Hunger haben 12, 35
hurry *(to be in a)* es eilig haben 21, 31

hurt, to weh tun 139; schmerzen 145; *(oneself)* sich verletzen 139
husband Mann *m* 93
hydrofoil Tragflächenboot *nt* 74

I

I ich 162
ice Eis *nt* 94
ice-cream Eis *nt* 54, 64
ice cube Eiswürfel *m* 27
iced tea Eistee *m* 61
ice pack Kühlbeutel *m* 106
ill krank 140, 156
illness Krankheit *f* 140
important wichtig 12
imported importiert 113
impressive eindrucksvoll 84
in in 14
included inbegriffen 20, 24, 31, 32, 40, 63, 80
indigestion Magenverstimmung *f* 141
inexpensive preiswert 35; billig 124
infect, to infizieren 140
infection Infektion *f* 145
inflammation Entzündung *f* 142
inflation Inflation *f* 131
inflation rate Inflationsrate *f* 131
influenza Grippe *f* 142
information Auskunft *f* 67, 155
injection Spritze *f* 142, 144, 145
injure, to verletzen 139
injured verletzt 79, 139
injury Verletzung *f* 139
ink Tinte *f* 105
inn Gasthaus *nt*, Gasthof *m* 22, 33
inquiry Auskunft *f* 68
insect bite Insektenstich *m* 108, 139
insect repellent Insektenschutz *m* 109
insect spray Insektizid *nt* 109
inside drinnen 15
instead statt 37
insurance Versicherung *f* 20, 79
insurance company Versicherungsgesellschaft *f* 79
interest *(on investment)* Zinsen *m/pl* 131
interested, to be sich interessieren 83, 96
interesting interessant 84
international international 133, 134
interpreter Dolmetscher *m* 131
intersection Kreuzung *f* 77
introduce, to vorstellen 92
introduction *(social)* Vorstellung *f* 92; *(letter)* Empfehlungsbrief *m* 130
investment Kapitalanlage *f* 131
invitation Einladung *f* 94
invite, to einladen 94
invoice Rechnung *f* 131
iodine Jod *nt* 109
Ireland Irland *(nt)* 146
Irish Ire (Irin) *m/f* 93
iron *(laundry)* Bügeleisen *nt* 119
iron, to bügeln 29
ironmonger's Eisenwarenhandlung *f* 99
Italy Italien *(nt)* 146
its sein 161
ivory Elfenbein *nt* 122

J

jacket Jackett *nt*, Jacke *f* 116
jade Jade *f* 122
jam Marmelade *f* 38, 120
jam, to klemmen 28, 125
January Januar *m* 150
Japan Japan *(nt)* 146
jar Glas *nt* 120
jaundice Gelbsucht *f* 142
jaw Kiefer *m* 138
jeans Jeans *pl* 116
jersey Strickjacke *f* 116
jeweller's Juwelier *m* 99, 121
joint Gelenk *nt* 138
journey Fahrt *f* 72
juice Saft *m* 38, 61
July Juli *m* 150
jumper *(sweater)* Pullover *m* 116
June Juni *m* 150
juniper Wacholder *m* 51
just *(only)* nur 16, 37, 100

K

kerosene Petroleum *nt* 106
ketchup Tomatenketchup *nt* 51
key Schlüssel *m* 26
kidney Niere *f* 138
kilogram Kilo(gramm) *nt* 120
kilometre Kilometer *m* 20
kind nett, freundlich 95
king-size extra lang 126
knee Knie *nt* 138
knife Messer *nt* 36, 61, 107
knock, to klopfen 155
know, to wissen 16, 26; kennen 96, 114

L

label Etikett *nt* 105
lace Spitze *f* 114
lady Dame *f* 155
lake See *m* 23, 81, 85, 90
lamb Lamm(fleisch) *nt* 45
lamp Lampe *f* 29, 106, 119
landmark Wahrzeichen *nt* 85
landscape Landschaft *f* 92
lane *(in town)* Gasse *f* 154
lantern Laterne *f* 106
large groß 20, 101, 118, 130
last letzte 13, 68, 72, 149, 150, 151
last name (Familien)name *m* 25
late spät 13
later später 135
laugh, to lachen 95
launderette Waschsalon *m* 99
laundry *(place)* Wäscherei *f* 29, 99; *(clothes)* Wäsche *f* 29
laundry service Wäschedienst *m* 23
laxative Abführmittel *nt* 109
lead *(theatre)* Hauptrolle *f* 86
lead-free bleifrei 75
leap year Schaltjahr *nt* 149
leather Leder *nt* 114, 118
leather goods Lederwaren *f/pl* 127
leather trousers Lederhose *f* 116
leave, to lassen 26, 96, 156; *(go away)* abreisen 31; abfahren 68, 74
leek Lauch *m* 50
left linke 13; links 21, 30, 63, 69, 77, 79
left-luggage office Gepäckaufbewahrung *f* 67, 71
leg Bein *nt* 138
lemon Zitrone *f* 37, 38, 53, 54, 60
lemonade Limonade *f* 61
lens *(glasses)* Glas *nt* 123; *(camera)* Objektiv *nt* 125
lentil Linse *f* 43
less weniger 14
let, to *(hire out)* vermieten 155
letter Brief *m* 132
letter box Briefkasten *m* 132
letter of credit Kreditbrief *m* 130
lettuce Lattich *m* 50
library Bibliothek *f* 81, 99
licence *(for driving)* Führerschein *m* 20, 79
lie down, to sich hinlegen 142
life belt Rettungsring *m* 74
life boat Rettungsboot *nt* 74
lifeguard Rettungsdienst *m* 90
lift Fahrstuhl *m* 27, 100; Aufzug *m* 155
light leicht 13, 54, 59, 101; *(colour)* hell 101, 112, 113, 126
light Licht *nt* 28, 124; *(cigarette)* Feuer *nt* 95
lighter Feuerzeug *nt* 126
lighter fluid Benzin fürs Feuerzeug *nt* 126
lighter gas Gas fürs Feuerzeug *nt* 126
light meter Belichtungsmesser *m* 125
light music Unterhaltungsmusik *f* 128
lightning Blitz *m* 94
like, to *(want)* gerne haben 12, 23; mögen 20, 38; *(take pleasure)* gefallen 24, 92, 102, 112
line Linie *f* 73
linen *(cloth)* Leinen *nt* 114
lip Lippe *f* 138
lipsalve Lippenpomade *f* 110
lipstick Lippenstift *m* 110
liqueur Likör *m* 59, 60
liquid Flüssigkeit *f* 123
listen, to hören 127
litre Liter *m* 75, 120
little *(a)* ein wenig 14
live, to leben 83; *(reside)* wohnen 83
liver Leber *f* 46, 138
lobster Hummer *m* 41, 44
local hiesig 36, 60
local train Nahverkehrszug *m* 66, 69
long lang 26, 62, 76, 77, 78, 116
long-sighted weitsichtig 123
look, to sehen 123; sich umsehen 100
look for, to suchen 12
look out! Vorsicht! 156
loose *(clothes)* weit 116
lose, to verlieren 123, 156; *(one's way)* sich verirren 12, 156
loss Verlust *m* 131
lost and found office Fundbüro *nt* 67, 156
lost property office Fundbüro *nt* 67, 156
lot *(a)* eine Menge 14; viel 162
lotion Lotion *f* 110
loud *(voice)* laut 135
love, to lieben 163
lovely (wunder)schön 84; herrlich 94
low niedrig 141
lower untere 69, 70

low season Vorsaison *f*, Nachsaison *f* 149
low tide Ebbe *f* 90
luck Glück *nt* 152
luggage Gepäck *nt* 18, 26, 31, 71
luggage locker Schließfach *nt* 18, 67, 71
luggage trolley Kofferkuli *m* 18, 71
lump *(bump)* Beule *f* 139
lunch Mittagessen *nt* 34, 80, 94
lung Lunge *f* 138
Luxembourg Luxemburg *(nt)* 146

M

machine Maschine *f* 114
mackerel Makrele *f* 41, 44
magazine Illustrierte *f* 105
magnificent großartig 84
maid Zimmermädchen *nt* 26
mail, to aufgeben 28
mail Post *f* 28, 133
mailbox Briefkasten *m* 132
main Haupt- 40, 67, 80
make, to machen 131
make a mistake, to *(bill)* sich verrechnen 31, 63, 102
make up, to machen 28, 71, 108
man Herr *m* 115, 155; Mann *m* 159
manager Direktor *m* 26
manicure Maniküre *f* 30
many viele 14
map Karte *f* 76, 105; Plan *m* 105
March März *m* 150
marinated mariniert 44
marjoram Majoran *m* 51
market Markt *m* 81, 99
marmalade Apfelsinenmarmelade *f* 38
married verheiratet 93
mass *(church)* Messe *f* 84
match Streichholz *nt* 106, 126; *(sport)* Wettkampf *m* 89
match, to *(colour)* passen 112
material *(fabric)* Stoff *m* 113
matinée Nachmittagsvorstellung *f* 87
mattress Matratze *f* 106
May Mai *m* 150
may *(can)* können 11, 12, 163
meadow Wiese *f* 85
meal Mahlzeit *f* 24, 143; Essen *nt* 34, 63
mean, to bedeuten 10, 25
means Mittel *nt* 74
measles Masern *f/pl* 142
measure, to Maß nehmen 114
meat Fleisch *nt* 40, 45, 46, 62
mechanic Mechaniker *m* 78
medical ärztlich 144
medical certificate ärztliches Zeugnis *nt* 144
medicine Medizin *f* 83; *(drug)* Medikament *nt* 143
medium *(meat)* mittel 47
medium-sized mittlere 20
meet, to treffen 96
melon Melone *f* 53
memorial Denkmal *nt* 81
mend, to flicken 75; *(clothes)* ausbessern 29
menu Gedeck *nt* 36, 39; Menü *nt* 39; *(printed)* Speisekarte *f* 36, 39, 40
merry fröhlich 151
message Nachricht *f* 28, 136
metre Meter *m* 112
middle Mitte *f* 69, 87, 150
midnight Mitternacht *f* 153
mild mild 52, 126
mileage Kilometergeld *nt* 20
milk Milch *f* 38, 61, 64
milkshake Milchmixgetränk *nt* 61
million Million *f* 148
mineral water Mineralwasser *nt* 61
minister *(religion)* Pfarrer *m* 84
mint Pfefferminz(e) *f* 51
minute Minute *f* 21, 153
mirror Spiegel *m* 115, 123
miscellaneous verschieden 127
Miss Fräulein *nt* 9
miss, to fehlen 18, 29, 62
mistake Irrtum *m* 62
mixed gemischt 50
modified American plan Halbpension *f* 24
moment Augenblick *m* 11, 136
monastery Kloster *nt* 81
Monday Montag *m* 150
money Geld *nt* 129, 130
money order Postanweisung *f* 133
month Monat *m* 16, 150
monument Denkmal *nt* 81
moon Mond *m* 94
moped Moped *nt* 74
more mehr 14
morning Morgen *m* 151, 153
mortgage Hypothek *f* 131
mosque Moschee *f* 84
mother Mutter *f* 93
motorbike Motorrad *nt* 74

motorboat Motorboot *nt* 91
motorway Autobahn *f* 76
mountain Berg *m* 23, 85
mountaineering Bergsteigen *nt* 89
moustache Schnurrbart *m* 31
mouth Mund *m* 138
mouthwash Mundwasser *nt* 109
move, to bewegen 139
movie Film *m* 86
movie camera Filmkamera *f* 124
movies Kino *nt* 86, 96
Mr. Herr *m* 9, 131
Mrs. Frau *f* 9, 131
much viel 14
mug Becher *m* 107; *(beer)* Maß *f* 56
muscle Muskel *m* 138
museum Museum *nt* 81
mushroom Pilz *m* 41, 50
music Musik *f* 83, 128
musical Musical *nt* 86
music box Spieldose *f* 121, 127
mussel Muschel *f* 41, 44
must, to müssen 23, 31, 95, 101
mustard Senf *m* 37, 51, 64
mutton Hammelfleisch *nt* 45
my mein 161
myself selbst 120

N

nail *(human)* Nagel *m* 110
nail brush Nagelbürste *f* 110
nail clippers Nagelzange *f* 110
nail file Nagelfeile *f* 110
nail polish Nagellack *m* 110
nail polish remover Nagellack-entferner *m* 110
nail scissors Nagelschere *f* 110
name Name *m* 23, 25, 79, 136
napkin Serviette *f* 36, 105, 106
nappy Windel *f* 111
narrow eng 118
nationality Nationalität *f* 25
natural history Naturkunde *f* 83
near nah 13
nearby in der Nähe 77, 84
nearest nächste 78, 98
neat *(drink)* pur 59
necessary nötig 88
neck Hals *m* 138; *(nape)* Nacken *m* 30
necklace Halskette *f* 121
need, to brauchen 29, 118, 137
needle Nadel *f* 27
negative Negativ *nt* 125
nephew Neffe *m* 93
nerve Nerv *m* 138
nervous system Nervensystem *nt* 138
Netherlands Niederlande *pl* 146
never nie 15
new neu 13
newsagent's Zeitungshändler *m* 99
newspaper Zeitung *f* 104, 105
newsstand Zeitungsstand *m* 19, 67, 99, 104
New Year Neujahr *nt* 151
New Zealand Neuseeland *(nt)* 146
next nächste 13, 65, 68, 73, 76, 149, 150
next time nächstes Mal 95
next to neben 14
nice *(beautiful)* schön 94, 152
niece Nichte *f* 93
night Nacht *f* 9, 24, 151
nightclub Nachtlokal *nt* 88
night cream Nachtcreme *f* 110
nightdress Nachthemd *nt* 116
nine neun 147
nineteen neunzehn 147
ninety neunzig 147
ninth neunte 148
no nein 9
noisy laut 24
nonalcoholic alkoholfrei 61
none kein 15
nonsmoker Nichtraucher *m* 70
non-smoking Nichtraucher- 36
noodle Nudel *f* 49
noon Mittag *m* 153
normal normal 30, 110
north Nord(en) *m* 77
North America Nordamerika *(nt)* 146
Norway Norwegen *(nt)* 146
nose Nase *f* 138
nosebleed Nasenbluten *nt* 141
nose drops Nasentropfen *m/pl* 109
not nicht 15, 163
note *(banknote)* Schein *m* 130
notebook Notizheft *nt* 105
note paper Briefpapier *nt* 105
nothing nichts 15, 17
notice *(sign)* Tafel *f*, Hinweis *m* 155
notify, to benachrichtigen 144
November November *m* 150
now jetzt 15
number Nummer *f* 25, 65, 134, 136; Zahl *f* 124, 147
nurse Krankenschwester *f* 144

O

occupation *(job)* Beruf *m* 93
occupied besetzt 13, 70, 155
October Oktober *m* 150
office Büro *nt* 22, 80
oil Öl *nt* 51, 75, 111
oily *(greasy)* fettig 30, 111
old alt 13
old town Altstadt *f* 82
omelet Omelett *nt* 64
on an, auf 14
once einmal 148
one eins 147
one-way *(ticket)* einfach 69
on foot zu Fuß 76
onion Zwiebel *f* 50
only nur 15
on time pünktlich 68
onyx Onyx *m* 122
open offen 13, 82
open, to öffnen 10, 17, 82, 108, 132; *(account)* eröffnen 130
opening hours Öffnungszeiten *f/pl* 82
opera Oper *f* 88
opera house Opernhaus *nt* 82, 88
operation Operation *f* 144
operator Vermittlung *f* 134
operetta Operette *f* 88
opposite gegenüber 77
optician Optiker *m* 99, 123
or oder 15
orange orange 113
orange Orange *f* 53, 64; Apfelsine *f* 53
orange juice Orangensaft *m* 38, 61
orangeade Orangeade *f* 61
orchestra Orchester *nt* 88; *(seats)* Parkett *nt* 87
orchestral music Orchestermusik *f* 128
order *(goods, meal)* Bestellung *f* 40, 102
order, to *(goods, meal)* bestellen 36, 62, 102, 103
ornithology Vogelkunde *f* 83
other andere 59
our unser 161
out of order außer Betrieb 155
out of stock nicht vorrätig 103
outlet *(electric)* Steckdose *f* 27
outside draußen 15, 36
oval oval 101
over über 14
over there dort drüben 69
overalls Overall *m* 116
overdone zu stark gebraten 62
overheat, to *(engine)* heißlaufen 78
overnight *(stay)* eine Nacht 26
overwhelming überwältigend 84
owe, to schulden 144
oyster Auster *f* 41, 43

P

pacifier Schnuller *m* 111
packet Packung *f* 120; Schachtel *f* 126
page *(hotel)* Page *m* 26
pail Eimer *m* 106, 128
pain Schmerz *m* 140, 141, 144
painkiller Schmerzmittel *nt* 109
paint Farbe *f* 155
paint, to malen 83
paintbox Malkasten *m* 105
painter Maler *m* 83
painting Malerei *f* 83
pair Paar *nt* 116, 118, 149
pajamas Schlafanzug *m* 117
palace Palast *m*, Schloß *nt* 81
palpitation Herzklopfen *nt* 141
panties Schlüpfer *m* 116
pants *(trousers)* Hose *f* 116
panty girdle Strumpfhalterhöschen *nt* 116
panty hose Strumpfhose *f* 116
paper Papier *nt* 105
paperback Taschenbuch *nt* 105
paperclip Büroklammer *f* 105
paper napkin Papierserviette *f* 105
paraffin *(fuel)* Petroleum *nt* 106
parcel Paket *nt* 133
pardon? Wie bitte? 10
parents Eltern *pl* 93
park Park *m* 82
park, to parken 26, 77
parking Parken *nt* 77, 79
parking disc Parkscheibe *f* 77
parking meter Parkuhr *f* 77
parliament Parlament *nt* 82
parsley Petersilie *f* 51
part Teil *m* 138
parting *(part)* Scheitel *m* 30
partridge Rebhuhn *nt* 48
party *(social gathering)* Party *f* 95
pass *(rail, bus)* Mehrfahrkarte *f* 72
pass *(mountain)* Paß *m* 85
passport Paß *m* 16, 17, 25, 26
passport photo Paßbild *nt* 124

pass through, to auf der Durchreise sein 16
pasta Teigwaren *f/pl* 49
paste *(glue)* Klebstoff *m* 105
pastry Gebäck *nt* 54
pastry shop Konditorei *f* 99
patch, to *(clothes)* flicken 29
path Weg *m* 85
patient Patient(in) *m/f* 144
pay, to (be)zahlen 31, 63, 68, 102, 136
payment Zahlung *f* 131
pea Erbse *f* 50
peach Pfirsich *m* 53
peak Bergspitze *f* 85
peanut Erdnuß *f* 53
pear Birne *f* 53
pearl Perle *f* 122
pedestrian Fußgänger *m* 79
peg *(tent)* Hering *m* 107
pen Feder *f* 105
pencil Bleistift *m* 105
pencil sharpener Bleistiftspitzer *m* 105
pendant Anhänger *m* 121
penicillin Penizillin *nt* 143
penknife Taschenmesser *nt* 106
pensioner Rentner(in) *m/f* 82
people Leute *pl* 93
pepper Pfeffer *m* 37, 51, 64
per cent Prozent *nt* 148
percentage Prozentsatz *m* 131
perch Barsch *m* 43
per day pro Tag 20, 32, 89
performance *(session)* Vorstellung *f* 87
perfume Parfüm *nt* 110
perhaps vielleicht 15
per hour pro Stunde 77, 89
period *(monthly)* Periode *f* 141
period pains Menstruationsbeschwerden *f/pl* 141
permanent wave Dauerwelle *f* 30
per night pro Nacht 24
per person pro Person 32
person Person *f* 32, 36
personal persönlich 17
personal call Gespräch mit Voranmeldung *nt* 134
per week pro Woche 20, 24
petrol Benzin *nt* 75, 78
pewter Zinn *nt* 122
pheasant Fasan *m* 48
phone Telefon *nt* 28, 78, 79, 134
phone, to telefonieren 134
phone booth Telefonzelle *f* 134
phone call (Telefon)gespräch *nt* 135, 136; Anruf *m* 136
phone number Telefonnummer *f* 96, 134, 135
photo Foto *nt* 124, 125
photocopy Fotokopie *f* 131
photograph, to fotografieren 82
photographer Fotograf *m* 99
photography Fotografie *f* 124
phrase Ausdruck *m* 11
pick up, to *(person)* abholen 80, 96
picnic Picknick *nt* 63
picture Bild *nt* 82; *(photo)* Foto *nt* 82
piece Stück *nt* 29, 52, 64, 120
pigeon Taube *f* 48
pill Pille *f* 141
pillow Kopfkissen *nt* 27
pin Nadel *f* 110; *(brooch)* Anstecknadel *f* 121
pineapple Ananas *f* 53
pink rosa 113
pipe Pfeife *f* 126, 127
pipe cleaner Pfeifenreiniger *m* 126
pipe tobacco Pfeifentabak *m* 126
place Ort *m* 25, 76
place of birth Geburtsort *m* 25
plaice Scholle *f* 44
plane Flugzeug *nt* 65, 159
plaster *(cast)* Gipsverband *m* 140
plastic Plastik *nt* 107
plastic bag Plastikbeutel *m* 106
plate Teller *m* 36, 62, 107
platform *(station)* Bahnsteig *m* 67, 68, 69, 70
platinum Platin *nt* 122
play *(theatre)* Stück *nt* 86
play, to spielen 86, 88, 89, 93
playground Spielplatz *m* 32
playing card Spielkarte *f* 105
please bitte 9
plimsolls Turnschuhe *m/pl* 118
plug *(electric)* Stecker *m* 29, 119
plum Pflaume *f* 53
pneumonia Lungenentzündung *f* 142
pocket Tasche *f* 117
pocket calculator Taschenrechner *m* 105
pocket dictionary Taschenwörterbuch *nt* 104
pocket watch Taschenuhr *f* 121
point, to *(show)* zeigen 11
poison Gift *nt* 109

poisoning Vergiftung *f* 142
Poland Polen *(nt)* 146
police Polizei *f* 78, 156
police station Polizeiwache *f* 99, 156
pond Teich *m* 85
pop music Popmusik *f* 128
poplin Popeline *m* 114
porcelain Porzellan *nt* 127
pork Schweinefleisch *nt* 45
port Hafen *m* 74; *(wine)* Portwein *m* 59
portable tragbar, Koffer- 119
porter Gepäckträger *m* 18, 71; *(hotel)* Hausdiener *m* 26
portion Portion *f* 37, 54, 62
possible möglich 137
post *(letters)* Post *f* 28, 133
post, to aufgeben 28
postage Porto *nt* 132
postage stamp Briefmarke *f* 28, 126, 132
postcard Postkarte *f* 105, 126, 132
poste restante postlagernd 133
post office Postamt *nt* 99, 132
potato Kartoffel *f* 48, 49
pottery Töpferei *f* 83
poultry Geflügel *nt* 48
pound *(money)* Pfund *nt* 18, 102, 130; *(weight)* Pfund *nt* 120
powder Puder *m* 110
powder compact Puderdose *f* 122
prawn Garnele *f* 44
pregnant schwanger 141
premium *(gasoline)* Super *nt* 75
prescribe, to verschreiben 143
prescription Rezept *nt* 108, 143
present *(gift)* Geschenk *nt* 17, 121
press, to *(iron)* dampfbügeln 29
press stud Druckknopf *m* 117
pressure Druck *m* 75
pretty hübsch 84
price Preis *m* 40, 69
priest Priester *m* 84
print *(photo)* Abzug *m* 125
private privat 91, 155
private toilet eigene Toilette *f* 23
processing *(photo)* Entwickeln *nt* 124
profession Beruf *m* 25
profit Gewinn *m* 131
programme Programm *nt* 87
prohibit, to verbieten 155
pronunciation Aussprache *f* 6
Protestant protestantisch, evangelisch 84
provide, to besorgen 131
prune Backpflaume *f* 53
public holiday Feiertag *m* 152
pull, to ziehen 155
pullover Pullover *m* 117
pumpkin Kürbis *m* 50
puncture Reifenpanne *f* 75
purchase Kauf *m* 131
pure rein 114
purple violett 113
push, to *(button)* drücken 155
put, to stellen 24
put through, to verbinden 28
pyjamas Schlafanzug *m* 117

Q

quality Qualität *f* 103, 113
quantity Menge *f* 14, 103
quarter Viertel *nt* 148
quarter of an hour Viertelstunde *f* 153
quartz Quarz *m* 122
question Frage *f* 10
quick schnell 13, 156
quickly schnell 79, 137
quiet ruhig 23, 25

R

rabbi Rabbiner *m* 84
rabbit Kaninchen *nt* 48
race course/track (Pferde)rennbahn *f* 90
racket *(sport)* Schläger *m* 89
radiator *(car)* Kühler *m* 78
radio *(set)* Radio *nt* 23, 28, 119
radish Radieschen *nt* 50
railway station Bahnhof *m* 19, 21, 67
rain Regen *m* 94
rain, to regnen 94
rain boot Gummistiefel *m* 118
raincoat Regenmantel *m* 117
raisin Rosine *f* 53
rare *(meat)* blutig 47
rash Ausschlag *m* 139
raspberry Himbeere *f* 53
rate Tarif *m* 20; *(exchange)* Kurs *m* 18, 130; *(inflation)* Rate *f* 131
razor Rasierapparat *m* 110
razor blade Rasierklinge *f* 110
read, to lesen 40
ready fertig 29, 118, 123, 125, 145
real echt 121
rear hinten, Hinter- 75

DICTIONARY Wörterverzeichnis

receipt Quittung *f* 103, 144
reception Empfang *m* 23
receptionist Empfangschef *m* 26
recommend, to empfehlen 22, 35, 80, 86, 88, 145
record *(disc)* Schallplatte *f* 127, 128
record player Plattenspieler *m* 119
rectangular rechteckig 101
red rot 59, 113
redcurrant rote Johannisbeere *f* 53
reduction Ermäßigung *f* 24, 82
refill *(pen)* Ersatzpatrone *f* 105
refund Rückerstattung *f* 103
regards Grüße *m/pl* 152
register, to *(luggage)* aufgeben 71
registered mail per Einschreiben 132
registration Anmeldung *f* 25
registration form Anmeldeschein *m* 25, 26
regular *(petrol)* Normal *nt* 75
religion Religion *f* 83
religious service Gottesdienst *m* 84
rent, to mieten 19, 20, 74, 89, 91; vermieten 155
rental Verleih *m* 20, 74
repair Reparatur *f* 125
repair, to reparieren 29, 118, 119, 121, 123, 125, 145
repeat, to wiederholen 11
report, to *(a theft)* anzeigen 156
require, to verlangen 88
reservation Reservierung *f* 19, 65, 69
reservations office Reservierungsschalter *m* 19; Platzreservierung *f* 67
reserve, to reservieren (lassen) 19, 23, 36
restaurant Restaurant *nt* 19, 32, 33, 35, 67
return *(ticket)* hin und zurück 69
return, to *(give back)* zurückgeben 103
reverse the charges, to ein R-Gespräch anmelden 134
rheumatism Rheumatismus *m* 141
rhubarb Rhabarber *m* 53
rib Rippe *f* 46, 138
ribbon Band *nt* 105
rice Reis *m* 49
right rechte 13; rechts 21, 30, 63, 69, 77, 79; *(correct)* richtig 13, 76
ring *(on finger)* Ring *m* 122
ring, to klingeln 155; telefonieren 134
ripe reif 52
river Fluß *m* 74, 85, 90; *(major)* Strom *m* 85
road Straße *f* 76, 77, 85
road assistance Pannendienst *m* 78
road map Straßenkarte *f* 105
road sign Verkehrszeichen *nt* 79
roast Braten *m* 45
roasted gebraten 47
rock Felsen *m* 85
roll *(bread)* Brötchen *nt* 38, 64
roller skate Rollschuh *m* 128
roll film Rollfilm *m* 124
roll-neck mit Rollkragen 117
romantic romantisch 84
room Zimmer *nt* 19, 23, 24, 25, 27, 28; *(space)* Platz *m* 32
room number Zimmernummer *f* 26
room service Zimmerbedienung *f* 23
rope Seil *nt* 107
rosary Rosenkranz *m* 122
rosé rosé 59
rosemary Rosmarin *m* 51
round rund 101, 117
roundtour Rundfahrt *f* 74
roundtrip *(ticket)* hin und zurück 69
rowing-boat Ruderboot *nt* 91
rubber *(material)* Gummi *m* 118; *(eraser)* Radiergummi *m* 105
rubber sole Gummisohle *f* 118
ruby Rubin *m* 122
rucksack Rucksack *m* 107
ruin Ruine *f* 81
ruler *(for measuring)* Lineal *nt* 105
rum Rum *m* 59
running water fließendes Wasser *nt* 23
rye Roggen *m* 38

S

safe *(not dangerous)* gefahrlos, ungefährlich 90
safe Safe *m* 26
safety pin Sicherheitsnadel *f* 111
saffron Safran *m* 51
sage Salbei *m* 51
sailing-boat Segelboot *nt* 91
salad Salat *m* 49, 50
sale Verkauf *m* 131; *(bargains)* Ausverkauf *m* 101, 155
sales tax Mehrwertsteuer *f* 24, 40, 102
salmon Lachs *m* 41, 44; Salm *m* 44
salt Salz *nt* 37, 51, 64
salty salzig 62

same selbe 40; gleiche 118
sand Sand *m* 90
sandal Sandale *f* 118
sandwich Sandwich *nt* 64; *(open)* belegtes Brot *nt* 64
sanitary towel/napkin Damenbinde *f* 109
sapphire Saphir *m* 122
sardine Sardine *f* 41
satin Satin *m* 114
Saturday Samstag *m*, Sonnabend *m* 150
sauce Soße *f* 48
saucepan Kochtopf *m* 107
saucer Untertasse *f* 107
sauerkraut Sauerkraut *nt* 50
sausage Wurst *f* 47, 64
scallop Jakobsmuschel *f* 44
scarf Halstuch *nt* 117
scenic route landschaftlich schöne Straße *f* 85
school Schule *f* 79
scissors Schere *f* 107, 110
scooter Motorroller *m* 74
Scotland Schottland *(nt)* 146
scrambled egg Rührei *nt* 38
screwdriver Schraubenzieher *m* 107
sculptor Bildhauer *m* 83
sculpture Bildhauerei *f* 83
sea Meer *nt* 85, 90
sea bass Seebarsch *m* 44
seafood Meeresfrüchte *f/pl* 43
season Jahreszeit *f* 149; Saison *f* 149
seasoning Würze *f* 37, 51
seat Platz *m* 69, 70, 87
seat belt Sicherheitsgurt *m* 75
second zweite 148
second Sekunde *f* 153
second class zweite Klasse *f* 69
second hand Sekundenzeiger *m* 122
second-hand *(books)* antiquarisch 104
second-hand shop Gebrauchtwarenladen *m* 99
secretary Sekretär(in) *m/f* 27, 131
see, to sehen 163; *(check)* nachschauen 11
sell, to verkaufen 100
send, to schicken 78, 132; senden 102, 103, 132
send up, to hinaufschicken 26
sentence Satz *m* 11
separately getrennt 63
September September *m* 150
service Bedienung *f* 24, 40, 63, 100; *(religion)* Gottesdienst *m* 84
serviette Serviette *f* 36
set, to *(hair)* legen 30
set menu Tagesgedeck *nt* 36, 40
setting lotion Haarfestiger *m* 30, 111
seven sieben 147
seventeen siebzehn 147
seventh siebte 148
seventy siebzig 147
sew, to nähen 29
shampoo Haarwaschmittel *nt* 30, 111
shape Form *f* 103
shape, to *(hair)* legen 30
share *(finance)* Aktie *f* 131
sharp scharf 52; *(pain)* stechend 140
shave, to rasieren 30
shaver Rasierapparat *m* 27, 119
shaving brush Rasierpinsel *m* 111
shaving cream Rasiercreme *f* 111
she sie 162
shelf Regal *nt* 120
ship Schiff *nt* 74
shirt Hemd *nt* 117
shoe Schuh *m* 118
shoelace Schnürsenkel *m* 118
shoemaker's Schuhmacher *m* 99
shoe polish Schuhcreme *f* 118
shoe shop Schuhgeschäft *nt* 99
shop Geschäft *nt*, Laden *m* 98
shopping Einkaufen *nt* 97
shopping area Geschäftsviertel *nt* 81, 100
shopping centre Einkaufszentrum *nt* 99
shop window Schaufenster *nt* 100, 112, 124
short kurz 30, 116, 117
shorts Shorts *pl* 117
short-sighted kurzsichtig 123
shoulder Schulter *f* 138
shovel Schaufel *f* 128
show *(theatre)* Vorstellung *f* 86, 87
show, to zeigen 11, 12, 76, 100, 101, 103, 119, 124
shower Dusche *f* 23, 32
shrimp Garnele *f* 44
shrink, to einlaufen 114
shut geschlossen 13
shutter *(window)* Fensterladen *m* 29; *(camera)* Verschluß *m* 125
sick *(ill)* krank 140, 156
sickness *(illness)* Krankheit *f* 140
side Seite *f* 30

sideboards/burns Koteletten *f/pl* 31
sightseeing Besichtigung *f* 80
sightseeing tour Stadtrundfahrt *f* 80
sign *(notice)* Schild *nt*, Aufschrift *f* 155
sign, to unterschreiben 26, 130
signature Unterschrift *f* 25
signet ring Siegelring *m* 122
silk Seide *f* 114
silver silbern 113
silver Silber *nt* 121, 122
silver plated versilbert 122
silverware Tafelsilber *nt* 122
simple einfach 124
since seit 14, 150
sing, to singen 88
single *(not married)* ledig 93; *(ticket)* einfach 69
single cabin Einzelkabine *f* 74
single room Einzelzimmer *nt* 19, 23
sinister unheimlich 84
sister Schwester *f* 93
six sechs 147
sixteen sechzehn 147
sixth sechste 148
sixty sechzig 147
size Format *nt* 124; *(clothes)* Größe *f* 114, 115; *(shœs)* Nummer *f* 118
skate Schlittschuh *m* 91
skating rink Eisbahn *f* 91
ski Ski *m* 91
ski, to skifahren 91
skiboot Skischuh *m* 91
skiing Skifahren *nt* 89, 91
ski lift Skilift *m* 91
skin Haut *f* 110, 138
skin-diving Tauchen *nt* 91
ski pole Skistock *m* 91
skirt Rock *m* 117
ski run Skipiste *f* 91
sky Himmel *m* 94
sleep, to schlafen 144
sleeping bag Schlafsack *m* 107
sleeping-car Schlafwagen *m* 66, 68, 69, 70
sleeping pill Schlaftablette *f* 109, 143
sleeve Ärmel *m* 117
slice Scheibe *f* 120
slide *(photo)* Dia *nt* 124
slip Unterrock *m* 117
slipper Hausschuh *m* 118
slow langsam 13
slow down, to langsam fahren 79
slowly langsam 11, 21, 135
small klein 13, 20, 24, 37, 62, 101, 118, 130
smoke, to rauchen 95
smoked geräuchert 44
smoker Raucher *m* 70
snack Imbiß *m* 63
snack bar Schnellimbiß *m* 34, 63, 67
snail Schnecke *f* 41
snap fastener Druckknopf *m* 117
sneakers Turnschuhe *m/pl* 118
snow Schnee *m* 94
snow, to schneien 94
soap Seife *f* 27, 111
soccer Fußball *m* 89
sock Socke *f* 117
socket *(outlet)* Steckdose *f* 27
soft weich 52, 123
soft-boiled *(egg)* weich(gekocht) 38
soft drink alkoholfreies Getränk *nt* 64
sold out ausverkauft 87
sole Sohle *f* 118; *(fish)* Seezunge *f* 44
soloist Solist *m* 88
some etwas, einige 14
someone jemand 95
something etwas 36, 54, 108, 112, 113, 125, 139
son Sohn *m* 93
song Lied *nt* 128
soon bald 15, 137
sore throat Halsschmerzen *m/pl* 141
sorry *(I'm)* Entschuldigung, Verzeihung 10; es tut mir leid 16
sort *(kind)* Sorte *f* 52, 120
soufflé Auflauf *m* 54
soup Suppe *f* 42
sour sauer 62
south Süd(en) *m* 77
South Africa Südafrika *(nt)* 146
South America Südamerika *(nt)* 146
souvenir Andenken *nt* 127
souvenir shop Andenkenladen *m* 99
Soviet Union Sowjetunion *f* 146
spade Schaufel *f* 128
spare tyre Ersatzreifen *m* 75
sparking plug Zündkerze *f* 75
sparkling *(wine)* Schaum- 59
spark plug Zündkerze *f* 75
speak, to sprechen 11, 135, 163
speaker *(loudspeaker)* Lautsprecher *m* 119
special Sonder- 20; Spezial- 37
special delivery per Expreß 132
specialist Spezialist(in) *m/f* 142
speciality Spezialität *f* 40, 60

specimen *(medical)* Probe *f* 142
spectacle case Brillenetui *nt* 123
spell, to buchstabieren 11
spend, to ausgeben 101
spice Gewürz *nt* 51
spinach Spinat *m* 50
spine Wirbelsäule *f* 138
spiny lobster Languste *f* 41, 44
sponge Schwamm *m* 111
spoon Löffel *m* 36, 62, 107
sport Sport *m* 89
sporting goods shop Sportgeschäft *nt* 99
sprain, to verstauchen 140
spring *(season)* Frühling *m* 149; *(water)* Quelle *f* 85
square viereckig 101
square Platz *m* 82
stadium Stadion *nt* 82
staff Personal *nt* 26
stain Fleck *m* 29
stainless steel rostfreier Stahl *m* 107, 122
stalls *(theatre)* Parkett *nt* 87
stamp *(postage)* Briefmarke *f* 28, 126, 132, 133
staple Heftklammer *f* 105
star Stern *m* 94
start, to beginnen 80, 87, 88; *(car)* anspringen 78
starter *(appetizer)* Vorspeise *f* 41
station *(railway)* Bahnhof *m* 19, 21, 67; *(underground, subway)* Station *f* 73
stationer's Schreibwarengeschäft *nt* 99
statue Statue *f* 82
stay Aufenthalt *m* 31
stay, to bleiben 16, 26; *(reside)* wohnen 93
steak Steak *nt* 46
steal, to stehlen 156
steamed gedämpft 44
stew Eintopfgericht *nt* 42
stewed gedämpft 47, 51
stew pot Schmortopf *m* 107
stiff neck steifer Nacken *m* 141
sting Stich *m* 139
sting, to stechen 139
stitch, to nähen 29, 118
stock *(supply)* Vorrat *m* 103
stock exchange Börse *f* 82
stocking Strumpf *m* 117
stomach Magen *m* 138
stomach ache Magenschmerzen *m/pl* 141
stools Stuhl(gang) *m* 142
stop *(bus)* Haltestelle *f* 72, 73
stop! Halt! 156
stop, to halten 21, 68, 70, 72
stop thief! Haltet den Dieb! 156
store *(shop)* Laden *m*, Geschäft *nt* 98
straight *(drink)* pur 59
straight ahead geradeaus 21, 77
strange seltsam 84
strawberry Erdbeere *f* 53
street Straße *f* 25, 82
streetcar Straßenbahn *f* 72
street map Stadtplan *m* 19, 105
string Bindfaden *m*, Schnur *f* 105
strong stark 126, 143
stuck *(to be)* klemmen 28
student Student(in) *m/f* 82, 93
study, to studieren 93
stuffed gefüllt 47
sturdy robust 101
subway *(railway)* U-Bahn *f* 73
suede Wildleder *nt* 114, 118
sugar Zucker *m* 37, 51, 64
suit *(man)* Anzug *m* 117; *(woman)* Kostüm *nt* 117
suitcase Koffer *m* 18
summer Sommer *m* 149
sun Sonne *f* 94
sunburn Sonnenbrand *m* 108
Sunday Sonntag *m* 150
sunglasses Sonnenbrille *f* 123
sunshade *(beach)* Sonnenschirm *m* 91
sun-tan cream Sonnencreme *f* 111
super *(petrol)* Super *nt* 75
superb prächtig 84
supermarket Supermarkt *m* 99
suppository Zäpfchen *nt* 109
surcharge Zuschlag *m* 68
surfboard Surfbrett *nt* 91
surgery *(consulting room)* Arztpraxis *f* 137
surname (Familien)name *m* 25
suspenders *(Am.)* Hosenträger *m/pl* 117
swallow, to schlucken 143
sweater Pullover *m* 117
sweatshirt Sweatshirt *nt* 117
Sweden Schweden *(nt)* 146
sweet süß 59, 62
sweet *(candy)* Bonbon *nt* 126
sweet corn Mais *m* 50

sweetener Süßstoff *m* 37, 51
swell, to schwellen 139
swelling Schwellung *f* 139
swim, to schwimmen, baden 90
swimming pool Schwimmbad *nt* 32, 90; *(open-air)* Freibad *nt* 9; *(indoor)* Hallenbad *nt* 90
swimsuit Badeanzug *m* 117
Swiss schweizerisch, Schweizer
Swiss army knife Schweizer Armeemesser *nt* 127
switch Schalter *m* 29
switchboard operator Telefonist(in) *m/f* 26
Switzerland Schweiz *f* 146
swollen geschwollen 139
synagogue Synagoge *f* 84
synthetic synthetisch 114
system System *nt* 138

T

table Tisch *m* 36, 107; *(list)* Tabelle *f* 157
tablet Tablette *f* 109
tailor's Schneider *m* 99
take, to nehmen 18, 24, 72, 77; *(time)* dauern 62, 72, 76, 102; *(bring)* bringen 18, 21, 96
take away, to *(carry)* mitnehmen 63, 102
talcum powder Körperpuder *m* 111
tampon Tampon *m* 109
tangerine Mandarine *f* 53
tap *(water)* Wasserhahn *m* 28
tape recorder Kassettenrecorder *m* 119
tax Taxe *f* 32; Steuer *f* 24, 40, 102
taxi Taxi *nt* 18, 19, 21, 31, 67
taxi rank Taxistand *m* 21
tea Tee *m* 38, 61, 64
team Mannschaft *f* 89
tear, to reißen 140
teaspoon Teelöffel *m* 107, 143
telegram Telegramm *nt* 133
telegraph office Telegrafenamt *nt* 99
telephone Telefon *nt* 28, 78, 79, 134
telephone, to telefonieren 133
telephone booth Telefonzelle *f* 134
telephone call (Telefon)gespräch *nt* 135, 136; Anruf *m* 136
telephone directory Telefonbuch *nt* 134
telephone number Telefonnummer *f* 96, 135, 136
telephoto lens Teleobjektiv *nt* 125
television *(set)* Fernseher *m* 23, 28, 119
television room Fernsehraum *m* 27
telex Telex *nt* 133
telex, to ein Telex schicken 130
tell, to sagen 12, 73, 76, 136, 153
temperature Temperatur *f* 90, 142; *(fever)* Fieber *nt* 140
temporary provisorisch 145
ten zehn 147
tendon Sehne *f* 138
tennis Tennis *nt* 89
tennis court Tennisplatz *m* 89
tennis racket Tennisschläger *m* 89
tent Zelt *nt* 32, 107
tenth zehnte 148
tent peg Hering *m* 107
tent pole Zeltstange *f* 107
term Ausdruck *m* 131
terminus Endstation *f* 72
terrace Terrasse *f* 36
terrible schrecklich 84
tetanus Wundstarrkrampf *m* 140
than als 14
thank you danke 9
that der, die das 10, 160
the der, die das 159
theatre Theater *nt* 82, 86
theft Diebstahl *m* 156
their ihr 161
then dann 15
there dort 13, 15
thermometer Thermometer *nt* 109, 144
these diese 160
they sie 162
thief Dieb *m* 156
thigh Schenkel *m* 138
thin dünn 113
think, to *(believe)* glauben 31, 63, 94
third dritte 148
third Drittel *nt* 148
thirsty, to be Durst haben 12, 35
thirteen dreizehn 147
thirty dreißig 147
this diese(r/s) 160
those die 160
thousand tausend 148
thread Faden *m* 27
three drei 147
throat Hals *m* 138, 141
throat lozenge Halspastille *f* 109
through durch 14

through train durchgehender Zug *m* 68, 69
thumb Daumen *m* 138
thumbtack Reißzwecke *f* 105
thunder Donner *m* 94
thunderstorm Gewitter *nt* 94
Thursday Donnerstag *m* 150
thyme Thymian *m* 51
ticket Karte *f* 87, 89; *(plane)* Flugticket *nt* 65; *(train)* Fahrkarte *f* 69; *(bus)* Fahrschein *m* 72
ticket office Fahrkartenschalter *m* 67
tide *(high)* Flut *f* 90; *(low)* Ebbe *f* 90
tie Krawatte *f* 117
tie pin Krawattennadel *f* 122
tight *(clothes)* eng 116
tights Strumpfhose *f* 117
time Zeit *f* 80, 153; *(occasion)* -mal 148
timetable Fahrplan *m* 68
tin *(can)* Büchse *f* 120
tinfoil Aluminiumfolie *f* 107
tin opener Büchsenöffner *m* 107
tint Tönungsmittel *nt* 111
tinted getönt 123
tire Reifen *m* 75, 76
tired müde 12
tissue *(handkerchief)* Papiertuch *nt* 111
tissue paper Seidenpapier *nt* 105
to zu 14
toast Toast *m* 38
tobacco Tabak *m* 126
tobacconist's Tabakladen *m* 99, 126
today heute 29, 150, 151
toe Zehe *f* 138
toilet paper Toilettenpapier *nt* 111
toiletry Toilettenartikel *m/pl* 110
toilets Toilette *f* 27, 32, 37, 67
toilet water Toilettenwasser *nt* 111
tomato Tomate *f* 50
tomato juice Tomatensaft *m* 61
tomb Grab *nt* 82
tomorrow morgen 29, 151
tongs Zange *f* 107
tongue Zunge *f* 46, 138
tonic water Tonic *nt* 61
tonight heute abend 29, 86, 87, 88, 96
tonsil Mandel *f* 138
too zu 14; *(also)* auch 15
tooth Zahn *m* 145
toothache Zahnschmerzen *m/pl* 145
toothbrush Zahnbürste *f* 111, 119
toothpaste Zahnpasta *f* 111
torch *(flashlight)* Taschenlampe *f* 107
touch, to berühren 155
tough *(meat)* zäh 62
tour Rundfahrt *f* 80
tourist office Fremdenverkehrsbüro *nt* 22, 80
tourist tax Kurtaxe *f* 32
towards gegen 14
towel Handtuch *nt* 111
tower Turm *m* 82
town Stadt *f* 19, 76, 105
town hall Rathaus *nt* 82
tow truck Abschleppwagen *m* 78
toy Spielzeug *nt* 128
toy shop Spielwarengeschäft *nt* 99
track *(station)* Gleis *nt* 67, 68, 69
tracksuit Trainingsanzug *m* 117
traffic *(cars)* Verkehr *m* 79
traffic jam Stau *m* 79
traffic light Ampel *f* 77
trailer Wohnwagen *m* 32
train Zug *m* 66, 68, 69, 70, 73, 159
tram Straßenbahn *f* 72
tranquillizer Beruhigungsmittel *nt* 109
transfer *(bank)* Überweisung *f* 131
transformer Transformator *m* 119
translate, to übersetzen 11
transport Transport *m* 74
travel, to reisen 93
travel agency Reisebüro *nt* 99
traveller's cheque Reisescheck *m* 18, 63, 102, 130
travelling bag Reisetasche *f* 18
travel sickness Reisekrankheit *f* 108
treatment Behandlung *f* 143
tree Baum *m* 85
tremendous außerordentlich 84
trim, to *(beard)* stutzen 31
trip Reise *f* 93, 152, 159; Fahrt *f* 72
trousers Hose *f* 117
trout Forelle *f* 44
try, to versuchen 135; *(sample)* probieren 60; *(clothes)* anprobieren 115
T-shirt T-Shirt *nt* 117
tube Tube *f* 120
Tuesday Dienstag *m* 150
tumbler Wasserglas *nt* 107
tunny *(tuna)* Thunfisch *m* 41
turbot Steinbutt *m* 44
turkey Truthahn *m* 48
turn, to *(change direction)* abbiegen 21, 77

turnip Kohlrabi *m* 50
turquoise türkisfarben 113
turquoise Türkis *m* 122
turtleneck mit Rollkragen 117
tweezers Pinzette *f* 111
twelve zwölf 147
twenty zwanzig 147
twice zweimal 148
twin beds zwei Einzelbetten *nt/pl* 23
two zwei 147
typewriter Schreibmaschine *f* 27, 105
typewriter ribbon Farbband *nt* 105
typing paper Schreibmaschinenpapier *nt* 105
tyre Reifen *m* 75, 76

U

ugly häßlich 13, 84
umbrella Regenschirm *m* 117; *(beach)* Sonnenschirm *m* 91
uncle Onkel *m* 93
unconscious bewußtlos 139
under unter 14
underdone *(meat)* blutig 47; zu roh 62
underground *(railway)* U-Bahn *f* 73
underpants Unterhose *f* 117
undershirt Unterhemd *nt* 117
understand, to verstehen 11, 16
United States Vereinigte Staaten *m/pl* 146
university Universität *f* 82
until bis 14
up hinauf 15
upper obere 69
upset stomach Magenverstimmung *f* 108
urgent dringend 12, 145
urine Urin *m* 142
use Gebrauch *m* 17
use, to benutzen 78, 134
useful nützlich 14
usual gewöhnlich 143

V

vacancy freies Zimmer *nt* 23, 155
vacant frei 13, 22, 155
vacation Ferien *pl*, Urlaub *m* 151
vaccinate, to impfen 140
vacuum flask Thermosflasche *f* 107
vaginal infection Scheidenentzündung *f* 141
valley Tal *nt* 85
value Wert *m* 131
value-added tax *(VAT)* Mehrwertsteuer *f* 24, 40, 102, 154
vanilla Vanille *f* 54
veal Kalbfleisch *nt* 45
vegetable Gemüse *nt* 40, 49, 50
vegetable store Gemüsehandlung *f* 99
vegetarian vegetarisch 37
vein Vene *f* 138
velvet Samt *m* 114
velveteen Manchester *m* 114
venereal disease Geschlechtskrankheit *f* 142
venison Reh *nt*, Hirsch *m* 48
vermouth Wermut *m* 60
very sehr 15
vest Unterhemd *nt* 117; *(Am.)* Weste *f* 117
veterinarian Tierarzt *m* 99
video cassette Videokassette *f* 119, 128
video-recorder Videorecorder *m* 119
view Aussicht *f* 23, 25
village Dorf *nt* 76, 85
vinegar Essig *m* 51
vineyard Weinberg *m* 85
visit Besuch *m* 92
visit, to besuchen 94, 144; *(look around)* besichtigen 84
visiting hours Besuchszeit *f* 144
vitamin pills Vitamintabletten *f/pl* 109
V-neck mit V-Ausschnitt 117
volleyball Volleyball *m* 89
voltage (Strom)spannung *f* 27, 119
vomit, to sich übergeben 140

W

waistcoat Weste *f* 117
wait, to warten 21, 95, 108
waiter Kellner *m* 26; Herr Ober *m* 36, 56
waiting-room Wartesaal *m* 67
waitress Kellnerin *f* 26; Fräulein *nt* 36
wake, to wecken 27, 71
Wales Wales *(nt)* 146
walk, to (zu Fuß) gehen 74, 85
wall Mauer *f* 82
wallet Brieftasche *f* 156
walnut Walnuß *f* 53
want, to *(wish)* wünschen 12
warm warm 94
wash, to waschen 29, 114

Inhaltsverzeichnis

DENMARK
SWEDEN
BALTIC SEA
NORTH SEA
Flensburg
Kiel
Rostock
Lübeck
Schwerin
Wilhelmshaven
Hamburg
Bremerhaven
EAST GERMANY
Oldenburg
Bremen
Elbe
NETHERLANDS
WEST GERMANY
Berlin
POLAND
Hannover
Braunschweig
Rhein
Weser
Magdeburg
Münster
Ems
Dortmund
Göttingen
Leipzig
Essen
Kassel
Düsseldorf
Dresden
BELGIUM
Köln
Erfurt
Aachen
Bonn
Karl-Marx-Stadt
Koblenz
Mosel
Wiesbaden
Main
Frankfurt
Bayreuth
Trier
Mainz
CZECHOSLOVAKIA
Saarbrücken
Mannheim
Nürnberg
Heidelberg
Rothenburg
Karlsruhe
Donau
Stuttgart
Baden-Baden
Isar
Neckar
Augsburg
FRANCE
Inn
Wien
Freiburg
München
Salzburg
Garmisch-Partenkirchen
Bodensee
Basel
Zürich
Kitzbühel
AUSTRIA
Innsbruck
Bern
Luzern
SWITZERLAND
ITALY
YOUGOSLAVIA

BERLITZ Books for travellers

TRAVEL GUIDES

They fit your pocket in both size and price. Modern, up-to-date, Berlitz gets all the information you need into 128 lively pages – 192 or 256 pages for country guides – with colour maps and photos throughout. What to see and do, where to shop, what to eat and drink, how to save.

AFRICA	Algeria (256 pages)* Kenya Morocco South Africa Tunisia
ASIA, MIDDLE EAST	China (256 pages) Hong Kong India (256 pages) Japan (256 pages) Nepal* Singapore Sri Lanka Thailand Egypt Jerusalem & Holy Land Saudi Arabia
AUSTRAL-ASIA	Australia (256 pages) New Zealand
BRITISH ISLES	Channel Islands London Ireland Oxford and Stratford Scotland
BELGIUM	Brussels
FRANCE	Brittany France (256 pages) French Riviera Loire Valley Normandy Paris
GERMANY	Berlin Munich The Rhine Valley
AUSTRIA and SWITZER-LAND	Tyrol Vienna Switzerland (192 pages)
GREECE, CYPRUS & TURKEY	Athens Corfu Crete Rhodes Greek Islands of Aegean Peloponnese Salonica/North. Greece Cyprus Istanbul/Aegean Coast Turkey (192 pages)
ITALY and MALTA	Florence Italian Adriatic Italian Riviera Italy (256 pages) Rome Sicily Venice Malta
NETHER-LANDS and SCANDI-NAVIA	Amsterdam Copenhagen Helsinki Oslo and Bergen Stockholm

*in preparation

RTUGAL	Algarve Lisbon Madeira
PAIN	Barcelona/Costa Dorada Canary Islands Costa Blanca Costa Brava Costa del Sol & Andalusia Ibiza and Formentera Madrid Majorca and Minorca
ASTERN UROPE	Budapest Dubrovnik & S. Dalmatia Hungary (192 pages) Istria and Croatian Coast Moscow & Leningrad Prague Split and Dalmatia Yugoslavia (256 pages)
ORTH AMERICA	U.S.A. (256 pages) California Florida Hawaii Miami

NORTH AMERICA	New York Canada (256 pages) Toronto Montreal
CARIBBEAN, LATIN AMERICA	Puerto Rico Virgin Islands Bahamas Bermuda French West Indies Jamaica Southern Caribbean Mexico City Brazil (Highlights of) Rio de Janeiro
EUROPE	Business Travel Guide – Europe (368 pages) Pocket guide to Europe (480 pages) Cities of Europe (504 p.)
CRUISE GUIDES	Caribbean cruise guide (368 pages) Alaska cruise guide (168 p) Handbook to Cruising (240 pages)

DELUXE GUIDES

combine complete travel guide, phrase book and dictionary in one book.
Titles available:
Amsterdam, Barcelona, Budapest, Florence, French Riviera, Madrid, Mexico, Munich, Paris, Rome, Venice.

SKI GUIDES

Top resorts rated, where to ski, colour maps:
Austria
France
Italy
Switzerland
Skiing the Alps*

BLUEPRINT GUIDES

Imaginative new large size guide with mapped itineraries, special interest checklists, selected restaurant and hotel recommendations, large-scale road atlas, all in full colour.

France, Germany*, Great Britain*, Greece*, Italy, Spain*.

MORE FOR THE $

Over $ 4'000 worth of discount coupons and gift certificates from the finest hotels and restaurants for each country covered.

France, Italy.

*in p

PHRASE BOOKS

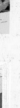

World's bestselling phrase books feature all the expressions and vocabulary you'll need, and pronunciation throughout. 192 pages, 2 colours.

Arabic	Hebrew	Russian
Chinese	Hungarian	Serbo-Croatian
Danish	Italian	Spanish (Castilian)
Dutch	Japanese	Spanish (Lat. Am.)
Finnish	Korean	Swahili
French	Norwegian	Swedish
German	Polish	Turkish
Greek	Portuguese	European Phrase Book
		European Menu Reader

All of the above phrase books are available with C60 or C90 cassette and miniscript as a "**cassettepak**".

Cassette and miniscript only are also available in the major languages as a "**phrase cassette**".

DICTIONARIES

Bilingual with 12,500 concepts each way. Highly practical for travellers, with pronunciation shown plus menu reader, basic expressions and useful information. Over 330 pages.

Danish	French	Norwegian
Dutch	German	Portuguese
Finnish	Italian	Spanish
		Swedish

TRAVEL VIDEO

ative
lar
40
a
ons.
l